I AM
JEWISH

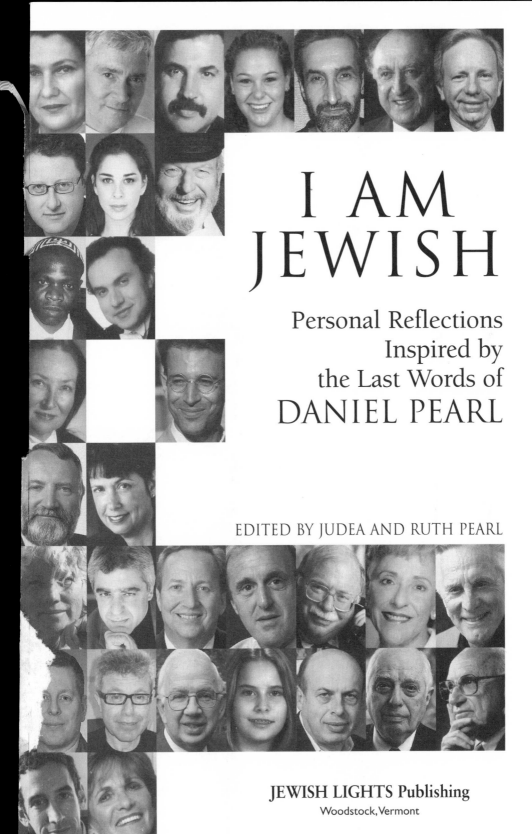

I AM
JEWISH

Personal Reflections
Inspired by
the Last Words of
DANIEL PEARL

EDITED BY JUDEA AND RUTH PEARL

JEWISH LIGHTS Publishing
Woodstock, Vermont

I Am Jewish:
Personal Reflections Inspired by the Last Words of Daniel Pearl

2004 First Printing
© 2004 by Judea and Ruth Pearl

All rights reserved. No part of this book may be reproduced or transmitted in any form or by any means, electronic or mechanical, including photocopying, recording, or by any information storage and retrieval system, without permission in writing from the publisher.

For information regarding permission to reprint material from this book, please mail or fax your request in writing to Jewish Lights Publishing, Permissions Department, at the address / fax number listed below, or e-mail your request to permissions@jewishlights.com.

Pages 251-260 constitute a continuation of this copyright page.

Library of Congress Cataloging-in-Publication Data
I am Jewish: personal reflections inspired by the last words of Daniel Pearl / edited by Judea and Ruth Pearl.
    p.   cm.
ISBN 1-58023-183-7
1. Jews—Identity. 2. Judaism. 3. Interpersonal relations—Religious aspects—Judaism. 4. Ethics, Jewish. 5. Pearl, Daniel, 1963–I. Pearl, Judea. II. Pearl, Ruth, 1935–
DS143 .I4 2004
305.892'4—dc22

                                      2003026052

10 9 8 7 6 5 4 3 2 1

Manufactured in Canada

Published by Jewish Lights Publishing
A Division of LongHill Partners, Inc.
Sunset Farm Offices, Route 4, P.O. Box 237
Woodstock, VT 05091
Tel: (802) 457-4000   Fax: (802) 457-4004
www.jewishlights.com

We dedicate this book to you, Danny,
for brightening our world with your magic,
for showing us the bold face of goodness,
for your precious gift—your words.

And to you, Adam,
to discover the garden where your father grew
and where he bloomed in boundless love for you,
to find freedom in his roots, and comfort in his words.

CONTENTS

Contents

Part III: Covenant, Chosenness, and Faith

PART IV: HUMANITY AND ETHNICITY

PART V: TIKKUN OLAM (REPAIRING THE WORLD) AND JUSTICE

CONTENTS

CONTENTS BY CONTRIBUTOR

Publisher's Note

This note will explain the overall approach to the book, the methodology used to gather the contributions for it, and the structure of it.

In our work with Judea and Ruth Pearl on this project in honor of their son, Daniel, the goal was to create an inspirational book that would encourage people to reflect on Danny's words, "I am Jewish," and the meaning of these words in their own lives.

Many Jews were particularly moved by Danny's words in which he affirmed his Jewish identity. Many were inspired to reflect on or analyze their feelings toward their lives as Jews.

The saying "two Jews, three opinions" well reflects the Jewish community's broad range of views on any topic. This book is an attempt to capture this richness of interpretation and to further inspire Jewish people to reflect upon and take pride in their identity. We began the project with confidence that, despite the diversity, common denominators would shine through clearly and distinctly—and they did.

In order to achieve our goals, we decided it was important to include input from highly respected leaders in all fields throughout the world. The invited contributors include top scholars, artists, entertainers, government officials, authors, media personalities, scientists, community leaders, rabbis, and others covering the entire religious, professional, and political spectrum.

We began by developing, in consultation with many people, comprehensive lists of potential contributors by geographic, occupational, and religious categories. After a careful analytical process, we invited several hundred people to contribute their thoughts to the book, keeping in mind that the interpretation of the words "I am Jewish" would vary widely with one's background, experience, and beliefs.

Although comprehensive in its coverage, this book was not intended to be a scientifically designed survey of Jewish thought and views, and we recognize that while our design was broadly inclusive, individual decisions on participation make for an idiosyncratic selection of people and their ideas. We wish we had been more successful in reaching people in Latin America and some other parts of the Sephardic world in particular.

Contributions range from major essays to a paragraph or a sentence, and they come from adults as well as youngsters. They are in the form of personal feelings, statements of theology, life stories, and historical reflections. Almost all contributions are original. A few have been previously published but were carefully selected by their contributors to represent their thinking on the question: What do you mean when you say, "I am Jewish"?

As you will see, clear themes did emerge. While many contributions contained more than one theme, we have organized the responses into five broad categories, reflecting what appeared to the editors to be the major theme of each statement. They have been integrated to provide a thought-provoking and inspiring diversity of opinion that we hope will lead to further discussion in the Jewish community in the United States and elsewhere.

The categories in which the responses have been organized reflect the major relationships of our lives.

- **Identity**—Our relationship to ourselves, how we define who we are in the most fundamental way.
- **Heritage**—Our relationship to family, community, culture, tradition, and our collective history.
- **Covenant, Chosenness, and Faith**—Our relationship to God, our understanding of the relationship between God and the Jewish people, and our understanding of Judaism as a religion.
- **Humanity and Ethnicity**—Our relationship to others who are not part of the Jewish people. How does a sense of particularism relate to the universal themes and teachings of Judaism?
- *Tikkun Olam* (**Repairing the World**) **and Justice**—Our relationship to the larger world, and what "I am Jewish" means for what we do with our lives as we address our responsibilities in the world.

We hope this book will motivate people throughout the Jewish community to think more about their lives as Jews and, in particular, have a profound effect on the way Jewish youngsters shape their identity in years to come.

S. M. M.

PREFACE

BACKGROUND

It took a few endless minutes for me to comprehend the meaning of the words the United States Consul General in Karachi was reading to me over the phone. It was a transcript of the videotape the Consulate had received a day earlier; it was taken in the last hours of our son's life, and the words were Danny's: "My father is Jewish, my mother is Jewish, I am Jewish."

It hit me right away that this sentence would strike an especially deep chord for Jews everywhere, though I could not fully grasp its scope or significance.

It was only a few weeks later that I came to realize that Danny left us a precious gift in those words—a faithful mirror in which we, Jews, can see ourselves. Danny had that mirror too; he was not alone on that fateful day.

Danny never concealed his Jewishness in his world journeys, and after he was abducted, we knew this might determine his fate. This awareness, however, did not prepare me for the brutality and the brazeness of his killers. I was especially repulsed by how those murderers, instead of hiding their anti-Semitic perversion, proudly displayed their motives in public, boasting in their deformity. But over time, steadily emerging from rage and pain there came for me a sense of pride at Danny's unyielding dignity in those critical moments. His dignity signified so vividly the victory of the eternal Jew over his perennial enemies, the victory of Danny over his killers.

It also became obvious to me that, with all their technical sophistication, the murderers made one essential miscalculation: making a spectacle of their contemptuous act would backfire and result in the opposite of whatever they sought to achieve. In particular, highlighting Daniel's identity as a Jew in front of millions of people around the world would forever associate Jews with the admirable qualities of Danny's character and Jewishness with his missions of peace-seeking and bridge-building.

Nonetheless, I did not deem that sort of victory satisfactory for my grandson, Adam, and his generation.

The burning question in my mind was how Adam would view his Jewish lineage. Would he take it as a genetic accident that may lead to tragedies like the one that befell his father, or would he embrace it as the fountain of his father's spirit, from which he, too, could draw strength, comfort, and direction?

Over the months following, we received ample indications that strength and mission would be the dominant elements of Danny's Jewish legacy.

Letters from Jewish children around the world invariably expressed a sense of pride and commitment, with no trace of fear or victimhood. For example, eight-year-old Evan from Berkeley, California, wrote to our daughter Michelle: "I read this poem 'I am a Jew' at my sister's Bat Mitzvah because Daniel Pearl was courageous when he said, 'I am a Jew, my father is a Jew, my mother is a Jew.' I think he was really brave to say that knowing he will probably be killed for it. I can't believe that this happened in my life and I even know his sister."

Another letter from Temple B'nai Shalom in East Brunswick, New Jersey, asked our permission to name their religious school after Danny. When we explained that Danny was not "religious" in the conventional sense, the rabbi insisted, "We want our children to have a model of what it means to be Jewish, and every mother I speak to says that she wants her son to be a Jew like Daniel Pearl."

We realized then that modern Jewish identity, as it is forged in homes and schools, is in dire need of a role model and a human face to give life to Jewish values and teachings, and to connect these to relevant events in our turbulent world. We came to realize that Daniel's face, coupled with the broad impact of his last words, could help fortify Jewish identity with the resilience needed to counter its adversaries' attacks. We saw in this potential yet another part of Danny's victory over his murderers: while they tried to sow fear and humiliation among Jews, Danny's words would lead to empowerment and pride and, eventually, to a stronger, more united Jewish people. We began to view the building of Jewish pride as a debt we owe our people for endowing us with the heritage, education, and support that has kept us strong in times of hardship and which helped shape Danny's spirit and personality, both heart and might.

THE BOOK PROJECT

We knew, however, that the commitment to strengthen Jewish identity is not shared by all fellow Jews. Many Jewish parents, especially in the secular section of the community, question both the meaning of their Jewishness and whether it is something worth preserving in a world where ethnicity is often considered a divisive relic of a bygone age.

An idea germinated. Danny's last words could also serve as a catalyst for fellow Jews to reflect upon, question, ponder, discuss, analyze, and hopefully clarify their own feelings about their Jewishness.

The seed of this idea was sewn by then twelve-year-old Alana Frey (see her contribution, page 73), who came up with an inspiring project for her Bat Mitzvah: to ask friends and relatives what being Jewish means to them, compile the answers in booklet form, and send the booklet to Adam Pearl, so that "he would have an understanding of his heritage and his father's words would always comfort him."

I was instantly intrigued by the power of Alana's idea. I first thought of continuing this theme on an ongoing basis through a series of Bar and Bat Mitzvah projects and then, when Adam becomes Bar Mitzvah age himself, we would edit and publish the contributions in book form. It later dawned on me that the theme was so powerful and timely that it could inspire contributions from a wide range of Jews from all walks of life and be of immediate benefit to the community as a whole. Such a book would provide both a valuable picture of how Jews define themselves and insightful new answers to the difficult question, "What does being Jewish mean to me?"

The question is not trivial. Is "being Jewish" some sort of a birthmark with which one is burdened or blessed for life? A genetic incident? How can one be proud of a genetic incident? Is it a religious belief? An ethnic loyalty? A commitment to a certain behavior or perspective?

An attitude? A collection of sweet childhood memories? A language to communicate with one's ancestors and decode their wisdom and experience? A key to the literary or ethical force of Bible stories? Most importantly, could a coherent, meaningful answer ever emerge from a community whose members view the question through such diverse prisms?

I sought the advice of Rabbi Harold Schulweis, and he not only endorsed the idea as timely and of great value, but also put me in touch with Stuart Matlins of Jewish Lights Publishing. Stuart received the idea with enthusiasm, and the result of our collaboration is told in the Publisher's Note.

To adhere to the central mission of this volume, we asked authors to minimize references to Danny's tragedy and to focus on the main question: "What does being Jewish mean to you?" I thought it would be appropriate, however, to make one exception to this rule by including my perception of what being Jewish meant to Daniel. This question was discussed in the remarks I made at a multi-faith memorial service at Congregation B'nai Jeshurun in New York City on Danny's first Yahrzeit, February 24, 2002. With the encouragement of the publisher, I include these remarks (slightly edited) in their entirety.

I AM JEWISH

History will record a tide of horror and madness that swept our planet in the beginning of the third millennium. The basic rules of civilization were violated, and all theories of cognition, common sense, and human values laid shattered and betrayed.

History will also record that, in the midst of this chaos, there was a young man who, in a moment of extreme crisis, looked straight in the eye of evil, and said: "My father is Jewish, my mother is Jewish, I am Jewish."

He did not say it under duress, nor did he say it with defiance or with gallantry. He said it in his usual matter-of-fact way, slightly irritated, as if saying: "How many times do I have to repeat myself? Two plus two equals four, and I am Jewish!"

He was not so naive as to ignore the venom that drooled from his captors' mouths each time he uttered the word "Jewish." Still, he repeated: "My father is Jewish, my mother is Jewish, I am Jewish." What did he mean by those eleven words?

The Challenge of Understanding

Danny was not a religious Jew. Judaism for him was the language of his extended family—a source of strength, commitment, and historical identity.

To Danny, "I am Jewish" meant "I must understand." Or in other words: "I am possessed with a historically baked obsession to understand and repair things, because my wandering ancestors, hardened by centuries of persecution and discrimination, have taught me to mistrust all dogmas and ideologies and to question authority and the status quo and conventional wisdom. So, as a Jew, I have inherited no other mental tranquilizer except that chronic urge to question and to understand.

"I understand suffering, because the suffering of my ancestors is etched on my consciousness.

"I understand justice, because I was distilled by injustice.

"I understand Muslims' suffering as well, for I have seen your people in Kosovo, I have worked with your carpet weavers in Iran, and I have sung with your pearl divers in Qatar.

"'I am Jewish' means I am reminding you of the challenge of understanding. So, let's come to our senses."

Humanity in Diversity

I tried to explain all this to the people of Pakistan in an open letter published a few months ago in Karachi.

When Danny said "I am Jewish," I wrote, what he meant in fact was: "I respect Islam precisely because I am Jewish, and I expect you to respect me and my faith precisely because you are, or claim to be, good Muslims."

In other words, "I come from a place where one's heritage is the source of one's strength, and strength is measured by one's capacity to accommodate diversity. Because it is only through diversity that we recognize common humanity.

"Look at our patriarch, Abraham! The first thing he does after his circumcision is to invite three strangers to sit down and have a chat. Remember?

"So let's have a chat. 'I am Jewish' means I am the litmus test of your faith and the fire test of your strength. Let's come to our senses."

The Founders of the Town

What I did not explain to readers in Pakistan was Danny's next sentence, the very last that he spoke freely: "Back in the town of Bnei Brak, there is a street named after my great-grandfather, Chayim Pearl, who was one of the founders of the town."

Why is he telling us this strange story about his great-grandfather from Bnei Brak? In that frantic race for nanoseconds, why does his mind stumble on this anecdotal, almost-forgotten story from our family archive?

As you can imagine, I have asked myself this question millions of times in the past year, and I would like to share my theory.

He chose this story because it carried three different messages simultaneously to three different audiences: First, to his family; second, to his captors; and third, to everyone in the free world.

To his family he said: "Behold, I am volunteering information that no one else knows. Why? Because I want to assure you that I am well, I am speaking freely, and I am not defeated."

To his captors he said: "Look, guys! I come from a place where a person is judged by the towns that he builds, by the trees that he plants, and by the wells that he digs. Not by the death and destruction that he brings to the world. So come to your senses."

At times I theorize that Danny had an even deeper message here, and that he tried to tell his captors something like this: "You know, my great-grandfather was angry, too; in fact, he had as many grievances in the Europe of 1924 as you have today in Pakistan. Yet, when he was struck on the head with an iron bar by a Polish peasant, and called 'dirty Jew,' he did not strap himself with explosives and go blow up a church. Instead, he crawled home, wiped his blood, and told his wife and four children, 'Start packing!' And he sold everything he had, bought a piece of sandy land in then British Palestine, and traveled to build a better life for his family and for their neighbors."

And I can almost hear Danny inviting his captors to come and have a look at Bnei Brak today, and saying: "Judge for yourself if such a miracle cannot happen in your part of the world. So come to your senses."

Finally, to the people of the free world, Danny said: "You know what? Despite all the protests and criticism that we hear around us, we are still the town builders in this world, not our critics.

"With all the images of the 'ugly West' and 'ugly America' and 'ugly Israel' that my captors and their intellectual supporters have labored to paint in the past few decades, we can be mighty proud of who we are: We are the town builders in the world.

"True, we have not been perfect. And our actions are occasionally stained with materialism, arrogance, selfishness, unilateralism, and other ills and maladies that we are constantly accused of practicing, but we are still the world's largest exporters of hope, pluralism, tolerance, equality, and basic freedoms; and our heritage is still the most reliable source of values, values to which there are no alternatives anywhere.

"So, let us continue to reach out for dialogue. But at the same time we must continue to demand unequivocally: Come to your senses."

Modern Jews of Courage

People ask us whether Danny was a hero or a martyr.

Danny loved life; he did not court death. Rejecting the shadow of death, he tried to sanctify life with the only weapon he had: "Come to your senses."

No! Modern Jews of courage do not accept martyrdom as an inevitable pattern of Jewish history. Modern Jews of courage see their duty in looking in the eyes of hate-carriers in the world, and reminding them that civilized society is founded upon certain principles, and repeating to them, again and again: "Come to your senses!"

Oh, Danny, Danny, where did you get the strength to demand so stubbornly that those thugs come to their senses? Could it be the stubbornness of your ancestors, carrying the torch of inquiry and compassion through centuries of dogma and estrangement? Could it possibly be that little street in Bnei Brak, named after your great-grandfather?

No! For us, Jews, the story of Daniel Pearl represents not a saga of martyrdom, nor a claim on victimhood, but a proud reminder of who we are and what we stand for, as well as a subtle reminder of who our adversaries are and what they stand for.

The Galvanic Effect of Betrayal

History will record that on February 21, 2002, another rule of common sense was shattered. The young man who kept on insisting "Come to your senses" was silenced—silenced by senselessness itself.

Many ask why the death of Daniel Pearl has touched and united so many people. After all, there were hundreds who lost their lives in terrorism-related violence in 2001, among them nineteen journalists.

Indeed, the special significance of Danny's death lies not in the fact that he was an innocent journalist and expectant father, killed in cold blood. The significance lies in the reasons for which he was murdered. Danny was killed for what he represented, and what he represented was each one of us. To his killers, he represented the ideals that every person in every civilized society aspires to uphold—openness, pluralism, understanding, freedom of inquiry, truth, respect for people.

And that galvanizes people into one community.

If you are an American, or a citizen of any democracy, it was your values and your freedoms that were targeted and abducted on that fateful night of January 23, 2002.

If you are a journalist, it was your hands that were chained in Karachi on that terrible night.

If you are a Muslim who struggles to lift his countrymen to new opportunities, it was your head that came under the gun in Karachi in January 2002.

If you are a Jew, it was your voice that reverberated from that dungeon in Karachi and blended with the voice of your ancestry in that ultimate affirmation of identity: "My father is Jewish, my mother is Jewish, I am Jewish."

If you are a decent person anywhere, it was your decency that was betrayed on February 21, 2002.

The Ultimate Revenge

People ask us if we do not seek revenge.

Yes, we do! Hatred killed our son, and hatred we will fight for the rest of our lives, with vengeance and tenacity.

In my letter to the people of Pakistan I made it quite clear: "The loss of Danny will forever tear my heart, but I cannot think of a greater consolation than seeing your children [in Pakistan] pointing at Danny's picture one day and saying, 'This is the kind of person I want to be. Like him, I want to be truthful and friendly, open-minded, and respectful of others.'"

This is our vision of revenge: fighting the hatred that took Danny's life. And the Daniel Pearl Foundation was created to support this vision. It may seem overly ambitious, I know, but it is not totally unrealistic, because the hatred that killed Danny also opened unique opportunities to fight hatred.

One opportunity is to take the legacy of a person who earned respect on both sides of the East/West divide and use it to lower the walls of ignorance that have allowed hatred to ferment to such heights. It is a unique opportunity because there are not many such legacies around. In other words, there aren't many faces which both a Muslim and a Westerner can point to and agree: "Here is a man of peace, an emissary of goodwill."

Coalition of the Decent

To utilize this opportunity we must galvanize people along a new frontier, one defined not along national or religious lines but along lines of decency and understanding. By building respect for diverse cultures and values, this "Coalition of the Decent" will strengthen its ranks and will stand up to rising cultures of hate, accusation, and deceit.

We have found an ocean of decency and goodwill all over the world to help us in this endeavor.

For example, on October 10, 2002, we celebrated Danny's thirty-ninth birthday in the form of a global concert called Daniel Pearl Music Day. Thousands of musicians in over one hundred concerts and eighteen countries around the world played for world harmony and took a stand for tolerance and humanity. This was a modest but significant beginning.

Among the many participants was Pakistan's number-one rock group, Junoon, who dedicated their performance in the United States to Danny. By this dedication, the Pakistani rock group has sent a symbolic message to their countrymen, which I read as follows:

"Here we come from Pakistan, a country where, to many people, the word 'Jewish' implies contempt (if not a license to kill), and here we are celebrating the life of a Jewish boy from Los Angeles, California, a descendant of a Hasidic Jew from Bnei Brak, Israel. Ask yourself why we do that! We do it because Daniel Pearl is a symbol of the new alignment, the 'Coalition of the Decent,' to which we belong and toward which we wish our country to develop."

It was merely a symbolic gesture, true, but lo and behold, when they returned to Pakistan, they were interviewed about their trip to the United States, and their participation in the Daniel Pearl Music Day was all over the news. If this jolted music fans in Pakistan to find out what Jews and Judaism are all about, then the world has gotten rid of another ounce of hate, and our vision has advanced one step closer toward realization.

The Troops of Peace

And this brings me to discuss a second component in the battle over hatred. Military battles are won in two parallel ways: by making your enemy weaker, and by making your troops stronger. The same applies to battles against hatred. In addition to curtailing ignorance in the world at large, we must empower the troops of peace here at home, and I consider your children and grandchildren to be the elite forces of these troops.

I consider these youngsters semiclones of Danny—talented, curious, principled, and friendly—and I tell myself: Look at the kind of hatred they will be facing when they grow up. They deserve encouragement. They deserve to be told, "You are OK. You are not the bloodthirsty baby-killing money-hungry imperialists that Danny's killers and their intellectual sympathizers on college campuses try to portray you as. No. You are Daniel Pearl's kin.

"Like him you will be traveling the world with a pen and a fiddle trying to make sense of what you see; like him you will make friends with thousands of strangers, Jews and non-Jews, and enrich their lives with humor, music, and new insights; and like him you will offer your humble contribution to *tikkun olam* by insisting, with all the stubbornness of your ancestors, 'I am Jewish! Come to your senses!'

"So, go ahead and repair the world. You can do it!"

———————————————————— ✡ ————————————————————

A FACE OF AN ERA

History recalls another Jewish person whose face and tragic end personified the horrors of an era. The name of that person was Anne Frank. Paralleling the impact of Anne Frank's diary in the early 1950s, the story of Daniel Pearl now inspires Jews and non-Jews alike to re-study the anatomy of anti-Semitism, to reflect on the consequences of fanaticism, to take pride in their heritage, and to stand up for tolerance and understanding everywhere.

The difference, however, is that the diary of Anne Frank was discovered after the Holocaust, while Danny's story came to public attention in time to prevent another one. This gives us the hope that, some day, I will be able to tell my grandson: "You see, Adam? Your father's legacy helped us win that battle! Humanity has triumphed!"

Judea Pearl
Los Angeles, California
www.danielpearl.org

PART I:

IDENTITY

 AVRAHAM BURG is a senior member of the Israeli Labor Party and one of the most charismatic members of Parliament. The youngest speaker ever in the history of the Knesset, he is a staunch supporter of peace in the Middle East.

"Judaism is like a chain of peace and existence that spans space and time, where each individual Jew is a different link."

I am Jewish. It began at birth purely by chance. It continues through my life as a great challenge and will end in the final moments of my life. What is most amazing, though, is that even after I am gone, Judaism will continue.

The fact that I was born a Jew—the fact that anyone is born a Jew—cannot be explained. We don't choose it, it chooses us. Judaism is like a chain of peace and existence that spans space and time, where each individual Jew is a different link. Our mission is to maintain the strength and continuity of Judaism, and each one of us has a role in shaping and continuing the future. In return it gives us meaning—an identity in this world. This identity as Jews, fighting for peace and existence, is what defines us. And this is why Judaism, more than any other ancient civilization, has survived the test of time. It is much more than a religion or a culture—it is an identity.

Jewish identity changed and adapted according to the contemporary needs of the last four thousand years. These identities, even in today's world, include the zealots and the assimilated, the devout and the runaways, and all the shades in between. There are so many kinds of Judaism, so many identities that have developed throughout time, yet the overall mission has been one of peace and existence.

Today's Jewish identity is unprecedented in our history. We are living in a time when the challenges of the past are fading and new, modern challenges are developing. The Holocaust, wars, pogroms, and persecution of the past still hang over our heads in heavy clouds, but I believe with complete faith that the days of war are nearly over and that peace is waiting for us just around the corner. But this peace is accompanied by a new kind of internal struggle for our identity.

We are the first generation to exist as the "new Jew." For hundreds of generations, Judaism was more than a set of laws governing religious and moral conduct. These generations were raised on the foundations of faith that we are God's chosen nation, that we were the expression of God's worth in this world, and in the name of this amazing deliverance we were willing to withstand any torture. There was no punishment that could uproot the real and great faith in God, the creator of the universe. Maybe we did not always understand God's ways, but we always believed in the complete justice of our faith, and we were determined to survive at any cost.

Our generation is working under completely different circumstances. For the "new Jew," this is a time of choice. This generation is the first in history that has the option of choosing to be Jewish and to remain a Jew. And, furthermore, the "new Jew" is the first generation to make these decisions knowing that the choice to abandon Judaism has no consequences. It is possible to choose not to be Jewish and, according to society, everything will be all right. There is little talk about breaking the chain. The focus, rather, is on personal choice rather than the well-being of the whole.

At the same time, the "new Jew" has emerged alongside the modern, Western gentile who is defined by the strong progressive values of open-mindedness, freedom, and equality for everyone—including the Jews. Until now, Judaism was always the "other" religion. It always stood apart from the majority. Our tradition teaches us that Abraham, the father of Judaism, was referred to not just by his name, but as Abraham the Hebrew in order to highlight his differences that separated him from the rest of the world: he was a Hebrew. Today Jews are integrating into Western civilization more and more and are seen as part of the whole, not as the other. The result is a relatively safe world where Jews can live among gentiles.

These modern circumstances for the Jews started developing after the Holocaust and since then have divided the Jewish nation into two major geographic centers: Israel and the United States. Today, seventy-seven percent of all world Jewry lives in one or the other of these locations. Both of these centers have distinctly different Jewish identities, yet they share the universal mission of continuing the Jewish chain.

The Jewish experience in Israel is quite different from that in the United States. In the United States, the average Jewish identity is exactly that of the "new Jew." No nation in the world stands for the values of personal freedom and equality like the United States does. This universal acceptance identifies everyone, first and foremost, as people and, secondarily, as Jews. American Jews get their identity internally as this community within humanity. This sounds like a utopia, but this environment introduced a completely new problem into Judaism. In a country where personal freedom is so highly valued, in a country where these values are widespread throughout the gentile community that lives and works among the Jewish community, the assimilation rate is quickly rising. The future of the American Jewish community is at risk. The generation of "new Jews" is now confronted with the challenge of preventing assimilation at such extraordinary levels. It is up to this group to find a way of surviving in such an accepting world, in a place without an enemy. The question is whether Judaism can maintain its structure without external pressure identifying it as the "other." And if this civilization is any indication of what the future holds for civilizations worldwide, what does that mean for the future of Judaism?

The Jews that live in Israel have a very different identity and a different challenge. These Jews have no problem with identity. As with past generations, they are seen by the outside world as something different. Israel is unique because it is a Jewish country. Their identity also comes from the fact that their main challenge has an external source. Consequently, Israel's Jews are forced to stick together. Israel is fighting for its existence and for peace. This peace is not just for itself as a nation, but also for the world as a whole. Jews in Israel represent more than just Judaism, they represent the Western world. The Middle East is the center of human civilization and has always been the focal point of global tension. The peace that soon will be realized will bring thousands of years of conflict between the Judeo-Christian world and the Muslim world to an end. Peace in the region will bring new relationships and possibilities for the Western-Muslim world. Israel, therefore, is not only fighting an enemy for survival, it is literally working toward world peace.

So how do I see my identity as a Jew? When my children ask me why we are Jewish I quote Maimonides, one of the greatest Jewish thinkers of all time. He said, "There is nothing between this world and the days of the Messiah except enslavement to Kingdoms." Maimonides is saying that humanity's future that lies in the days of the messiah will not be full of wonders that change the world as we know it. There will be no great technology, no fabulous creations from the outside, no angels with wings, and no notices from God and the rabbis on every corner. There will only be a better humanity. No one will be enslaved, no nation will conquer another, human beings will not suppress each other, and freedom will be a universal value.

Maimonides continued:

> The sages and the prophets did not yearn for the days of the Messiah, not in order to control the entire world, not in order to control paganism, and not so that the other nations will regard them as their authority, and not in order to eat, drink and to rejoice, but rather in order to be available for studying Torah and its wisdom. And they will not have an oppressor and one who limits their activities ... and at the same time there will not be hunger nor war, and no jealousy nor competition, that good will be greatly bestowed, and all the wonderful delights will be available like dust.
> —Mishneh Torah Hilchos Melachim

During this time of a fixed world there will be mostly good. It will be a period of intellectualism and morality that the world has never before witnessed. This is Maimonides' Jewish vision of the future, and it is for this reason that I am Jewish and refuse to sever my link in the chain. Judaism has the responsibility of bringing peace to the world, and I am Jewish.

 RUTH R. WISSE is Martin Peretz Professor of Yiddish Literature and a professor of comparative literature at Harvard University. Her books include *The Modern Jewish Canon: A Journey Through Language and Culture, If I Am Not for Myself: The Liberal Betrayal of the Jews*, and *A Little Love in Big Manhattan: Two Yiddish Poets.*

"We may choose to live as Jews, visibly and vitally, or else slip anonymously into the gentile mainstream."

Words depend on the context within which they are uttered. During the course of my normal life, whether "I am a Jew" or not is usually either obvious or irrelevant or both at once: obvious at the kosher butcher shop, irrelevant at the bank; obvious in the synagogue, irrelevant in the subway. When I teach Yiddish literature at the university, I use the first person pronoun to refer to us students, not us Jews. While my own interest in Yiddish may have been inspired by my Jewishness, some of my non-Jewish students were drawn to the subject by the desire to master an unfamiliar culture. Being Jewish may be the point or beside the point of the passion for literary studies. The American way of life affords us the freedom to live as we please, within the bounds of the law. We may choose to live as Jews, visibly and vitally, or else slip anonymously into the gentile mainstream.

Since I have always enjoyed being a Jew it never occurred to me to live otherwise. I appreciate the tough-mindedness of the Jewish religious tradition that knows how hard it is to achieve a mature civilization; I admire my ancestors who brought Jewish civilization to such a high level of maturity. Although I don't follow all the requirements of Halakhah, my observance is higher than that of my parents whose observance was lower than that of their parents. I love the cycle of the Jewish year, particularly the contrasted experiences of Rosh Hashanah and Passover. The culture and history of the Jewish people engages much of my intellectual energy. And the pleasure of being a member of the Jewish community usually outweighs its frustrations.

Most of all I cherish those of my fellow Jews who settled and who maintain the State of Israel, which I consider the highest manifestation of the human spirit in modern times. Jews always tried to take full responsibility for their actions in every human sphere, but not until we reclaimed responsibility for our political life could we provide a haven for Jews in danger. The more Hebrew I learn to speak and read, the longer and more often I am in Israel, the more friends and relatives I acquire in the country, the greater my debt to its defenders. The achievements of Israel depend entirely on the patience of its defenders, for it is the only democracy in the world that has had to fight for its life from inception to the present. Not since the Romans crushed the second Jewish commonwealth have Jewish soldiers been able to protect the Jewish polity from its enemies. It goes unappreciated that these defenders of Israel are also the front line of defense for the democratic world.

The presence of enemies introduces a different context for the affirmation of Jewish identity. Jean Paul Sartre believed that the presence of anti-Semites required that Jews embrace their identity, for they would otherwise become inauthentic—foils of their adversaries and escapists from their existential condition. In 1942, at the height of the Nazi slaughter of the Jews of Europe, the Soviet Yiddish poet Itsik Feffer wrote a poem titled, "I Am a Jew." Feffer was a colonel in the Red Army, a member of the Communist Party, and an agent for the Soviet secret police. In the preceding years, he had obeyed Stalinist dictates to avoid all Jewish national expression. But the rules changed once Germany invaded Russia, and Feffer's poem came out as subtle as a drum:

> Pharoah and Titus, Haman made their aim
> To slay me in their times and lands,
> Eternity still bears my name

Upon its lands.
And I survived in Spain the rack,
The Inquisition Fires, too.
My horn sounded this message back:
"I am a Jew!"
   —Itsik Feffer, translated by Joseph Leftwich

Every stanza ended with the same refrain of defiant Jewish self-affirmation. Not surprisingly, six years later, when Stalin ordered the arrest of Feffer, among other prominent Jews, on capital charges of anti-Soviet treachery, the poem was brought as evidence of Feffer's Jewish nationalist propaganda. At the trial a fellow defendant protested: "There cannot be anything criminal in the phrase 'I am a Jew.' If I approach someone and say, 'I am a Jew,' what could be bad about that?"[1] His comment was just, but, under the circumstances, naive. When the goal of aggressors is the ruin of the Jewish people, an otherwise unexceptional statement of fact acquires powers of resistance. This resistance became manifest when Soviet Jewry took up where Feffer left off in proclaiming, "We are Jews." Many claimed the right to live as Jews by immigrating to the Jewish homeland.

No Jew should have to affirm his identity in response to a knife at his throat. No regime or leader should seek aggrandizement at the expense of the Jewish people or deny us the same rights that they claim for themselves to land, to peace, to national existence. But as long as our enemies threaten, it is unutterably shameful to ignore their presence. Those of us who live outside Israel should be confronting its defamers no less vigorously than the Israel Defense Forces resist invaders and terrorists. I consider it my highest duty and priority as a Jew to oppose the propaganda war against the Jewish state, which has been waged with increasing sophistication and resources by Arab leaders who should have been improving their own societies. Precisely because America allows me the choice to be or not to be a Jew, I am free to expose our attackers for as long as it takes them to stop their attacks.

---

1. *Stalin's Secret Pogrom: The Postwar Inquisition of the Jewish Anti-Fascist Committee*, ed. Joshua Rubenstein and Vladimir P. Naumov, trans. Laura Esther Wolfson (New Haven: Yale University Press, 2001), p. 158.

Joshua Malina was tapped by Aaron Sorkin to fill the shoes of White House speechwriter in the Emmy Award–winning series *The West Wing.*

"Judaism is the foundation of my identity."

For me the statement "I am Jewish" is no different from the statement "I am." Judaism is the foundation of my identity, the fixed base upon which all other aspects of my self are balanced—actor, husband, father, American.

"I am Jewish." It is an assertion of identity that has caused so many of our people throughout history to be hated, exiled, killed. That Daniel Pearl was murdered for embodying the truth of his final statement is a terrible tragedy. But nothing can truly extinguish the light of identity. And in a real way, his statement allows me to say that although I never met him, he was my brother.

Irwin Cotler is a Canadian Member of Parliament and professor of law. He is an international human rights lawer and has defended political prisoners all over the world for the past twenty-five years.

"I am a Jew. My mother is a Jew. My father is a Jew. We all met at Sinai."

Daniel Pearl's last words, "My father is Jewish, my mother is Jewish, I am Jewish," were not just a statement of fact; under the circumstances, they were a courageous assertion of identity. And they have inspired me to reflect upon my own identity—on my parents' contribution to it—and, most importantly, the values imparted to me that underpin this identity.

My father—of blessed memory—was a lawyer with the soul of a poet, for whom being a lawyer was a *melitz yosher*—a counsel for the public good; was my first teacher in relating life to law and law to life; taught me *Pirkei Avot*—the Ethics of our Fathers—when I could not yet appreciate their profundity, but sensed their significance; and instilled in me—as my mother exemplified in her daily conduct—the core values that inform my Jewishness, indeed my identity, and which found subsequent expression in my writings and advocacy alike.

These values include:

1. **The Danger of Assaultive Speech**—the notion that, as my mother would remind me, "Life and death are on the tip of the tongue." And so while I was growing up where the schoolyard refrain was, "Sticks and stones may break my bones, but words will never hurt me," I learned early that words can hurt, "that one must guard one's tongue"; and that, as I was to later understand, words can wound, they can maim, they can kill.

2. **Importance of *Zachor* (Remembrance)**—I was taught early of the horrors of the Holocaust—that there are things in Jewish history too terrible to be believed, but not too terrible to have happened. Each victim, as my parents cautioned me, was not part of an abstract statistic of "six million Jews," but each one had a name, an identity—each one was a universe—thereby imparting in me the related teaching that "whoever kills a single person it is as if he/she killed an entire universe; but whoever saves a single person, it is as if they saved an entire universe."

   But while *zachor* is often identified with Holocaust remembrance, for my parents it went to the core of what Jewish identity is all about. For what does it mean to say—as my parents would recite and remind me every Passover Seder—that in every generation each one must see himself or herself as if we too came out of Egypt—as if we too experienced the oppression of slavery, and the exaltation of liberation? And they always added the universalizing ethic that we should therefore never forget the importance of treating the stranger—the *ger*—as an equal.

3. **"Do not Stand Idly By While the Brother's Blood Is Being Shed."**—It should not be surprising that my education in

Holocaust remembrance would lead inexorably to a third value: the responsibility "not to be a bystander to evil." The *Pirkei Avot* instructed: Where people avert their eyes from evil, our responsibility must be to confront it—to stand up and be counted—which later found expression, I suspect, in my advocacy on behalf of oppressed Jews, and, indeed, oppressed peoples; and to write of a "Duty to Protect" under International Humanitarian Law, and the need for humanitarian intervention in the Balkans, Rwanda, East Timor, and the like.

4. *Pidyon Shevuyim* (**Redemption of the Captives**)—Again, the notion of "not standing idly by"—of the duty to protect—very much underpins the duty to intervene to save those in captivity—a value which allows us to even transgress the Sabbath for that purpose—and is probably the single most important value accounting for my defense of political prisoners over the years. Regrettably, despite the heroic efforts of Daniel Pearl's family and friends to redeem him from captivity—thereby sanctifying this value—he was not saved.

5. **Women's Rights**—One might acknowledge the importance of women's rights as human rights while questioning what Jewish teaching inspired it. For me, it reverts once again to the lessons of liberation from Egypt, and to the notion that it was "due to the righteousness of women that the Jewish People were liberated from Egypt," a teaching replete with commentary and instruction, but like the preceding values and lesson, space does not permit elaboration.

6. **Jewish People, a Prototypical "First Nation" or Aboriginal People**—One of the most enduring of my parental teachings—and at the core of my identity—is the notion that Jews are not simply atomized individuals in the here and now, but that we are part of a People—a covenental people who came together at Sinai—a people with an Abrahamic religion that we share with Christians and Muslims; with an aboriginal land that we share with another indigenous people, the Arab nation; with an aboriginal Torah—or Bible—that inspired the New Testament and the Koran.

In a word, if I can paraphrase my parents' teaching, the Jewish People are among the only people in the world today who still inhabit the same land, embrace the same religion, study the same Torah, speak the same aboriginal language—Hebrew—and hear the same name—Israel—as we did 3,500 years ago.

I am a Jew. My mother is a Jew. My father is a Jew. We all met at Sinai.

 LAWRENCE H. SUMMERS took office as the twenty-seventh president of Harvard University on July 1, 2001. In 1999 he was confirmed by the United States Senate as Secretary of the Treasury, where he served as the principal economic adviser to President Clinton and as the CFO of the United States government.

"It would have been inconceivable a generation or two ago that Harvard could have a Jewish president."

In September 2002, I made the following remarks at morning prayers on the Harvard University campus, which speak to Daniel Pearl's final words:

> I am Jewish, identified but hardly devout. In my lifetime, anti-Semitism has been remote from my experience. My family all left Europe at the beginning of the twentieth century. The Holocaust is for me a matter of history, not personal memory. My experience in college and graduate school, as a faculty member, as a government official—all involved little notice of my religion.
>
> Indeed, I was struck during my years in the Clinton administration that the existence of an economic leadership team, with people like Robert Rubin, Alan Greenspan, Charlene Barshefsky, and many others, that was very heavily Jewish passed without comment or notice—it was

something that would have been inconceivable a generation or two ago, as indeed it would have been inconceivable a generation or two ago that Harvard could have a Jewish president.

Without thinking about it much, I attributed all of this to progress—to an ascendancy of enlightenment and tolerance. A view that prejudice is increasingly put aside. A view that while the politics of the Middle East was enormously complex, and contentious, the question of the right of a Jewish state to exist had been settled in the affirmative by the world community. But today, I am less complacent. Less complacent and comfortable because there is disturbing evidence of an upturn in anti-Semitism globally.

I would like nothing more than to be wrong. It is my greatest hope and prayer that the idea of a rise of anti-Semitism proves to be a self-denying prophecy—a prediction that carries the seeds of its own falsification. But this depends on all of us.

 RABBI ZALMAN M. SCHACHTER-SHALOMI, the inspiration of the Jewish renewal movement, is widely recognized as perhaps the most important Jewish spiritual teacher of the second half of the twentieth century. He is on the faculty of religious studies at Naropa University.

"If I, as an individual, do not have a good reason to continue to live as a Jew, then collectively the Jewish people has a problem—assimilation."

Horace M. Kallen—a friend of Professor Mordechai Kaplan, the creator and guiding spirit of the Reconstructionist movement—once said that a Jew is one of eleven and a half million people in search of a definition. Like Kallen, most Jews will ponder the question *"Mi hu*

Yehudi?" "Who is a Jew?" at some point in their lives. Debates about this have been so inflammatory and so frequently unproductive that it is tempting to abandon them altogether. Nevertheless, as difficult and vexing as this question is, we still need to address it. Most of us want a definition that fits our way of life, but which excludes people whose beliefs differ from our own. It is as though we say: "Up to where I sit on the continuum is still an honest way to be a good Jew. But those on the other side are really just hypocrites." Whether it's a matter of nationality, ethnicity, or race, I am hungry for an opportunity to direct my energies toward an understanding of what it means to be a Jew, because then I will know the best way to live as one.

When I was the chairperson of the Department of Judaic and Near Eastern Studies at the University of Manitoba, I was invited to sit on a panel that addressed the question "Who is a Jew?" Also taking part was a city councilor who was trusted and accepted by all segments of the community. This councilor was so popular that whenever he ran for office he was sure to be elected. In his ward, the fact that he was a Communist was irrelevant.

We participated on this panel discussion at a time when Daniel Rufeisen, the Jew turned Carmelite monk, was applying to become an Israeli citizen under the Law of Return. Rufeisen's was the case that first raised the question of *mi hu Yehudi* for public debate. When my turn came to make a statement, I said that Rabbi Joseph Albo, a great teacher and author of the *Sefer ha-Ikkarim (Book of Core Principles),* wrote that to be a Jew it is necessary for a person to adhere to three things: belief in one God, belief that God cares what people do, and belief that God rewards and punishes people as an expression of divine care.

The councilor, I said, does *not* believe in those three principles, while Daniel Rufeisen does believe in them. Thus, according to Rabbi Joseph Albo, Daniel Rufeisen is more deserving to be recognized as a Jew than is the councilor.

Everyone in the audience became furious at the suggestion that their beloved representative might not count as a Jew while the traitorous convert should be counted. Finally someone said, "But, the councilor's children will marry Jewish children." The only thing I could say at that point was to promise them that the celibate monk's children would also not marry any gentiles.

THE ACCUSATIVE "JEW"

The word "Jew" is such a peculiar word. It is a descriptor that gets applied in different ways. Its meaning is only clear from its context— for instance, it could be used to describe someone's cultural heritage, religious practices, ancestral lineage, or theological beliefs. And any one or more of these common contexts may have nothing to do with the person being described. Think of how many people you know to whom the term "Jew" applies in one context but applies only marginally, if at all, in at least one of the others.

When I say, "Zalman is a Jew," "Jew" is in the accusative declension. It's like saying, "A piano is an instrument." What can be learned from such a statement? Is "Jew" a nationality, or a race, or a religion? The statement does not say much more than that I am a member of some larger class or kind, presumably of people. The problem with using "Jew" as a noun is that, as a noun, it objectifies. It locks me in, describing me without really communicating any essential aspects of me other than the "accidental trait" of my existence.

When I hear the word "Jew" used as a noun by someone who doesn't smile and look as Jewish as me, then I immediately wonder if this person is an enemy. When someone I know wants to talk to me about the fact that I'm a Jew, he will usually ask, "You're Jewish, aren't you?" The adjective with its "ish" ending is somehow preferable to the noun. It is not so accusatory. It's like being blonde or brunette. "What I am is American. But I am a Jew*ish* American."

Yet the adjective "Jewish" is also very limited. We usually use adjectives in three ways: as a base form, as a comparative, and as a superlative. For example, we might say, "Reform is Jewish, Conservative is Jewish*er,* and Orthodox is Jewish*est.*" However, that is nonsense. It simply does not describe the moves a person makes to become more or less Jewish. It is evident that "Jewish," the adjective, also does not tell us very much about our own volition. And what we will and commit to be is the most important consideration.

Suppose that I drop my concern about it being derogatory and use the word "Jew" as a verb, comparable to "practice" or "engage." If someone suggested that he was a better Jew than I am, I might inquire, "How often do you 'Jew'? If you 'Jew' many times a week, then you may in fact be a better Jew than I am." But what if I "Jew" with more energy, and put more thought into it? Is it frequency of practice that makes someone a good Jew, or the intensity and thought that goes into that practice?

One of the more significant and often exciting questions that we can ask ourselves is: "What benefit do I get from being a Jew, from 'Jewing' regularly and with intensity?" It remains the most real of all questions. And perhaps that very reality is why the asking can cause such discomfort.

If I, as an individual, do not have a good reason to continue to live as a Jew, then collectively the Jewish people has a problem— assimilation. If I live and interact with the environment in a functional, efficient way, then I no longer will keep myself separate from that same environment. If, on the other hand, I keep myself apart from the environment by saying, "Because I am a Jew, I cannot let myself blend in too much with what is around me," then it costs me more to be a Jew than it would cost me if I were not a Jew.

An observant Jewish man might wear a *yarmulke* at home, but he takes it off when he goes to work. Instead of having a beard, which many traditional men believe is a crucial part of Jewish observance, this man shaves with an electric razor. He goes out to lunch with colleagues and clients. How does he justify this behavior? Usually, the reason is something like: "I need to make a living and I don't want hassles about my Jewishness to interfere. I need to look like everyone else. But this is not a big problem, because my *yiddishkeit,* my Jewishness, is safe, deep in my heart. My business life is just on the outside, and when I am finished with work I go home, where I can be fully a Jew."

This approach will inevitably lead to assimilation, whether in his own life or in the lives of his children.

A *SHEYNER YID!* (A BEAUTIFUL JEW!)

People used to talk about being a Jew in a very different way. Our *zeydes* (grandfathers) and *bubbes* (grandmothers) might have said:

"Do you know Moishe?"

"Moishe? Who's Moishe?"

"You don't know Moishe? Moishe. The one who limps on one leg."

"Moishe who limps on one leg?"

"Moishe. Who limps on one leg. He's cross-eyed. He has a wart on his nose."

"Moishe who limps on one leg, is cross-eyed, and has a wart on his nose? Don't know him."

"Come on! Moishe! You don't know Moishe? The one who has the bent back, the wart on the nose, limps on one leg, crossed eyes."

"Oh, him! A *sheyner Yid!* A beautiful Jew!"

A point is finally reached where they can agree and confirm that Moishe is, indeed, a beautiful Jew. Then they are no longer talking about his bent back, crossed eyes, limping leg, and bewarted nose. They have moved from talking about Moishe's problems to the recognition that he is an exemplar of that quality which we call *Yisrael,* a *Yid*—a Jew.

The deeper levels of meaning that arise from a more cognitive perspective on what it means to be Jewish demand that we do our philosophical homework and ask ourselves what is our place in the fabric of the planet's life. Reason alone will not help us when the going gets tough. Here we need to pray and connect with the Divine and see ourselves as being a spark of the Living God. I need to fan the hidden spark in my soul, and always try to be a *sheyner Yid.*

THE RIGHT HONOURABLE THE LORD WOOLF was appointed Lord Chief Justice of England and Wales in 2000. From 1987 to 2000 he served as president of the Central Council of Jewish Social Services.

"To say with pride and confidence, regardless of the consequences, 'I am Jewish.'"

Throughout his life—at school, at work, and socially—a Jew is faced with situations where it can be convenient, more comfortable, and tempting to avoid identifying himself as a Jew. I have always hoped that when it mattered, I would not be tempted to take the convenient and comfortable course. I am afraid I have not always but usually observed my own standards.

I have been fortunate. I have never been faced with the ultimate challenge, as Danny was. I find it impossible to say, with certainty, how I would react to the challenge that Danny faced. What I can say is Danny's example would make it easier for me and for all Jews, now and in the future, to react in the way they would want to: to say with pride and confidence, regardless of the consequences, "I am Jewish."

I am grateful for the inspiration he has provided.

ANGELA WARNICK BUCHDAHL is the first Asian American in North America to be ordained as a rabbi or invested as a cantor. She graduated from Hebrew Union College and serves Westchester Reform Temple in Scarsdale, New York.

"At that moment I realized I could no sooner stop being a Jew than I could stop being Korean, or female, or *me*."

My father is a Jew and my mother is a Korean Buddhist. As the child of a mother who carried her own distinct ethnic and cultural traditions—and wore them on her face—I internalized the belief that I could never be "fully Jewish" because I could never be "purely" Jewish. My daily reminders included strangers' comments ("Funny, you don't look Jewish"), other Jews' challenges to my halakhic status, and every look in the mirror.

Jewish identity is not solely a religious identification, but also a cultural and ethnic marker. While we have been a "mixed multitude" since biblical times, over the centuries the idea of a Jewish race became popularized. After all, Jews have their own language, foods, and even genetic diseases. But what does the Jewish "race" mean to you if you are black and Jewish? Or Arab and Jewish? Or even German and Jewish, for that matter? How should Jewish identity be understood, given that *Am Yisrael* reflects the faces of so many nations?

Years ago, after a painful college summer of feeling marginalized and rejected as a Jew while living in Israel, I called my mother to declare that I no longer wanted to be Jewish. I did not look Jewish, I did not carry a Jewish name, and I no longer wanted the heavy burden of having to explain and prove myself every time I entered a new Jewish community. My Buddhist mother's response was profoundly simple: "Is that possible?" At that moment I realized I could no sooner stop being a Jew than I could stop being Korean, or female, or *me*. Judaism might not be my "race," but it is an internal identification as indestructible as my DNA.

Jewish identity remains a complicated and controversial issue in the Jewish community. Ultimately, Judaism cannot be about race, but must be a way of walking in this world that transcends racial lines. Only then will the "mixed multitude" truly be *Am Yisrael*.

A. B. YEHOSHUA, novelist and playwright, is one of Israel's most widely read authors.

"To be a Jew means to belong to a national group that can be left or joined, just as any other national group is left or joined."

We discover an astonishing fact in the classic halakhic definition. According to the Halakhah, nothing is said about the Jew's conduct, his thoughts, or basic principles of behavior. There is nothing indicating his homeland or language, or even the nature of his affiliation to a specific collective (such as maintaining solidarity with the Jewish people). A Jew is nothing more than a child of a Jewish mother, not even of a Jewish father. Is this biological fact really so compelling and binding? Not at all! Jews are not a race and never viewed themselves as such. They viewed themselves only as a people. According to the halakhic definition, a Jew, the son of a Jewish mother, who converts to Christianity ceases to be a Jew. That the Halakhah enables someone not born of a Jewish mother to become a Jew also indicates that the Jews do not constitute a race.

To be a Jew means to belong to a national group that can be left or joined, just as any other national group is left or joined. Countless Jews have abandoned the Jewish people, and the struggle now and in all generations against assimilation indicates that it is possible to leave the Jewish people, that the individual is not compelled to retain his membership in it.

We are now approaching the root of the matter. If we delve deep into the logic of the religious definition we see at its base another definition: A Jew is someone who identifies as a Jew.

Someone born of a Jewish mother is no longer considered a Jew if, for example, he converts to Christianity or to Islam. It is of no importance where the Jew goes. What matters is his desire to leave. It must be understood that in the past, when everyone had a religious identification, Judaism ruled that passing to any other religion turns the Jew into a non-Jew. But today, when the individual is not obliged to maintain a religious identity, a person can leave the Jewish people without having to pass through a religious corridor, even if according to the Halakhah it seems that he must. The determining factor is not the technical step of formal religious conversion but his desire no longer to identify with the Jewish people. A Jewish atheist can become a non-Jewish atheist; the passage through another religion is a dispensable formality.

The same holds for joining the Jewish people. The determining factor is the act of identification, free will, and not the formal conversion, which may be altogether meaningless for the convert who, let us assume, is a confirmed atheist. These religious corridors (for entry and exit) may be good as a salve for the conscience of religious establishments, but they are irrelevant and meaningless for someone who wants to enter or leave, and does so as a freely chosen act.

The definition I am proposing, that a Jew is someone who identifies as a Jew, is not one I would want to be maintained always, but this definition has been the realistic, correct, and genuine definition until now. It is the base definition underlying the halakhic definition. The halakhic definition, born in the recesses of Jewish history, was suited to a world and situation in which religion was the decisive element of a person's identity. The secular identity taking shape before our eyes in the world and in Israel (which always existed as a potential) exposes the deep and true definition at the foundation of the halakhic definition, that which declares that a Jew is someone who identifies as a Jew.

All the pseudo-Sartrean theories that would base Jewish self-identification on the existence of the Gentile (in the best circumstances) or the anti-Semite (in the worst circumstances), who forces the Jew to identify as such, are ridiculous. I don't need the Gentile's perception or the anti-Semite's hostility to establish my Jewish identity. Even if there weren't an anti-Semite in the world I would still want to identify as a Jew. How demeaning to present Jewish identity and belonging as a kind of trap from which there is no escape. Hundreds of thousands of Jews have left the Jewish people for good, as a matter of their own choosing, and have been lost forever among other peoples. To be a Jew is a matter of choice. This element of freedom in the act of Jewish identification has of late been obscured, but it is an element of tremendous importance, for it brings with it responsibility. If I identify as a matter of free choice I assume certain responsibilities. When young people repeatedly ask, as they have been doing with increasing frequency since the Yom Kippur War: Is it possible to cut one's ties with the Jewish people? Is it possible to carry out a "disengagement of forces" with the Jewish people? Or, in the words of a soldier, is it possible to be just a person?—to all of these questions my answer is clear: It most definitely is possible. But if a person decides to identify as a Jew he assumes responsibility for his identification, since his decision was freely made. I do not ignore the social, cultural, and family influences on a decision about identification, but these are not sufficient to determine the identification. It requires willed choice. The dimension of freedom, which always formed part of Jewish identification and which has recently been obscured by notions of Jewish "fate" and by the experience of the Holocaust, needs to be highlighted once again. The sense of freedom immediately lightens the sense of responsibility. A man is capable of mighty actions if he has a sense of freedom, while feeling coerced only depresses and incenses him.

The element of freedom in the act of identification is also what makes possible change and reinterpretation of Judaism. I do not dismiss those who think only of continuity, who want to keep alive the "ember" they imagine has been passed on to them. But no less legitimate is the desire of those who want to introduce change in Judaism, with which they identify as an act of free will.

MICHAEL CHLENOV is an anthropologist living in Moscow. He is a professor at the Moscow Maimonides Academy and the Moscow State University, and chairman of Va'ad, the Federation of Jewish Organizations and Communities of Russia.

"Judaism is a tool of resistance wherever you come across words, behavior, events that you feel are evil."

When I was a kid, my father explained to me that "Judaism is a tool of resistance." I didn't understand what he meant then. During the rest of my long life I learned more and more about Jews and Judaism. Some parts of our heritage I accepted easily, others with reluctance, some others I did not accept at all. But in comprehending Judaism as a whole, I became convinced of my father's words. Yes, Judaism is a tool of resistance. Wherever you come across words, behavior, or events that you feel are evil, you almost automatically react with three simple words: "I am Jewish!" That means you are not ready to be part of evil. Even if you will be murdered, as Daniel Pearl, blessed be his memory, was, by these words you resist, you are not part, you are not with. Remember Mordechai, who said that he would not kneel before Haman because he was Jewish.

DANIEL SCHORR is a senior news analyst at National Public Radio. He has covered the news for more than six decades.

"We Jews are searchers for truth."

I have been first a Jewish journalist, and then a Jew in journalism. For seven years, until inducted into the Army in 1942, I worked for the Jewish Telegraphic Agency in New York. That involved everything from interviewing Bruno Walter, a Jewish conductor, to editing dispatches from Europe that told of the dark night descending over the Jews. Released from the Army in 1945, I decided that journalism would be my lifelong vocation. But not Jewish journalism, which I found too limiting. The hunt for the Jewish Angle was frustrating. So I became a Jew in journalism. I went to the Netherlands, first as a "stringer" (freelancer) for, of all things, the *Christian Science Monitor,* then later the *New York Times.* In 1952 I applied for a staff position with the *Times* and was tentatively accepted. Then the appointment was mysteriously canceled. Two years later, a shame-faced foreign editor, Emanuel Friedman, and assistant managing editor, Ted Bernstein, invited me to dinner to confess to me that the appointment had been canceled because I was Jewish. Executive editor Turner Catledge had decided to freeze the hiring of Jews as correspondents because of a need to maintain flexibility in covering the Middle East.

And so, in 1953, on the invitation of Edward R. Murrow, I joined the staff of CBS News, first as State Department correspondent, and later at the United Nations, in Moscow, where I opened the CBS bureau, and in Germany. My CBS bosses asked me whether, as a Jew, I anticipated any personal conflicts in working in Germany. I said I thought not. And indeed, I had no great problem. In fact, I came to admire the way the new generation of Germans sought to win their way back into civilized society.

The matter of being Jewish arose only once in my six years in Germany. As the time neared to leave, I was invited to lunch by an official of the Government Information Office, who said he had to ask me a delicate question. The president of the Federal Republic was prepared to confer on me a decoration, the Grand Cross of Merit, but needed my assurance that I would not reject it. I was amused and touched. The mighty German government stood in fear of a Jewish journalist. (My wife, a refugee from Germany, had some reservations about my accepting a German award, but that is another story.)

Oddly enough, it was in the United States, to which I returned in 1966, that I was made aware of anti-Semitism in high places. Assigned by CBS to cover Watergate, I learned of Oval Office conversations in which President Nixon, Chief of Staff H. R. Haldeman, and adviser John Ehrlichman indulged in anti-Semitic invective, sometimes singling out "that son-of-a-bitch Dan Schorr."

I was a pretty good Watergate reporter, winning three Emmy awards. Did being Jewish have anything to do with it? We Jews are searchers for truth, sometimes called investigative reporting. Also, having grown up poor in the Bronx, I had a need to prove myself to the *goyim*. There! I've said it. But would a Jewish ethic ever cause me to kill a story that I had unearthed? It happened once, and I tell about it in my memoir, *Staying Tuned,* from which I quote:

> My last major assignment in Poland was to produce, in 1959, an hour-long documentary, "Poland—Country on a Tightrope," for Ed Murrow's *CBS Reports* series. This gave me a production team and the time and resources for a deeper look at Poland—its people, its schools, its fast-decollectivizing farms.
>
> And Oswiecim ... Auschwitz.
>
> In 1959 not many from the West had visited Auschwitz, and I was not prepared for what I would see and try to capture on film. I have always tried to separate my Jewish heritage from my reporting, but keeping emotion under control in Auschwitz, where members of my family may have died, was not easy.
>
> I had to read parts of my script several times, trying to control a catch in my throat and sound detached as I reported, "Here was the greatest death factory ever devised ... where a million died ... pushed through these gas chambers at a rate of sixty thousand a day ... their bodies efficiently moved out and lifted mechanically into brick ovens ... after their clothes and hair and gold teeth had been removed.... For many, there was no room in the ovens, and they were buried in open pits ... now these stagnant ponds. If you run your hand along the bottom, you will pick up human ashes and fragments of bone."
>
> I interviewed a guide, Tadeusz Szymanski, who had Auschwitz number 200,314 tattooed on his forearm, asking whether he found it painful to be working there. He said, "When some of my friends were carried off to be executed, they shouted, 'Remember us and avenge us!' So

I am here to see that they are remembered."

As we talked, a group of young Poles passed, ushered along by a woman who also had an Auschwitz tattoo. She sounded so remarkably matter-of-fact: "Here stood a crematorium…. Here was where people were pushed into a room, and then the doors were sealed, and the gas—so-called Cyclon B—was released. In most cases they died in ten minutes."

A young Polish girl gulped. Mostly they just stood and stared, and no one asked any questions.

While working on this Polish documentary, I ran into what may have been the greatest ethical dilemma of my career. Our little CBS cavalcade of three rented cars, carrying the camera crew, the producer, and a Polish interpreter, was driving through a small town in eastern Poland, not far from the Soviet border, when we espied a strange sight. It was a caravan of about ten horse-drawn wagons, carrying a few dozen people and piled high with their possessions. Stopping to talk to them, I discovered that they were Polish Jews and that I could converse with them in the Yiddish that I had hardly used since childhood.

They had come across the border in the Soviet Union and were on their way to a railway station, bound for Vienna and from there to Israel. Our camera was soon set up in the muddy road, and I interviewed them in Yiddish. They could not tell me, however, how it was that they were permitted to travel to Israel. Out of consideration for Arab opinion, Russia and its satellites officially banned emigration to Israel.

Back in Warsaw the next day I consulted the Israeli minister, Shimon Amir, a chess-playing friend of mine.

"They told you they were on their way to Israel, and you have that on film?" he asked.

"Yes," I said. "But how is it possible?"

"All right, since you know this much, I will tell you the rest, and then you will decide what to do."

He explained that the Jews came from a part of

Poland that had been annexed by the Soviet Union, that there were several thousand more caught on the Soviet side who had survived the war and the Holocaust and were desperately anxious to leave. Israel had negotiated a delicate secret arrangement with the Soviet and Polish governments. The Jews would be "repatriated" to Poland with the understanding that they would almost immediately leave the country—bound for Israel.

"But there was one condition attached to the agreement," said Amir. "The arrangement must remain a secret. If any word becomes public, the Soviets will immediately cancel the arrangement."

"So," my friend concluded, "you can decide, Mr. Schorr. Put this on television, and you condemn thousands of Jews to remaining in the Soviet Union."

Each evening, my cameraman would pack up the cans of film we had shot that day and ship them by air to New York, later to be assembled with narration for our documentary. But I held back the reel with the Jewish interviews. It stayed on my desk in the hotel next day, and the next day and the next. I would have liked to have consulted Murrow, but could not do so over an open telephone. I never decided, exactly, that for humanitarian reasons I would practice self-censorship. I simply kept postponing the decision until it was too late. After a while, my camera crew stopped asking about it.

This was a profound violation of my journalistic ethic that a reporter has no right to interpose himself between information legitimately acquired and the public he serves. Once before I had done so—in the case of a Dutch queen. This seemed even tougher.

My *CBS Reports* program, "Poland—Country on a Tightrope," went on the air, documenting the political chill settling over Poland as Gomulka came to terms with his Soviet bosses. Auschwitz was in my film. But not the caravan of Jews making their way to Israel.

When next I was in New York, I brought the reel of

film with me and went to see Murrow. He had strong pro-Israel sympathies himself. When he was sick, my Zionist mother had a tree planted in Israel in his name as a prayer for his recovery. His first question to me was, "How is my tree doing?"

I then produced the can of film and explained how, against all my principles, I had withheld it. All he said was, "I understand."

STEFANIE STOLER, 19, Hamburg, Germany

Being Jewish is very important and not easy for me at the same time. Growing up and living in Germany, my Judaism has shaped me incredibly and gives me strength as well as a feeling of belonging. Being and feeling Jewish makes me happy, although I sometimes tend to be afraid of expressing it in a total non-Jewish, often not very understanding world.

MAUREEN LIPMAN, CBE, is a leading British entertainer, writer, and actress.

"To know, to talk to myself, to contradict, to question."

I am Jewish because on a blistering Saturday night in July with a party (Brazilian theme) next door—to which I'm invited—I am sitting here typing these words, curious to see what I'll say.

I am Jewish because when a fraud is unmasked, or an act of terror or ill will is reported, my first instinct is to scan the report to see if his name is Abromovitz. My second feeling is relief when his name is ethnically different from mine.

I am Jewish because when I am needed to protest against the obscenity of chained women in our community, or to protest on behalf of a Nepalese asylum seeker or the despotic military rule in Burma, I turn up for them all.

I am Jewish because when my mother despairs telephonically because my wonderful children either have no partners or non-Jewish ones I defend their choices vigorously and berate her for caring only what others think. Then, in the bath or over Sabbath candles or on a long walk with a friend, I wish for miracles like Jewish grandchildren, Jewish in-laws, and the approbation of people I don't even know.

I am Jewish because the rising tide of anti-Semitism alarms and bewilders me and even more alarming is that sometimes I almost understand it. And recognize the innate racism in myself.

I am Jewish because in my schooldays in the north of England, in the fifties, I felt different and was proud to be different, because it meant extra days off and fascinating food and a whole extra set of friends and not going to morning assembly. Except I rather liked the hymns and wondered if I was also missing something on account of my "differentness."

I am Jewish because when I learn that seventeenth-century Jews had to wear yellow identification badges and return to the ghetto by curfew, I am both furious and resigned. It's the resigned bit, I know, that is the one I have to fight.

I am Jewish because I really look forward, on a Friday night, to going to bed with *The Jewish Chronicle* and reading the names chosen in the "Births" column. I'm particularly warmed when I come across "*Mazel tov!* and welcome to Kimberly Savannah India Tuchbedirber, long-awaited sister for Crispin St. John and Sebastian Jolyon ... named in loving memory of *Bubbe* and *Zeyde,* Miriam and Shlomo Goldblatt."

I am Jewish because when, as Mother in the film *The Pianist,* I put a pan of chicken soup down on the table in the family dinner scene, I realized it was the fourteenth time I'd done a variation of that action in thirty-five years as an actress. Which is fourteen times more often than I've sipped champagne in a punt, entered the Forest of Arden in a pair of tights, hunted to hounds, or glided through French doors cooing, "Croquet on the lawn, anyone?"

Furthermore, when, on the first day of rehearsals for the National Theatre's production of *Oklahoma!,* we were asked to introduce ourselves, my response was, "My name is Maureen Lipman and I'm playing Aunt Eller because Trevor Nunn is doing the whole show Jewish and renaming it *Oyklahoma!!*" For a moment some people believed it.

I am Jewish because I am rendered legless by the Marx Brothers, illogically proud of Steven Spielberg, understanding of Winona, defensive of Woody, amused by Billy Crystal, and slightly bemused by the United Kingdom success of Jackie Mason.

I am Jewish because when I visited Yad Vashem I came out dry-eyed and determined, but when I visited Auschwitz I came out dragging my bones, weighed down by a depression breathed in from grief embedded in the fabric of the walls.

I am Jewish because I must go and prepare food for my husband but I cannot stop creating words on a page. I am curious to know, to talk to myself, to contradict, to question.

MIKE WALLACE is senior correspondent on *Sixty Minutes* and has been a reporter for CBS News for forty years.

"But I'm an American reporter, a Jew who believes in going after facts on the ground."

Occasionally down the years I've winced at being labeled a "self-hating Jew" because my reporting from the Middle East was perceived as tainted by hostility toward Israel. It wasn't true, of course, but I figured it came with the territory, meaning that I was deemed biased because I reported accurately what was happening on the other side, with the Palestinians.

And it turned out that every once in a while it was helpful to me as a reporter, for the fact that I am Jewish and not in the pocket of the Israelis seemed to appeal to movers and shakers in Cairo and Damascus and Riyadh, who were willing to talk to me on the record with some candor.

I've worked the Middle East beat since the 1950s, back in the days of Moshe Dayan, Golda Meir, Menachem Begin, Anwar Sadat,

Yasir Arafat, Mu'ammar Gadhafi. My relations with all of them, with the sole exception of Begin, were cordial and straightforward. But when I questioned Begin in a fashion that I thought reasonable and he found belligerent, our conversation was brought to an end by the intervention of Ezer Weizman, his defense minister, who shortly afterward took me for a friendly drink at a nearby bar.

My eyes had first been opened to Israeli/Palestinian realities by two pioneering figures from that part of the world. Back in the fifties, Reuven Dafne, a Romanian Israeli, and Fayez Sayegh, a Palestinian Christian, two friends of mine, gave me a primer course on the complicated subject, for which I remain grateful.

I have long admired the courage and determination of the Israelis and sympathized with their yearning for a secure state. I have similar feelings about the Palestinians. But I'm an American reporter, a Jew who believes in going after facts on the ground, as Daniel Pearl did, and reporting them accurately, let the chips fall where they may.

NATAN SHARANSKY, founder of the Israel for Immigration Party, spent nine years in a Soviet prison prior to emigrating in 1986. He is now the Minister of Jerusalem and Diaspora Affairs.

"Only a person who is connected to his past, to his people, and to his roots can be free, and only a free person has the strength to act for the benefit of the rest of humanity."

There were more than a few Jews among the leaders of the Bolshevik Revolution, just as there have been more than a few Jews among the leaders of many other movements that have sought to save mankind. They believed with all their souls that the way to redeem humanity and create a better world was to achieve absolute equality. All human beings are equal, and equality means no differences. All human beings should therefore be identical. Ethnicity, class, religion, and national characteristics belonged to an old and decaying world. The time for such distinctions had passed. The Jewish revolutionaries wanted to release the iron reins that held each person to his tribe, that tied each Jewish man and woman to a unique heritage and culture, and to create a new man—Homo sovieticus.

While these were assimilated Jews, a very Jewish aspiration was the basis for their actions. They wanted to be a light to the gentiles. To have influence, to lead, to mend the world. The way to do that, as they understood it, was to leave their villages, the *shtetls,* to erase their particularist Jewish identity, to meld utterly into their surroundings in order to create the new man who would live in the better world they so longed for.

I was one of the millions of new human beings in the Bolshevik experiment, which was successful far beyond its makers' expectations. Section five in my identity papers informed me that I was a Jew, but I hadn't a clue as to what that meant. I knew nothing of Jewish history, language, or customs, nor had I even heard of their existence. My father, who loved to tell stories, would sometimes tell us tales from the Bible. We heard about Joseph and his brothers, about Samson and Delilah, but they were stories just like all his other stories. No one told us that these were the history of our nation, no one thought to mention that these stories were connected to us in any way. Like all Soviet Jews of my generation, I grew up rootless, unconnected, without identity.

With our Jewish identity lacking positive content, only anti-Semitism gave it any meaning at all. To be a Jew was to be hated and discriminated against, to have fewer options. To be a Jew was to have a perpetual problem. We were weak, and we sought ways to escape our fate. Excelling at science, art, or chess were all ways to run away from that mysterious, inexplicable Jewishness. It not only failed to give us strength, identity, and meaning, but was actually a burden and interfered with our lives.

The strength arrived, unexpectedly, from a far-off land and war. The stellar Israeli victory in the Six Day War enabled us to stand tall. People suddenly treated Jews differently. Even the anti-Semitic jokes changed. They were no longer about the cowardly, mendacious Jew.

They were about the upstart, brave, and victorious Jew.

It was through the war that I became aware of the Jewish state, and of the language and culture it embodied. I was suddenly exposed to the existence of the Jewish people, to the existence of tradition and culture. I was no longer a disconnected individual in an alienating and hostile world. I was a person with an identity and roots. I felt that I had a history, a nation, and a country behind me. That I had, at the end of the earth, a homeland. That I belonged. That feeling was my companion through years of struggle for human rights, in the framework of the Zionist movement, and through long years in prison. Even in solitary confinement I believed that the Jewish people and the State of Israel would fight for me. I was not alone. I was arrested a few months after the Entebbe operation. The operation signified that Israel was prepared to go any distance to save its citizens, and it made a huge impression on me. During my years in prison, every aircraft in Siberia's skies sounded to me like the rescue force coming to liberate me. True, I was not rescued by an airplane or a bold military mission, but I was certainly released from my prison by the Jewish people and the State of Israel. I truly was not alone.

Identity and a sense of belonging give life strength and meaning. A person who has his Jewish identity is not enslaved. He is free even if they throw him in prison, even if they torture him. For me and for my colleagues in the Zionist movement, Jewish identity was a source of pride, and pride gave us the strength to fight. At first for our own self-respect, and afterward for our national honor, and in the end for the destruction of the evil Communist empire and for freedom throughout the world.

The Jews who led the Bolshevik Revolution believed that rubbing out their Jewish identity was the way to redeem the world. In practice, they lent a hand to one of the cruelest regimes mankind has known. Instead of being a light to the gentiles, they brought a great darkness on the world. Slashing off their roots did not create a new, strong, and free man. Instead, it trampled on human dignity and turned the individual into a slave and chattel. We have learned that liberation in fact depends on strengthening identity, on returning to one's roots. Only a person who is connected to his past, to his people, and to his roots can be free, and only a free person has the strength to act for the benefit of the rest of humanity.

Daniel Pearl's last words testify that he was a man who knew where he came from. He was not alienated from his identity. Only such a man could have been free and brave enough to take upon himself the important and dangerous mission during which he was murdered. The freedom that beat within him, the freedom that came from within his identity, is what gave him the strength to leave his land and his family and to do what he thought was right and important, for the sake of the rest of the world.

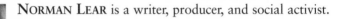

NORMAN LEAR is a writer, producer, and social activist.

"A 'cultural Jew' ... total Jew."

I identify with everything in life as a Jew. The Jewish contribution over the centuries to literature, art, science, theater, music, philosophy, the humanities, public policy, and the field of philanthropy awes me and fills me with pride and inspiration. As to Judaism, the religion: I love the congregation and find myself less interested in the ritual. If that describes me to others as a "cultural Jew," I have failed myself. My description, as I feel it, would be: total Jew.

DAVID HOROVITZ is the editor of *The Jerusalem Report* newsmagazine and author of *A Little Too Close to God: The Thrills and Panic of a Life in Israel* and the new *Still Life with Bombers: Israel in the Age of Terrorism.*

"I am Jewish, and it colors everything I've done, do, and will do."

Sometimes I say it differently. Sometimes I say, "I'm a journalist from Israel." But it comes down to the same thing: I am Jewish, and it colors everything I've done, do, and will do.

It means I was born into a family with a rabbinical heritage that my beloved Uncle Markie spent years tracing back through the ages. When my mother was single-handedly raising my sister and me, it gave her the framework on which to construct our lives. It determined the school I went to, and that there would be little punch-ups some days with the kids from the other school down the road, the non-Jewish school, on the way to the underground station after lessons. The Jewish thing, and that unmistakably Jewish name that came with it, Horovitz, meant I knew, very early on, that I wasn't completely English, or that even if I was back then, I was something else as well.

It meant I learned to read Hebrew, and went to Israel for a short school trip, and felt connected, if not immediately at home. It kept me coming back to Israel, the country seeping into me, resonating somewhere within me.

It's because she is Jewish that my wife-to-be was sitting in a political science class at the Hebrew University in Jerusalem, the fourth daughter of the sole Holocaust survivor of a big, boisterous, decimated Hasidic family from Lodz. My father-in-law, orphaned by the Nazis, had set her life on its course to Jerusalem because he knew that in Israel, like nowhere else on earth, we Jews get to choose our own fate, rather than rely for our survival on the tolerance of others. His family in Poland had depended on such tolerance, and been wiped out.

It's why I've stubbornly insisted, thus far at least, on raising my children here, even through months and years when, simply because we are Jewish and intent on survival, closing the front door in the morning meant entering a grisly lottery: going out into the world in the certainty that today, every day, significant numbers of people were dreaming of killing us, and some of them were going to try. Stubborn. Perhaps, as a father and a husband, even irresponsible. But not irresponsible as a Jew.

I see myself as one of the fortunate heirs to the centuries of Jewish tradition—a tradition of relentless questioning and self-examination. That's why I was drawn to journalism and that's why I was drawn to Israel, where the questions and the constantly reexamined arguments truly matter, where our national destiny is still unresolved and we Jews here, all of us, help shape it.

Not long ago, at an international conference in Jordan, I spotted a white-robed Saudi prince alone on a plump sofa overlooking the Dead Sea. "I'm a journalist from Israel," I told him. "Perhaps we could speak for a while." He looked up and nodded benign assent. He had read my nametag, confirmed that I am Jewish, and that was the filter through which he looked at me as we talked. And it was, as ever, the prism through which I looked at him.

 Kitty Dukakis is a social worker, assisting refugees since 1981, and a member of the United States Holocaust Memorial Council. She is also a dancer and has been a modern dance instructor since 1953.

"More than matzo balls, chopped liver, and chicken soup."

I have felt Jewish since my earliest memories.

My father, a musician who passed away at ninety-four, was born to Russian immigrant parents who arrived in Boston at the turn of the twentieth century. My Poppa (grandfather) was a left-handed tailor and also a conductor on the streetcars in Cambridge and Somerville, where they lived. He was not a very religious man, but proud of his Jewish background. My Boby (grandmother) was very traditional and went to synagogue until she couldn't walk anymore. In her old age, she would stand on street corners with a *pushke* (charity box) collecting money for Hadassah. I remember when I was very young sitting with her in the balcony of her old *shul* (synagogue) and expressing unhappiness that my male first cousins were allowed to be downstairs.

My mother's biological father was Irish, and her mother was a Hungarian Jew who was the oldest of nine children. She was adopted by wealthy German Jews, who were not religious at all, and she began to learn about Judaism and its traditions after she married my dad.

My immediate family did not belong to a synagogue, so my

understanding of my religion and its traditions came from Shabbat and other traditions at my grandparents' and aunts' homes. Growing up, my neighborhood was mostly Jewish, as were the grammar and high school I attended. When I went to Israel in 1978, bringing a mixed group of Christians and Jews from Massachusetts, I had a profound and spiritual experience.

Being Jewish for me is more than matzo balls, chopped liver, and chicken soup, though food and the generosity that go with it are very much a part of who I am. I love the Jewish traditions and was brought up to believe that fairness with all people was sacred.

Jamie Sistino, 19, Charleston, South Carolina

Growing up in an interfaith household, being actively Jewish was a choice for me. Judaism now can be seen throughout all of my actions in my life. Being Jewish is who I am before anything else. Before I am an American, or a girl, or from South Carolina, I am Jewish.

 **Thomas L. Friedman** is a three-time Pulitzer Prize–winning columnist for the *New York Times*. He is the author of *From Beirut to Jerusalem, The Lexus and the Olive Tree: Understanding Globalization,* and *Longitudes and Attitudes: Exploring the World After September 11.*

"A very important part of my identity, but not the only part of my identity."

I have to confess, I always had a hard time reading the stories about Danny Pearl's abduction. It was just too close to home for me. I did not know Danny. Our career paths never crossed, but it was always clear to me that our dreams and passions must have. We were both American Jewish young men who loved journalism and had a particular passion and interest in the Arab and Muslim worlds. We both pursued those passions and interests without regard to the inherent dangers our biographies contained. After all, we were not just reporters. We were not just American reporters. We were reporters operating in the Muslim world in an age when the Arab-Israeli conflict had made the statement "I am Jewish" a potentially dangerous thing.

How did one deal with that? I always found that the best way to approach this situation was first of all to be totally honest about who you are: "I am Jewish" is something I said many times to people over the years, without fear of attack. My experience was that people were more curious than hostile when they met a Jewish reporter, and they respected you more when you made clear that you are as proud of your own faith as they are of theirs. They also tend to want to engage you more, and argue with you more, because they sense that you are not just a reporter but also a participant somehow in their drama. They sense that you are not just passing through, that you have stakes in the outcome of this story, and that often attracts people more than repels them.

When I visited Saudi Arabia a few months after 9/11, after writing very critical articles about the Saudis, I was always struck by how many Saudis, who were not prepped to meet me, greeted me with some variation of "You know, I hate everything that you write. Would you come to my home for dinner so I can get some friends together to talk to you?"

And that gets to another survival mechanism I use to defuse my "I am Jewishness"—try to be a good listener. People tell me that Danny was a very good and sympathetic listener. I am not surprised. Being a good listener is the greatest survival strategy, not to mention secret, to good journalism. It has never failed me. Because no matter how hostile people might be to you or your point of view, when you show them the respect of listening, they will eventually be disarmed. Listening is the foundation of all good journalism, and the best bulletproof vest in a dangerous environment.

But then there is one other survival mechanism I adopted. And that is denial. You tell yourself that if you listen hard enough, if you try to be fair, and are honest and up front about who you are, no one will want to do you harm just because of who you are, or who your parents are, or what your religion is. After all, you're just a journalist representing your newspaper, not your faith. That denial is critical, albeit reckless, because without it you would never really be able to operate in some situations, like a bad neighborhood in Karachi.

Unfortunately, Daniel's ordeal is a reminder that denial is just that—denial of an underlying reality. And the reality is the huge contrast in the role religion plays in the life of a Western correspondent and many of the people he or she may be covering.

For me, the phrase "I am Jewish" means what I suspect it meant to Daniel—a very important part of my identity, but not the only part of my identity. I see myself as an American, a journalist, a *New York Times* columnist, a husband, a father, a man of the world, a Jew. The last is by no means least. My faith defines not only the pathway I choose to connect with God, but also, just as important, a big part of my cultural and communal root system. Being Jewish is a big part of my olive tree, the thing that anchors me in the world. But it is not the only root. Because being an American is also very much part of my olive tree. "American Jew," "Jewish American," "American Jewish writer for the *New York Times*," it doesn't matter how you put it. They all capture me, and they are all important. They all locate where I've been and where I'm going.

Danny, I suspect, was also a multidimensional person, who found himself caught up in a one-dimensional world, a world where the only identity that mattered was religious identity. In that sense, if "I am Jewish" were indeed Danny Pearl's last words, they said so much more about his murderers than they did about him. For Danny too, religion was just one part of his rich identity, a proud and important part, no doubt, but just one part of who he was. But for his captors it was everything. Because they were men full of hate, full of intolerance, full of bile, for whom religious identity was all-defining—the key to explaining friend and foe, good and bad, who shall live and who shall die. They were barren, impoverished, one-dimensional people. They had to torture Danny to reduce him to their one-dimensional level. They had to squeeze every other bit of identity out of him. So when they got him to say "I am Jewish" as his last words, in truth they got him to reveal only a little bit about himself, but everything about themselves.

It is precisely because Danny was Jewish, and so many other things, that his memory lives on, and it is precisely because his kidnappers were hateful, and nothing else, that no one remembers who they were or what they even stood for.

BERNICE RUBENS is a Booker Award–winning novelist and American Blue Ribbon Award–winning documentary filmmaker.

"We hear a joyous cry of survival."

I was born in Wales and when people ask me if I am Welsh, I say, "I'm Jewish, and that's enough to be getting on with." It sounds as if being Jewish is a burden, and in a way, it is. But it's also a blessing.

Let's consider first the burden, that constant niggle of anti-Semitism. Many reasons have been suggested for this bigotry: economic, religious, and social. But it is something more. Something far more difficult to fight. It is man's perennial and neurotic need to scapegoat. Over the years, the target of this need has varied. American Indians, blacks, homosexuals, Armenians, asylum seekers, but in the span of history, the Jews are high in the pecking order. And especially now, with Israel open to virulent criticism. Out come those innate anti-Semites who have at last found a respectable label for their racism. They call it anti-Zionism and that passes as viable.

But the blessings of being Jewish are legion. Our historical bequest is sublime. I have inherited a fragmented but highly creative exile and, since 1948, a home. I don't know that I want to settle there. I prefer the creative spur of exile. It sanctions my outsiderness and puts my identity excitedly at risk. I'd sooner travel in transit from one exile to another. I do not want to arrive. But wherever I am I shall be Jewish, and that sound will inform every syllable I write. I am blessed with a long ancestry of wisdom, prophecy, and promise, a line of overwhelming creative achievement, courage, humor, and, above all, a dogged and chronic permanence, the greatest legacy of all.

Daniel Pearl's last words were a cry of bewilderment and pain. But in their echo we hear a joyous cry of survival.

LEON BOTSTEIN has been president of Bard College since 1975. He has been the music director of the American Symphony Orchestra since 1992, and was also recently appointed the music director of the Jerusalem Symphony Orchestra. In addition, he is co-artistic director of the Bard Music Festival and artistic director of the American Russian Young Artists Orchestra.

> "Being Jewish represents an inspiration to assert genuine individuality, to resist reductive group labels, and to transform one's life from the ordinary to the extraordinary.... In Judaism, learning is prayer."

Being Jewish is a matter of fact and, for most of us, a consequence of birth. External perception of the meaning of being Jewish inevitably engages the dialogue one has with oneself about the indelible facts of one's being. My generation has been, historically speaking, lucky. We were born after the Holocaust. In my case, being born in Europe as a child of Russian and Polish Jews who emigrated to the United States shaped my own relationship to my identity as a Jew. Nonetheless, for all American Jews of my generation, the decline in overt anti-Semitism in America since the 1950s and the current nearly universal status of Jews as middle class and white did not make being Jewish entirely unremarkable to others. What has changed in my lifetime is that, as a result of the success of integration and acculturation, Jews have become all too normal, too typically complacent, lazy, and unengaged with learning and public service. This process of normalization has accelerated as we have become more privileged. Predictably, Jews have become too allied with a narrow conservative view of social justice and have broken with a traditional historical alliance with the poor and the oppressed against the entrenched vested interests in government and the marketplace.

Indeed, being Jewish has become on the one hand more and more peripheral and incidental among those fully at home with

American life. On the other hand, for others, being Jewish has become entirely a matter of religious conviction. Furthermore, over the course of time, being Jewish in the American diaspora has become quite distinct as a source of identity from being a Jew in Israel, or better yet, an Israeli. And for those of us who would wish Israel to become more consistently a secular democracy, Israel's place in the world, particularly recently, has changed the dynamics between the Jewish state and the diaspora.

Consequently, those of us for whom being Jewish is consistent with agnosticism or even atheism, and who are Zionists but critical of most recent Israeli governments with respect to the role of religion in politics and the Palestinians, find ourselves in a place of loneliness, even among American Jews. In political terms, we are isolated from the neoconservative right and from the anti-Zionist left. In the diaspora, the revival of a radical fundamentalism within Judaism has split the unity of the community. Intolerance among the denominations is rampant. The religious revival in America has marginalized those for whom being Jewish is a matter of secular cultural traditions. For us, community membership in the synagogue should create the ideal place for rational and severe skepticism, innovation, debate, and learning, not superstition or blind adherence to tradition and ritual.

However, the idealism of Daniel Pearl reminds us that being Jewish represents an inspiration to assert genuine individuality, to resist reductive group labels, and to transform one's life from the ordinary to the extraordinary. That transformation depends on learning, the life of the mind, and the cultivation of idealism. In Judaism, learning is prayer, for it celebrates the human capacity for language and thought. Perhaps being Jewish in one's own way carries the danger of loneliness, but the traditions of Judaism and patterns of Jewish identity provide the unique chance to use the solitude of thought and study to reconfigure loneliness into the struggle for truth and justice.

PART II:

HERITAGE

 SHIMON PERES was born in Belorussia in 1923 and immigrated to Israel at the age of eleven. He worked closely with David Ben-Gurion and filled numerous positions in the service of his country in almost every sphere of government and public service. He was awarded the Nobel Peace Prize in 1994.

"I am a son of this people, a nation that is adamant about remembering the past, inspired by its heritage, receptive to change, undaunted by the great prophecy that forges the destiny of the Jewish people, as in the words of the verse: 'old from new produce.'"

The language of the Jewish people has no brother; its religion, no sister; its history, no family. The question I ask myself is, why? And the answer is not simple. Let's examine, for a start, the matter of the language. It is interesting to note that it is the only ancient language that was revived in the Mediterranean. The Egyptians do not speak in the language of hieroglyphics; the Syrians do not speak Assyrian; the Iraqis do not speak Babylonian; the Greeks do not speak ancient Greek; and the Italians do not speak Latin.

What I find riveting, as a Jew, is the enormous tension, or colossal bridge, that straddles the ancient past—deep, obdurate, rebellious—and the future—demanding, unpredictable, conditional, regenerated, revolutionary, and even somewhat brazen. I am moved by this tension, by the fact that I am a son of this people, a nation that is adamant about remembering the past, inspired by its heritage, receptive to change, undaunted by the great prophecy that forges the destiny of the Jewish people, as in the words of the verse: "old from new produce." I sometimes feel as one that must wander on foot along the lanes of history and soar on the wings of my imagination to a new destination; this destination might be distant, but the objective can in turn give birth to yet another new destination.

I feel that this tension prevents me from sinking into a sense of complacency. For creative faculties, and revolutionary deeds, emanate from a feeling of imperfection. They stem from the need to break new ground, seek an as-yet-uncharted path, that exists in some undefined location—something that is fueled by ancient values and new challenges, and provides a ray of hope to every person who wishes to climb to an ever-higher peak. I feel like a man who hungers for such a goal, and Judaism generates my appetite. Judaism is not a religion, it is a faith. It is not governed by any hierarchy imposed by the Almighty God, and all men, who in any case have been created in His image, can communicate directly with Him. As such, there is no need to separate faith from state. The essence of a Jewish state is that it is, first and foremost, a state that is founded on faith—a state that is distinguished by spiritual faith, and not necessarily a state that is controlled by a religious apparatus.

The Ten Commandments on which Judaism hinges also constitute the cornerstone of Western Civilization. Judaism was first to contest idolatry and slavery. It also spoke against superiority of race, color, nationality, or man. If superiority does exist, it is in matters of the spirit and not in the dominions of power. Sovereignty is moral, priority is intellectual, equality is human.

Our history has not been paved with joyful events. Quite the contrary. It has been a history of trials and tribulations, and the price we paid put faith to the test. I do not think that Judaism simply consists of a collection of rigid laws to be accepted and hallowed. It represents an assortment of ethnic challenges that spur man's discontent and fuel his perennial quest for perfection. This ideal does not come attired in a single garment, nor is it a final goal. It can be compared to Jacob's ladder: You climb one step after the next and gaze at the sky in the awareness that it is distant and unattainable. Yet the process of climbing the steps makes you feel you are in communion with God.

Possibly, if Judaism was more conciliatory toward Jesus, Christianity would never have been born. Some contend that Christianity is the consequence of a Jewish mistake. And had it not been made, today we would have counted hundreds of millions of Jews, instead of only fourteen million. We paid dearly for our obstinacy, but maybe this price enabled us to take huge steps forward in the annals of mankind, and while physically bruised and wounded, we have remained spiritually whole. And despite the fact that our body practically did not develop, it nevertheless managed to carry on its shoulders the weight of our faith, whose power is manifestly greater than the size of the shoulders that support it.

My biography as a Jew is imbued with awe and reverence for Jewish history. I was born in a small town in White Russia. It was totally Jewish—not a single *goy* lived there. Therefore, I experienced the taste of Jewish isolation from the moment I was born. Two synagogues built from wood graced the town, as well as the *tarbut* (culture) school, where classes were conducted in Hebrew. My forebears—grandfather and grandmother—were extremely religious. My parents were already secular. The person who had the most impact on me in my childhood was my grandfather, may his soul rest in peace, Rabbi Zvi Melzer. He taught me, from when I was five years old, a page of Gemara every day. I used to go along with him to synagogue. On Yom Kippur he led the prayers (he had an impressive voice), and when it was time for *Kol Nidre,* all the worshipers, and I among them, spread the *tallit* over our heads. It was then that I was struck by a great sense of fear, because I suddenly found myself alone, with all my sins, in front of the Almighty God.

My mother, who was a librarian, introduced me to Shalom Aleichem on the one hand and to Dostoyevsky on the other. As a youngster I read *Crime and Punishment,* and again I was overcome with fear—this time out of anxiety for interrelations among people. Shalom Aleichem calmed the agitation with a wise smile that stemmed from the Jewish soul.

Until World War II, half the town's population immigrated to *Eretz Yisrael,* including many members of my family. The second half was annihilated by the Nazis. A quarter of the town's residents, my grandfather among them, were packed into the synagogue, and while wearing their *tallit,* were set on fire and burned alive by the Nazis.

I was eleven when I immigrated to Israel. I was captivated by the blue skies, the Hebrew letters, and sunburnt pioneers. I wanted to resemble them. I was sent to the Ben Shemen Youth Village to study agriculture and make ready to become a *kibbutznik*. I spent some time in two *kibbutzim*, one in the Jezreel Valley and the other in Lower Galilee. I reaped wheat, led herds to pasture, constructed houses, lived, together with my companions, in tents open to the wind, and felt I was a participant in the creation of a state. I saw how a desert assumed a green mantle. My life seemed perfect. Then the riots started, and the war, and I was caught up by them, and into them, drawn into completely new and different worlds.

Of three million Jews who left eastern Europe between 1882 and 1914 (when World War I broke out), only fifty thousand immigrated to Israel. What a historical mistake! And despite everything, even this meager wave of immigration exercised a miracle: For the first time in history, a people who left, or was banished from, their country, was revived and started gathering in the land of their forebears. Never had such an extraordinary event been witnessed until then, nor did it take place since, with any other people.

Eretz Yisrael was desolate, devastated, its land reluctant and tired, land with practically no water. Despite the lack of experience, and infertility of the soil, the standard of agriculture that developed in Israel is today perceived by many to be the highest in the world. Not only did the desert bloom, but new and amazing cooperative frameworks were also built, such as the kibbutz and *moshav*, that encapsulated a distinctive type of social phenomenon never previously seen.

And as the barren land was being tilled, war broke out. Israel was attacked by forces that were far superior—both in numbers and in arms—whereas the barely born state was desperately short of arms, and its army practically nonexistent. The land of the Jews was attacked five times, and all five ended in victory. Once again, a people lacking in military tradition, and in the face of an unequal balance of strategic military power, created an army which, in this case as well, is recognized as one of the best in the world.

I saw the ploughs and I saw the rifles. And nowadays, I see modern microscopes in universities that shed light on atoms invisible to the naked eye, making it possible to build a whole new world. What could be more fulfilling, more riveting, more just, than to be a part of such a people? Truthfully, there were moments when it seemed that all was lost, that everything had vanished. And then there were other instances, when it appeared that all the problems had been resolved. Yet the former did not happen, and neither did the latter. The road ahead is still very long and hard, but inspiring nevertheless. We stopped being slaves in Egypt's house and moved into a home that is independent, democratic, and Jewish—in our land.

What propels us? Not marshals and not religion. We are propelled by tremendous faith that tells us that a new genesis is possible, one that will create a better world inhabited by better people: created in the image of God and lovers of humankind.

I feel like a man who has donned biblical sandals and is moving forward with a people inspired by its faith, part of a process of renewal and revival, walking on without fear. A people that fights without despairing, remembering and advancing at one and the same time.

CYNTHIA OZICK is the author of five novels and seven collections of short stories and essays. She has just completed a new novel to be published in 2004.

"To be a Jew is to be old in history, but not only that."

If we blow into the narrow end of the shofar, we will be heard far. But if we choose to be Mankind rather than Jewish and blow into the wider part, we will not be heard at all.

The Jewish Idea is characterized by two momentous standards. The first, the standard of anti-idolatry, leads to the second, the standard of distinction-making—the understanding that the properties of one proposition are not the properties of another proposition. Together, these two ideals, in the form of urgencies, have created Jewish history. To be a Jew is to be old in history, but not only that; to be a Jew is to be a member of a distinct civilization expressed through an oceanic culture in possession of a multitude of texts and attitudes elucidating these concepts.

For the Jewish intellectual who defines himself as a Jew through the slogan of "I am an outsider"; and for the Jewish intellectual who disbelieves what Mark Twain calls "evil joy," and what biblical metaphor names Amalek, I offer these thoughts: A moment may come when it is needful to be decent to our own side, concerning whom we are not to witness falsely or even carelessly to prove how worse we are. Without such loyalty—not always a popular notion among the global sentimentalists—you may find that you are too weak in self-respect to tell the truth or to commit yourself to the facts. The responsibility of Jewish intellectuals ought to include this recognition, or it is no responsibility at all. Thinkers are obliged above all to make distinctions, particularly in an age of mindlessly spreading moral equivalence. "I have seen the enemy and he is us" is not always and everywhere true; and self-blame can be the highest form of self-congratulation.

RUTH PEARL is a graduate of the Technion-Israel Institute of Technology and holds a master's degree in electrical engineering. She has worked as a computer consultant and is currently CFO and secretary of the Daniel Pearl Foundation.

"Empowerment to question, zeal for honesty, reverence for learning, and deep commitment to create a better world for the next generation."

Growing up as a Jewish child in Baghdad left me with recurring nightmares of being chased by a knife-wielding Arab in the school's stairway while two thousand schoolmates screamed hysterically. The screaming was a real and frequent occurrence triggered by sudden noise or a minor accident in a chemistry lab, a consequence of the trauma from the June 1941 looting and massacre of one hundred eighty Jews in Baghdad. I also remember my parents' night vigils waiting for my two brothers to come home after their outings. Indeed, one time my father had to bail them out of jail with a bribe after they were arrested not far from home, just for being Jewish.

All that changed when we left for Israel in 1951. My acclimation to Israel was amazingly easy and natural, though my nightmares continued for many years. In Israel, one does not have to be an observant Jew to feel Jewish, an atmosphere that suited me perfectly. By the time my husband and I arrived in the United States in 1960 for postgraduate studies, I was a proud and secure Jew and did not expect anti-Semitism to ever touch my life.

I was raised in a moderately religious home and community, and I absorbed many of the attitudes and values from my Jewish heritage, such as empowerment to question, zeal for honesty, reverence for learning, and a deep commitment to create a better world for the next generation. I tried to pass along to my children "my" ethical Judaism: a guilt-free, pragmatic religion with open-mindedness at its core.

My security and sense of justice were shattered with the murder of my son, Daniel.

Like many generations before us, we are now embarking on a new war against anti-Semitism and fanaticism. More than ever before, I am conscious of my Jewishness and my obligation to contribute to its preservation, for I feel bonded to people who share my values and my commitments. Driven by the vision of Danny—a proud Jew who continues to inspire people with his values and dignity—we will win this war, as did our ancestors for many generations.

 **LARRY KING,** Emmy Award–winning host of CNN's *Larry King Live,* has conducted more than 40,000 interviews in his broadcasting career. He is the founder of the Larry King Cardiac Foundation, which has raised millions of dollars for needy children and adults, and established a $1 million journalism scholarship at George Washington University's School of Media and Affairs for students from disadvantaged backgrounds.

"We are small in number; our impact has been incredible."

First and foremost, I had nothing to do with being Jewish. Fortunately for me, my parents, Eddie and Jennie from Minsk and

Pinsk in Belorussia, respectively, happened to be Jewish themselves. I say fortunately because despite many of the trials and tribulations Jews have faced over the years, I still consider it kind of a blessing to be Jewish.

Now, let's get this straight: I am not religious. I guess you could say I am agnostic. That is, I don't know if there is a God or not (if there is I sure have a lot of questions for him—or her). But I'm certainly culturally Jewish. I love the Jewish sense of humor. The shtick of the Jewish comedian burns in me. I love a good joke. I don't mind jokes about Jews told by Jews. Jewish humor has become universal.

The Yiddish language has many words now in daily use in other cultures all over the world. Is there, for example, a better word than "chutzpah"? It means "gall," but actually it's more than gall. Here's a good illustration of chutzpah: The Jewish women's organization Hadassah that raises money for Israel opens a fund-raising office in Libya. See what I mean by beyond gall?

And it's funny, even though I don't observe all the dietary laws, certain things have stayed with me since early childhood. For instance, I cannot eat meat with a glass of milk. The very thought of it turns my stomach. Jewish dietary laws prescribe that you don't mix the two. That is almost inbred in me. I don't observe the Jewish holidays, but I do admit to a certain reverence on Yom Kippur and Rosh Hashanah because it gives me a chance to reflect about my late parents. They were observant Jews. (Where did I go wrong?)

My father died when I was nine and a half and he was forty-three. My mother raised my younger brother and me, never remarrying. She was the classic Jewish mother. My Jewish name is Label, and so to her I was always Labela. I could do no wrong. Everything was for her children. That is Jewish to the core. I used to say that if I blew up a bank, killing four hundred people, my mother would say, "Perhaps they made a mistake in his checking account."

Judaism is both a religion and a race. It's an imprint I carry with me everywhere. I was taught to hate prejudice. I was taught the values of loyalty—the values of family. Even though I was not fortunate enough to go to college, I was certainly embedded with strong Jewish values of education and learning, no matter what the form. It is said that if you call a Jewish man in the middle of the night and ask him if you woke him up, he would say no, he was reading a book. The joke on the other side is, why do Jewish women never open their eyes during intercourse? It's because they can't stand to see someone else having pleasure. I throw in these little trinkets because they are so Jewish. We are small in number; our impact has been incredible.

I once asked a noted author, the late Harry Golden, if he ever regretted being Jewish. And he said no because when he dies there are only four possible leaders in the afterlife. They would be Moses, Christ, Karl Marx, and Sigmund Freud. And they were all Jewish so he figured he was on the right team from the start.

I remember how proud I was on my trip to Jerusalem with my brother a few years back. Seeing all of the street signs in Hebrew, feeling a sense of identity and belonging. We wandered no more …

One vivid memory of that trip is when I was standing by the Western Wall, known as the famous Wailing Wall, where Jews from all over the world go to pray. A rabbi standing near me was *davening* (the Jewish form of prayer) when he looked up and said: "What's with Perot?" It was a funny incident, really hitting me, showing the impact of CNN all over the world. Also on that trip I had the opportunity to visit many Israeli leaders, including spending a day with Yitzhak Rabin, who was campaigning to be prime minister, a job he would eventually win.

Again, having no strong religious affiliation, I must say the trip really hit home to me. The very flavor of Jerusalem stayed with me long after I left. I liked all the people of the region, including the many Palestinians I met. I felt a sense of belonging and I thought a lot about my late parents, who would have loved to step on that soil.

I'll close with classic Jewish humor. A Jewish grandmother takes her grandson to the beach. He goes in the water and disappears from view. His grandmother falls to the ground crying: "God save him." Suddenly, the boy washes to shore safe, alive, and breathing. The woman looks at the heavens and says: "He had a hat."

SARAH ROSENBAUM, 15, Coto de Caza, California

When I say that I am Jewish, I am identifying myself as part of a tradition, connected to our foremothers and fathers, and carrying on to the future a culture, a religion, a way of life. I feel pride, and am overwhelmed with joy when I declare that I am part of this incredible people, our people Israel.

W. MICHAEL BLUMENTHAL has had a distinguished career in business, government service, and education, including serving as the sixty-fourth secretary of the United States Treasury. In 1997 he accepted an invitation from the city of Berlin to become president and CEO of the Berlin Jewish Museum.

"While still young, I wondered whether my Jewish heritage was only a burden to be borne, rather than a privilege and blessing to be acknowledged with pride. Today I know better."

I was born a German Jew and escaped at the last moment from the Nazi Holocaust—to Shanghai, one of the few places that would accept Jews in 1939. Eighteen thousand fellow Jewish refugees survived a difficult life there, including two and a half years in a Japanese-run ghetto. As a postwar immigrant to the United States, I came to a country in which anti-Semitism was still an active force in many places.

Without strong religious anchors there was a time when, while still young, I wondered whether my Jewish heritage was only a burden to be borne, rather than a privilege and blessing to be acknowledged with pride. Today I know better.

The Jews are the oldest intact biblical people on the face of the earth. Through the ages, they have survived in a hostile environment, clinging stubbornly to their traditions and faith, even in the face of untold hardships. Millions paid for it with their lives, but others kept the heritage.

The Jewish religion is the foundation for the sum total of ethical and moral values of the Western world. Jewish men and women, wherever they lived, have contributed enormously to every facet of human life. It is a tradition and a heritage to be cherished and valued. For me, to be a part of it has become the source of a deep sense of satisfaction—and obligation.

"I am Jewish," I now say with pride. I view this as a sign of gratitude to those who came before me, as a precious duty, and as an admonition to my children and grandchildren. May they too say it with pride and joy, and never forget it!

 TAMARA PEARL holds a master's degree in psychology, works as a homeopath, and serves as vice president of the Daniel Pearl Foundation.

"A school of alchemy that knows how to transmute pain and horror into life-affirming substance."

What being Jewish means to me has changed throughout my life and again since my brother Danny was murdered.

In my childhood, being Jewish meant being part of a large tribe, a big family all over the world with a common culture, history, language, humor, and food. But it also meant being identified as part of a group that has been persecuted and killed throughout history for being who they are.

I remember going with my father to demonstrations for the plight of Soviet Jews. I remember knowing that my relatives were killed in the Holocaust, just for being Jewish. This produced a shame in me, a feeling that there might be some fault with us if so many people hate us and want to kill us.

Danny never felt that way—he was always deeply secure and comfortable about who and what he was. His deep inner calm radiated a palpable light to all who met him. He loved life more than anyone I know, and he lived life to the fullest. Throughout his travels and his explorations he maintained a strong faith in humanity, a deep respect for people, and a healthy sense of humor about himself and human nature.

These are qualities that no band of murderers could ever change. Even in the face of so much hatred he didn't doubt himself, and he maintained his dignity—we can see it in his eyes. The way he said, "I am Jewish," and the family story he told about our great-grandfather, conveyed: "I am Jewish, and if you have a problem with that, that is your problem. Yours! Not mine. If you harm me, that is your illness and your shame!"

He had his truth and his convictions and he never succumbed to their twisted attempts to use his heritage to justify their crime. Instead, his light accentuated the darkness of their hatred. I realized that the shame I had been feeling as a result of Jewish suffering belonged to those who caused the suffering and those who have allowed it to occur.

My feeling toward being Jewish changed dramatically after Danny's death, both as a result of his unyielding dignity throughout the ordeal and as a result of the deep wisdom and spiritual insight that Judaism offered me in my healing.

Now, to me, being Jewish means being heir to a spiritual, cultural, and long-standing mystical tradition that gives me the tools to survive and flourish in such a world. We as a people have had no choice but to develop these tools through the ages. Being Jewish means being an apprentice to a school of alchemy that knows how to transmute pain and horror into life-affirming substance. Even the mourner's *Kaddish* affirms life.

Being Jewish, to me, means respecting life. It means loving heartily, laughing loudly, inquiring deeply, debating voraciously, standing up for justice, and choosing to experience life with all its ramifications. And it means acquiring dignity, even while facing adversity.

SPENCER NEWMAN, 10, Miami, Florida

When I say I am Jewish it means to me that I have people taking care of me. It means family.

 SYLVIA BOORSTEIN is a founding teacher at Spirit Rock Meditation Center in Woodacre, California, and leads Mindfulness workshops and training courses nationwide. She is the author of four books, including *That's Funny, You Don't Look Buddhist: On Being a Faithful Jew and a Passionate Buddhist.*

"The unequivocal sense I have of being Jewish is fundamentally a kinship bond."

On a weekday winter morning early in 2003, with war in Iraq seeming imminent, I participated—as a teacher at Spirit Rock Meditation Center in the Buddhist tradition—in an interfaith prayer service. All of the major faith traditions were represented, and although each presenter was opposed to going to war, the contributions to the shared liturgy were not partisan. Everyone spoke, and offered prayers, on behalf of restraint, honest communication, and the forgiveness of grievances that would be necessary for building a lasting peace.

I was the last speaker. I spoke about being the granddaughter of immigrants who came to America because they believed in democracy. I said that I believed, as they had, that speaking up for what I felt was right was a patriotic act. When I finished, I backed up into the group of previous speakers who had gathered around me for the end of the service, and stepped, quite literally, on the toes of one of the several rabbis in the group.

"Whoops," I said. "I'm sorry."

"It's all right," the rabbi replied. "We consider you one of us, you know."

"I *do* know," I responded. "I do, too."

I teach a meditation called Mindfulness, a practice that the Buddha taught of paying balanced and focused attention in order to cultivate clarity of mind and kindness. And it has never occurred to me that I was anything but Jewish. Being Jewish is intimately and instinctively what I feel myself to be.

Perhaps the interfaith prayer service came to mind when I needed, for this essay, to articulate what "I am Jewish ..." means to me, because my earliest childhood memories conflate living in a family that was passionately Jewish and passionately political. My parents were not religious, but they loved being Jews. They loved their relatives. They loved talking about the news. They were devout about speaking out about what they valued, and they included me in their discussions. I learned early that any racial or religious slur pained them, and I also understood, when I was quite young, why we did not go into a store that had a picket line outside. In 1944, in our neighborhood that had Thomas E. Dewey signs displayed in nearly every window, my mother proudly wore large, dangling earrings that said FDR on them. She was barely five feet tall; I thought she was brave, and I loved her.

Voting, in my family, felt like a religious act. I remember walking with my parents and my grandmother to the polling place that was several blocks from where we lived in the same way (and in fact on the same streets) that we walked together to *shul* on Yom Kippur.

I stood in the voting booth with my mother, curtain drawn, and looking up, watched her pull levers. She voted slowly and deliberately, not a party-line vote. Once, having pulled a lever to vote for a Far Left candidate running for New York City councilman, she looked down at me and said, "Don't tell Daddy." That moment, in my memory, feels sacramental. I count it as my initiation into my role as a grown-up, independent, socially responsible Jewish woman.

The meditation I teach emphasizes working to keep one's mind free of anger and other confusing emotions by responding, with deliberate care, to whatever is happening. I know, from my own experience, that assigning blame and holding grudges makes reconciliation impossible and that anger and bitterness, in me, cause me to suffer. When I teach, I often hear myself say, "It's painful for me, as I am sure it is for all of you, to see how much suffering there is in the world these days. It's hard to keep a peaceful heart, but I am determined to do it. I need a peaceful heart so that I'll see clearly what can be done *and* have the courage and the energy to do it." Especially in these last several years, with more news available of troubles in the world, I find myself saying, "If I sound more intense, more eager to talk about political activism than you've known me to be in the past, it's because these are intense times. And I have the blood of the prophets in my veins, and their voices in my ears." I am pleased with how proud I feel when I announce my lineage.

And, I also wonder whether, even more than the particular traits that I know I learned from my family, the unequivocal sense I have of being Jewish is fundamentally a kinship bond. I grew up in a family that worried about, and rejoiced with, Jews whom I did not know but who seemed, somehow, part of my greater family. Some of my father's cousins survived the war in Poland by fleeing their small village and hiding in the forest for two years. In 1946, they stayed at our house in Brooklyn on their way to Canada, where they had been granted entrance visas. I sat at the edges of their conversations and listened to stories. They spoke in Yiddish, a language I understand because my grandmother, who lived with us, spoke it with my parents. The cousins gave me a child's gold ring that they'd brought with them from Poland, and I wore it for many years. I don't recall the moment in which I realized the ring must have belonged to a child who died. I do remember my parents coaching them on what they wanted to be able to say as they made their way, by train, across Canada. "I'm sorry. I don't understand you. I don't speak English." When I recall their voices, heavily accented, practicing those sentences, I cry.

And I remember, in 1948, sitting on the living room floor in front of the Magnavox radio listening, with my mother and father and grandmother, to the partition vote in the United Nations. "Paraguay votes 'Yes.'" The radio switched to "live from Tel Aviv" and even through the static we could hear people singing "Hatikvah." My mother started to cry. If I close my eyes, I can hear and see the scene now exactly as it was.

My life and my work and my children's families are full of diversity and I welcome it. And, I notice Jewishness. I do it spontaneously. When I hear about Jews doing wonderful things, I am proud. When they do ignoble things, I am embarrassed. I feel protective about Jews, as I would about family. A particular joy of my work teaching Mindfulness has been teaching it to Jews in Jewish community centers, in synagogues (including the one in which I am a regular congregant), and in rabbinic training programs. The nonparochial nature of Mindfulness practice makes it universally accessible, and it has been wonderful for me to have knowledgeable Jews rephrase the instructions for meditation so that they become uniquely Jewish. I love all of my teaching, but it is especially pleasurable for me to feel that I've learned something valuable that I am able to share with my family.

DAVID J. AZRIELI, architect and developer, is president of Canpro Investments Ltd., which develops, builds, and manages shopping centers and office buildings in North America, and established the first enclosed shopping mall in Israel. He won the Prime Minister's Jubilee Award in 1998 for his contributions to the Israeli economy.

"To accept a Jewish identification is to embrace much more than belief alone."

To accept a Jewish identification is to embrace much more than belief alone—it is to accept responsibility that you are part of something bigger and greater than yourself. It is to accept that you are part of a history, a tradition, and a people that emphasizes learning; a people that is often gifted with talents that contribute to society at large.

MARTIN PERETZ taught social theory and politics at Harvard University for more than three decades. He has been editor in chief of *The New Republic* since 1974.

"This is the lesson of Israel, the lesson that Zionism spoke to the exiles. Jewish meaning is made out of life, not out of martyrdom."

Would it not have been preferable had Abraham actually consummated the Akedah, the sacrifice of his son, and that his hand had not been stayed by the Angel? Then Isaac would have died, like Jesus later on, for the as-yet-uncommitted sins of the believers, and they might have been spared the afflictions that accompanied them through history. But that is not what happened. So the Jews were left with the specter of an interrupted ritual that has nonetheless haunted His people always, and—especially in modern times—separated them from what many thinking Jews saw as a capricious and cruel God. The binding has, then, been a continuous theological problem for them ... and a psychological one, too. I remember as a child trembling at the story of the binding of Isaac.

The sacrifice of Jewish sons and daughters can by now be counted in the many millions. And, because the chroniclers of 1096 and 1146 and of other disasters can be believed, some modest number of these children was certainly killed by their own fathers and mothers so that their blood not be shed by the unstoppable swords of the pious and savage Christian Crusaders who swept through Europe on their way to the Holy Land.

During the last century and a half, many of these innocent prey were not faithful to the ancient faith or, for that matter, even to symbolic traditions. Many of them were doubters, moderns, innovators, troublemakers. Or, as the Yiddish poet Yakov Glatstein put it more starkly,

> Now the merest child rebels
> Against his word.

But this did not mean that they had ceased being Jews. Many would still affirm with this same poet, "The God of my unbelief is magnificent." Others wouldn't. They had believed in what another Yiddish poet, Aaron Zeitlin, characterized as a "geometric god."

> A god that cannot change its own creation ...
> A god without horror or miracle,
> A god coldly heretical ...
> Who is incapable
> Of making it his concern
> Whether I die or live,
> Or burn
> In every fire until
> The final generation.

But this belief or disbelief, whatever you call it, would not save them either. Nothing would. Not even the secular gods, some already dead, some still alive.

We Jews count our victims of the world's true religions in the millions, pious men and women, for the most part, but skeptics and even the altogether unconcerned among them. And we had come to believe somehow that the Holocaust was our last act, a somber finale drowned in blood.

> ... just as we all stood together
> at the giving of the Torah at Sinai,
> so did we all die together in Lublin.

But we didn't all die. We are, in fact, very much alive.

A teacher of mine, Marie Syrkin, a great woman of letters and a vibrant Jew, explained,

> If you cannot be David,
> You will be Samson.
> One thing is sure,
> You will not be Isaac.
> You will not walk trustingly toward the altar.
> You know
> No ram will appear.

This is the lesson of Israel, the lesson that Zionism spoke to the exiles. Jewish meaning is made out of life, not out of martyrdom. Of course, Israel still struggles with the Jew-hatred of its neighbors and counts its dead now, incident by incident, only in the single and double digits, innocent lives all.

Daniel Pearl, whom I did not know, could have been any one of us. When he was so viciously murdered by fanatic Muslims—alas, more and more Muslims in this world seem to be fanatics!—I felt that he could have been my brother. Of course, this is because we shared a common past. We belonged to the same people. I sensed this, really, as soon as I'd heard of his disappearance into the darkness of Pakistan. But I did not really know. As Daniel Pearl's wife, Mariane, has pointed out, however, it was a *Washington Post* reporter who confirmed for the world that he was a Jew. In that part of the world, this small piece of information was what she called a "death sentence." She was right. I asked myself exactly what kind of Jew he might be. And I answered intuitively that probably he could comfortably say with me, "The God of my unbelief is magnificent." In that macabre setting, his recitation, to his killers and in front of a video camera, of the Jew that he was and had been for generations, before the sword of militant Islam cut his throat, was a pronouncement of gentle faith. But there is a stern lesson in his death: Do not walk trustingly toward the altar. No ram will appear. Be heavily armed and resolute. Besides: Do not rely on those who loudly proclaim themselves men and women of good will. Many of them bear poison, especially when they treat with Jews and with the Jewish nation.

 RABBI SHERWIN T. WINE is the founder of the movement of Humanistic Judaism, the founding rabbi of the first congregation of Humanistic Judaism, The Birmingham Temple, and currently dean of the International Institute for Secular Humanistic Judaism in Detroit, Michigan. He is the author of many articles and several books, including *Judaism Beyond God* and *Staying Sane in a Crazy World*.

"United through space and time by shared ancestry, shared culture, and shared historical memories."

When I say that I am Jewish I affirm the fact that I am part of an extraordinary people who began as a nation in ancient Judea and have become, over the centuries, an international family. This family is united through space and time by shared ancestry, shared culture, and shared historical memories. Because of persistent persecution, being Jewish is no ordinary identity. It also involves a shared social fate. We are a provocative people.

Our family is extraordinary because its history did not conform to conventional development. Very early in our history, we became an urbanized bourgeois people. With small exceptions, we have remained an urbanized bourgeois people. The consequence of this condition is that literacy, verbal skills, and intellectual activity became essential parts of Jewish culture. In ancient times, these skills were directed to religious endeavors. But, in modern times, they have been liberated. Over the past two centuries, there has been an explosion of Jewish activity that has transformed the secular world of science and the arts. From Einstein to Freud, the modern world bears the mark of Jewish innovation. Being a peripheral and ambitious people, we are often less reluctant to challenge the established ideas of the nations among whom we live. That is why we are provocative.

Our family enjoys the bonds of shared ancestry. But it is also open to anybody who wishes to join. Since there is no single set of ideas that define Jewish identity, joining the Jewish people means loving the Jewish people, Jewish culture, and Jewish achievement—and the willingness to identify with the history and social fate of the Jewish people.

The meaning of Jewish history and the Jewish experience offers us guidance for how to lead our lives as individuals. The implication of Jewish history is a way of life that we call the *life of courage*. The story of the Jews is a story of survival against overwhelming odds—in which the key to survival has not been the kindness of the fates but rather the courage and determination of brave men and women. Living courageously means that we do not expect outside magical powers to bring justice to the world. It means that the responsibility for justice is ours—and that the power for justice, however limited, is ours. As for our own personal happiness and fulfillment, the responsibility and power are also ours.

Living the life of courage as a Jew also means that we celebrate our history. The holidays and ceremonies of the Jewish people do not honor mysterious powers that never seem available to help us when we need them. They celebrate the power of brave people to confront a dangerous world and to live their lives with justice and dignity.

JADE RANSOHOFF, 7, Tampa, Florida

To me, "I'm Jewish" means having fun being a Jew. It's a miracle to be Jewish. Just like the Red Sea parting and the oil lasting for eight days.

WENDY WASSERSTEIN is a playwright. She is the author of *The Heidi Chronicles*, *The Sisters Rosensweig*, and *An American Daughter*.

"Distinctly Jewish voices: funny, ironic, yearning, sometimes self-deprecating, sometimes grandiose, but always with a great heart."

I made my stage debut in second grade, in 1957, as Queen Esther at the Yeshiva of Flatbush in Brooklyn, New York. As I recall, I wore one of my mother's striped sheets tied around me as a toga, and a birthday crown. I have no idea who played my cousin Mordechai, or the evil Haman, but to this day I am convinced that I have a life in the theater because of Queen Esther.

In later years, I wrote a play called *The Sisters Rosensweig* about Jewish identity. My friend Martin Sherman, the Jewish author of the play *Bent*, said to me, "Wendy, the thing is, these are all voices you remember from your childhood in Brooklyn." Those voices I remember were distinctly Jewish voices: funny, ironic, yearning, sometimes self-deprecating, sometimes grandiose, but always with a great heart.

My grandfather Shimon was a Yiddish playwright. He came to this country in 1928. He was an actor in Yiddish plays in Pittsburgh, and ultimately, was the principal of a Hebrew school in Paterson, New Jersey. According to my mother, my grandfather knew Menasha Skulnik and Molly Picon, the great practitioners of Yiddish theater in America at that time. Also according to my mother, my grandfather walked past the synagogue deliberately on High Holy Days. I have no idea whether that is true or not, but that story has always contextualized my religious practice.

When I was a student at the Yeshiva of Flatbush, my mother, Lola, served the children hamburgers with string beans and butter sauce, a deliberate kosher violation. She told the rabbi's children, who appreciated the sweetness of the beans, that it was really lemon juice. In my childhood mind, I thought a burning bush or flying hand would come through our window in Flatbush at any moment.

And yet, in many ways, those dinners seemed to me at the heart of why I consider myself Jewish. My sense of identity comes directly from the creativity of my mother and her profound sense of family. My mother, who had to be convinced by me to celebrate Passover yearly, used to bang on televisions and tell who exactly was Jewish. I remember distinctly her explaining to me that she didn't care what anybody said, but that Senator Barry Goldwater was Jewish. I didn't even know Jews lived in Arizona at that time.

I am often asked if I consider myself a woman writer or a Jewish writer. I am also often asked if I think my work is "too New York" to be appreciated in the rest of the country, or the world. My answer is: If I am not a Jewish or female writer, then I have no idea who I am. And as for being "too New York," I know what that is a euphemism for. I now have a four-year-old daughter. When I define myself, I am happily now not only a Jewish female writer but also the ultimate form of Judaism: a Jewish mother.

SARAH SILVERMAN is a comic, actress, and writer. She is very pretty.

"Remember the guy who smashed all the idols in the idol store?"

Remember the guy who smashed all the idols in the idol store? His mother had a heart attack when she saw the mess, but I'm sure she bragged about it later. That's us. That's me. I am Jewish.

MOSHE KATSAV was born in Iran and immigrated to Israel when he was five years old. He has served as president of the State of Israel since 2000.

"To be a Jew means to belong to a nation whose people are linked to each other spiritually and emotionally, to belong to a group that shares a common magnificent past, one tradition, and a common destiny and fate."

The late Daniel Pearl, of blessed memory, by stating "I am a Jew" to his terrorist captors before being murdered, proclaimed his affiliation to a religious and national entity and his being part of Jewish history. This declaration encompasses a way of life, beliefs, and views. To be a Jew means an outlook on worldwide issues, founded on Jewish principles based on the Bible.

To be a Jew means to belong to a faith, which gave humanity the belief in one God and universal values, that has accompanied humankind since the founding of the nation 3,313 years ago at Mount Sinai, when we sanctified our faith and received the Ten Commandments.

To be a Jew means to belong to a people who showed determination and steadfastness and who withstood many afflictions and tribulations for thousands of years.

The Jew belongs to a nation which lost its independence when the First Temple was destroyed 2,690 years ago and the people of Israel were expelled and exiled to Babylon.

He belongs to a nation which the Persian empire tried to annihilate 2,480 years ago. The Purim miracle occurred and the Jews were saved.

He belongs to a nation which the Hellenist empire, 2,166 years ago, tried to convert and did not succeed. The Jewish People then revolted under the Maccabeans against the Greeks and in so doing prevented the loss of independence.

He belongs to a nation which lost its independence a second time, 1,933 years ago, to the Roman Empire, resulting in the exile of the Jewish People from its country.

He belongs to a nation which for two thousand years experienced continuous suffering, expulsion, forced conversions, exiles, inquisition, and, worst of all, the terrible Holocaust by the Nazis and their collaborators. The Jewish People rose up from the ashes and succeeded in reviving and obtaining sovereignty and independence in its homeland.

No event in the history of mankind is similar to that of the Jewish People.

Fifty-six years ago, the Jewish People succeeded in reestablishing its State, a democratic, modern, and liberal country with advanced scientific and technological achievements, a country that bases its national life on the vision of the prophets of Israel and on the moral values that Judaism has given humanity.

Judaism emphasizes the value of communal life and mutual solidarity. "All Israel is responsible for one another" is the key phrase outlining a way of life. To be a Jew means to care for the weak and the needy.

Social justice and concern for the weak are cornerstones of Judaism and of the Torah of Israel, and we see a straight line between concern for the weak and our possession of the Land of Israel. "Justice, justice shall you pursue that you may thrive and inherit the land." In other words, in order for the Jewish People to live successfully in its historical homeland, it must take care of the weak, the orphan, the widow, and the disabled, as social justice is the basis of our life in Israel and the beginning of our redemption.

In the Bible there are many references and laws dealing with social justice and concern for the weak, including the commandments of *digest* (a poor man's share of the crop), *peah* (leaving the corner crops for the poor), forgotten sheaves, the *shmitta* year (the seventh year during which the land must be uncultivated), and the jubilee year (for the redemption of people and land). It is even stated that "charity is equal to all the commandments of the Torah." The State of Israel, as a Jewish democratic country, is also an advanced welfare state, confronting social needs.

There is no conflict between Judaism and Christianity and Islam.

After all, Christianity is based on Judaism and the Bible. The festivals and Jewish tradition were sanctified in the life of the Jewish nation before Christianity appeared, and Christianity is also based on them. During my last meeting with His Holiness the Pope in the Vatican, he quoted the Prophet Jeremiah and said to me that Jews are the elder brothers of Christians.

Likewise, regarding Islam: When the Jews were persecuted and expelled from Europe, approximately five hundred years ago during the Middle Ages, the Muslim world absorbed the exiled Jews. The cooperation between Judaism and Islam resulted in a period of great cultural development for all humanity. During those times, great collections of writing, meditations, and culture—in commentaries, law, Jewish thought, and communal life—were created.

The prayer book and the Bible, on which our national and religious life are based, bound thousands of Jewish communities, cut off from each other for thousands of years and scattered throughout the world. In this way, Judaism and the Jewish People were maintained.

The prayers in synagogue are meant for religious and worship purposes, but they are also an expression of appreciation of Judaism's magnificent past, thanks to which we survived as a nation. The synagogue is also a place where moral principles and rules of behavior are imparted to the congregants; in this way, a combination of religious prayer, honoring the past, and the acquisition of moral principles was created.

Every Jew feels a spiritual bond and an emotional attachment to Judaism even if, in the era of globalization, he hardly knows the basic concepts of Judaism; even if in his bookcase there are no books dealing with the Jewish faith, the Jewish People, or Jewish culture and history.

The values of Judaism are universal and humane values and certainly in all sectors and parts of the nation—Sephardic, Ashkenazi, Ultra-Orthodox, Reform, Conservative, Orthodox, Israelis, and diaspora Jews are all linked and joined to each other and to these values.

Judaism, therefore, is focused on social justice and concern for the weak. Judaism is faith, a world outlook, universal values, laws governing man's conduct toward his fellow man and his conduct toward God. Judaism is linked to life.

To be a Jew means to belong to a nation whose people are linked to each other spiritually and emotionally, to belong to a group that shares a common magnificent past, one tradition, and a common destiny and fate. The Jewish People are the sons of one father. They are one big family.

In conclusion, I wish to quote Professor Erwin Radkowski, the chief scientist of the American Atomic Energy Commission in the 1960s, which built the first nuclear-powered submarine, the *Nautilus*. When asked how he recommends improving one's thinking ability, his reply was: "Study a page of the Gemara [commentary on the Jewish Oral Law] every day."

AMANDA, Marietta, Georgia

When I say I am Jewish, I feel as if no matter where I am I will always have a home in Israel. Even if I'm not accepted anywhere else, I will be accepted in Israel because I am Jewish and Israel is the land of the Jewish people. When I say I am Jewish, I feel like I am part of one huge family.

 LORD GREVILLE JANNER is a former president of the Board of Deputies of British Jews. He is a vice president of the World Jewish Congress, founder president of the Commonwealth Jewish Council, and president of the Inter-Parliamentary Council Against Anti-Semitism.

"I hope that I, as a leading, proud, and active Jew, am not getting paranoid…. We should recognize the new and sad realities—and fight back, with heads held high."

Thinking about Daniel Pearl's last words, my mind flashed to a meeting in the lobby of the House of Lords, shortly after the end of the

Iraq War. I was approached by a tall, stooped, gray-haired Tory peeress. She looked down at me and crooked her index finger.

"Well, we've dealt with Saddam Hussein," she announced. "Your lot are next."

"My lot?" I queried.

"Yes. You cannot go on persecuting the Palestinians forever, you know."

"I'm not persecuting anyone."

"You know what I mean," she said.

"Yes," I replied. "I know precisely what you mean." And I walked off.

Since 9/11, open anti-Semitism has leaped back into European life. Bad in the United Kingdom, but not nearly as bad as in France and other parts of Europe. So why has this happened? "I" have always been an active, open, proud Jew. But now it's "you".... Why?

First, there's the Far Right. It has always been there, but since the war and the Holocaust, it has generally not felt it appropriate to attack "Jews." That is changing. True, they direct their main venom at the Muslims. Happily, our Jews do not seek to take shelter behind that attack. I tell my Muslim colleagues and friends that we Jews know that when the new Nazis win local authority seats on the basis of hatred for Muslims, asylum seekers, and foreigners ... if the Far Right wax fat on them ... then we Jews are next.

Reason two, then. Today, we have some one and a half million Muslims in the United Kingdom. There are maybe eight million in France. Numbers are growing. As a Jew, all four of whose grandparents were immigrants, I relate to them. I work to create the best relations between their community and ours. But it has become increasingly tough, especially since 9/11. Most of our British Muslims are from Pakistan and Bangladesh. Their first overseas religious focus is usually on Kashmir. But they identify with the Muslims of the Middle East in general and of Palestine in particular.

During the war, at the UN's so-called antiracist conference in Durban in 2002, I watched the Muslim parade, with banners reading "DEATH TO THE JEWS." I saw the same on a Muslim march in London. My work in the Muslim world has become much more difficult, both organizationally and personally. As a Jew, I want our

Muslim community to be integrated into the United Kingdom. As a Jew, I wish to help. But the problems are growing.

So the third reason for anti-Semitic growth is without question the miseries of the Middle East. Those Jews who do not identify with Israel are still regarded as part of "your lot." The distinction between anti-Zionism and anti-Semitism is often blurred. I have even met an anti-Semite who was pro-Israel, believing (he told me) that it was good to have a Jewish state because Jews in Britain and elsewhere could and should go and live there. In the main, though, you can say that, as a Jew in politics, I have deep gratitude to—and no problems with—my colleagues who are pro-Israel, even if they, like myself, simply disagree with some of the policies of Israel's government, as we do with some of our own. But the anti-Semites are almost without exception anti-Zionist. After all, Israel is the Jewish state ... I am a Jew ... and when the baroness spoke of "your lot," that meant me.

As a Labour peer, I am sad that the next category of open growth of anti-Jewish attack comes from the Left—and not just the Far Left, either. Until recently, it was not acceptable for left-wingers to make anti-Semitic attacks. But now, that has changed. True, they may be dressed up as anti-Israel or anti-Zionist, but "we people" are the ones under attack. The woman who went for me was from the Right. Which reminded me of President Eisenhower's great comment that "decent people travel in the center of the road. There's a gutter on each side."

Sadly, the anti-Israel bias of *The Independent* and *The Guardian* and other left-wing media has spilled over into the BBC. This formerly truly independent, decent public service has become a vehicle for anti-Israel attacks, too often spilling over into anti-Jewish, in comment and spin.

I often think of Henry Kissinger's wry comment: "I know that I am paranoid, but that don't mean I ain't got enemies!" I hope that I, as a leading, proud, and active Jew, am not getting paranoid. The Jewish part of my public and political life is, I believe, still respected by the vast majority of my non-Jewish colleagues, whether or not they agree with my views. As a Jew, I believe that we must recognize the change in the climate ... that we must not curl up in our shells and retreat to our communal and religious sanctuaries ... that we must continue to serve the countries in which we live ... but that we should recognize the new and sad realities—and fight back, with heads held high.

So I salute the memory and the words of Daniel Pearl—and I weep for his loss.

 **Alana Frey** is an eighth-grade student in Rockville Centre, New York. Besides being an honor student, she is also a singer and actress who has performed onstage at Madison Square Garden, Carnegie Hall, and local community theaters.

"I learned how similar and different we all feel as Jews."

In my Hebrew school, every student has to do a special project prior to her or his Bat/Bar Mitzvah. One night about three months before my Bat Mitzvah, my family was sitting in our usual Sunday night restaurant talking about what kind of project I could do, hopefully one that would have a positive effect on people and be different from the standard ones done.

With the tragedy of September 11 and the subsequent murder of Daniel Pearl, I thought that I could do something special not only for me, but also for Daniel's family, more specifically, his newborn son, Adam. I wanted the project to inspire his son with his father's own last words, "I am Jewish." If I could show him how his father's words inspired pride in others, then he would have an understanding of his heritage and his father's words would always comfort him.

The project started and grew into a booklet. I sent out a questionnaire and received many e-mails and letters from members of my temple, relatives, friends, my parents' friends and colleagues, along with some of my father's former high school students. Some were historical essays from immigrants, Holocaust survivors, and regular American Jews. Some people sent personal reflections and experiences and others just wrote a recipe—Jewish of course. Some people chose to donate to the Daniel Pearl Foundation (an option I also gave in my questionnaire) along with their written contribution or instead of one. By reading everyone's entries, I learned how similar and different we all feel as Jews, and that some people live a whole different Jewish experience than I do. The booklet was completed and on my Bat Mitzvah morning was placed outside of our sanctuary. Everyone received a copy. After the ceremony, we sent the booklet to Daniel's father, Judea Pearl, for this was the real reason for this effort. Hopefully, Adam Pearl will read it along with this book.

Personally, I love being Jewish, my family, and the history that my parents' parents share. My Grandma Lola is a Holocaust survivor who was in the concentration camps in Poland; my Papa Kurt is a Jewish survivor from the war who helped keep his family from being captured. On the other side of my family, my departed Papa Mickey, a Bronze Star recipient, liberated a concentration camp, and my Mama Ivy enlisted in the United States Army Signal Corps. My family understood the meaning of Judaism and its responsibilities; all four of them were eager to help and survive. Clearly it was not an easy time for them, but just as it is not easy for the family of Daniel Pearl, their love and spirit along with their religion helped them get by day after day.

This project has had a strong effect on me. I have been in contact with Daniel's family, and their support has kept my project alive. Also, I live in a town where the majority of people are not Jews. My project has in a way made me a teacher of my heritage. Since many of my closest friends are not Jewish, I enjoy and love explaining Judaism to them (even the little things about our customs and traditions). For instance, I had some non-Jewish friends over once when I was eating *hamantashen,* and I enjoyed how curious they were about them. They were so interested listening to the story of Purim. Explaining our differences makes us appreciate each other more. Shouldn't that be the message of "I am Jewish"?

Although I have completed my basic Hebrew school education, I am proud to say that I will be furthering my studies in Judaism at our local Hebrew high school. A year ago I would have definitely said that there was no way I would go to Hebrew high, but now there is no doubt in my mind that I want to go. One of the reasons I've changed my mind is because of the project's effect on our congregation, my family, and, most important, the Pearl family. It made me realize how special and what a gift being Jewish really is. It made me realize that Daniel Pearl's words stir emotion in all Jews. So what began as a project of inspiration for Adam Pearl turned out to be an inspiration for me.

Itay, 22, Haifa, Israel

I am Jewish means for me that I am a part of the Jewish people, connected throughout our common history and past. It also means that I'm connected to the rest of the Jewish people around the world, and that we share a future together. In some way, everything that happens to a Jew wherever he is because of his being a Jew, is my business, too.

Richard Dreyfuss is an Academy Award–winning actor and a social activist. Three of his films are included in the American Film Institute's list of the greatest one hundred films.

"The really interesting stuff was in the history, the debates, the great arguments between Jews and about Jews."

What was it that Daniel Pearl's killers could not afford to hear? That he was an American, a journalist, a Westerner, a Jew? That there is justice and ethics in the world? What is it that they loathed? The Jewish mobility of mind? The curiosity? The courage? The humor?

Mankind thrives on tales, relies on epics and myths and stories of great size, to measure against and see man, reflected, in the most honest way.

The Jewish tale is so complex and interesting, profound and eccentric, full of intellectual rigor and suppleness of mind.

I am a passionate Jewish agnostic who has always believed that we are the chosen people. So, go figure. Say that it's God, say that it's the complexities of history. Say that it's a mystery. Say that it's a metaphor, whatever, but I believe that the Jews are chosen to illuminate the human condition, good and bad; that means we can see in the Jews the state of man, his condition, his aspiration, his folly. Mankind's great and foolish behavior is contained within the Jews ... from Sinai to Chelm, from Judah Maccabee to Shabtai Tsvi.

As a kid I found all the rituals, the prayers, the acts of faith in synagogue or home to be inaccessible. I was unmoved by them; I didn't have a Bar Mitzvah. My dad talked me out of it. Told me the really interesting stuff was in the history, the debates, the great arguments between Jews and about Jews. And sure enough, it was in the ocean of fascinating and mysterious stories I discovered in my temple's classes that I really did find answers for questions that I needed to answer. That did reveal to me secrets, that told me who my mother and father were, and why, and who I was, and where I came from; the Jewish story offered me glimpses of heroism and dignity and allowed me to listen in on the ancient discussions of the nature of right and wrong. That offered me a look at the world and my place within it, that connected me to yesterday and tomorrow, to Jews here and everywhere. I am enormously proud. I declaim my membership in this club. The weird ones of the world, those who are often pictured holding a gun to the head of a bound American journalist, these come and go, for millennia. Deservedly so. The Jew, the One they try so hard to kill, he remains, for millennia. Forever. Deservedly so. Pretty impressive.

ROALD HOFFMANN is a theoretical chemist at Cornell University and a writer of poetry, nonfiction, and plays. He was awarded the Nobel Prize in Chemistry in 1981.

"A looking to the future. Out of the past."

To be Jewish is to be born in 1937 in a little town in Polish Galicia, Złzoczów, and be given the Hebrew name of Israel ben Hillel Safran.

And the secular name of Roald Safran (after Roald Amundsen). To grow up Jewish in that place, in that time of war—if one survived—is also to be named, in time, Roald Margulies, and Roald Hoffmann.

In Złoczów there once lived a great Hasidic rabbi, Yekhiel Mikhal, the Maggid of Złoczów. Martin Buber retells the following story:

> The maggid of Złoczów was asked by one of his disciples: "In the Book of Elijah we read: 'Everyone in Israel is in duty bound to say: When will my work approach the works of my fathers, Abraham, Isaac and Jacob.' How are we to understand this? How could we ever venture to think that we could do what our fathers could?"
>
> The rabbi expounded: "Just as our fathers invented new ways of serving, each a new service according to his own character: one the service of love, the other that of stern justice, the third that of beauty, so each one of us in his own way shall devise something new in the light of the teachings and of service, and do what has not yet been done."
>
> —from *Tales of the Hasidim: The Early Masters*

To "do what has not yet been done," "in the light of the teachings and of service." A looking to the future. Out of the past. Oh, it's not a sufficient definition of being Jewish. But perhaps something to which a Jew, observant or not, on the anguished yet proud line from Yekhiel Mikhal to my father to Daniel Pearl, could aspire.

 **VIDAL SASSOON,** who revolutionized hair, is founder of the Vidal Sassoon International Center for the Study of Antisemitism at the Hebrew University of Jerusalem.

"Humble yet proud of a heritage that has dignified me."

I am Jewish, humble yet proud of a heritage that has dignified me even as others have tried to destroy my race. I was twenty years old in 1948 when the Palmach/Haganah accepted me as a soldier in

Israel's War of Independence. The experience changed the course of my life. I am a Jew who believes that, though small in numbers, we have a powerful moral influence on the world, and in the words of Hillel, "If not now, when?"

IDA HAENDEL, violinist, plays with all the major orchestras in America, Canada, and Europe, and tours with them around the world. She is the recipient of the Sibelius Prize, and was given by the English Queen the title of "Commander of the British Empire" for her outstanding service to music.

"I was born here [Israel] thousands of years ago. This is where I belong."

I am by nature a perennial optimist, which is probably the influence of the eternal art of music. In the past, the Jewish people were not particularly regarded as brave or heroic. That all changed with the Holocaust and the incredible uprising of the Jewish ghetto in Warsaw. Poland, the country of my birth, where anti-Semitism was so rife, was surprisingly very supportive of me. Neither my parents, my older sister, nor I experienced any animosity or antagonism as Jews. On the contrary, the Polish government had the greatest respect for talent in general, and toward me in particular as a child prodigy. I was encouraged by the ministers in the Cultural Department and received a subsidy that enabled my father to bring me to London, where the renowned Hungarian violin pedagogue, Professor Carl Flesch, resided. Eventually we moved to England, which became an asylum for my family during the frightful war years. London was the niche where I spent my childhood. We became British citizens.

Almost immediately after the war, my father received a request from the Palestine Philharmonic Orchestra in Tel Aviv, founded by the great Jewish-Polish violinist Bronislaw Huberman, to bring me to Palestine. At the time, most members of the orchestra were Polish Jews from the Warsaw Philharmonic, and they knew me as a child prodigy. My London manager pointed out the danger of bringing a teenaged girl to war-torn Palestine. My father, an artist painter by profession, a slim delicate man of average height, became a giant, with the bravery of a David in front of Goliath. Not for a moment did he hesitate. He booked a cabin on a tiny Greek ship and brought me to Palestine.

This was the beginning of yearly visits to perform with the Palestine Philharmonic Orchestra. (When the State of Israel was declared, the orchestra changed its name, for obvious reasons, and became the Israel Philharmonic Orchestra.) My association and devotion to the orchestra continues to this day, and I join them whenever they need me. I played in the country's darkest hours as well as in its glorious, triumphant moments.

Now, when there is such turmoil in the world, the true hero is a man called Daniel Pearl and young generations of men and women like him. When Daniel Pearl so proudly proclaimed "I am Jewish" to the world, he described it all with this short, powerful statement. The Jewish nation will never be destroyed, nor defeated. No amount of brutality or genocide will ever accomplish it. As for myself, when I was interviewed in Israel not too long ago and asked the question, "Why do you keep coming back here all the time, taking such risks? What is the motivation and attraction?" my reply was, and still is: I was born here thousands of years ago. This is where I belong.

DANIEL LIBESKIND, a Polish-born American architect, designed the Jewish Museum in Berlin, among many other projects. He is the recipient of the Hiroshima Art Prize, an award given to an artist whose work promotes peace. Currently, Libeskind is the master plan architect for the World Trade Center redevelopment in New York City.

"Not the forgetting of the origin, but its maintenance as a living flame."

Jewish tradition, as opposed to other traditions, is not the forgetting of the origin, but its maintenance as a living flame. This flame burns with freedom and joy. In this sense, being Jewish is to have the possibilities of the world permanently open to the wonder of life. The joy, optimism, and creativity of Jewishness demarcate the horizon of the eternal in time.

JACKIE MASON was raised on the Lower East Side of Manhattan surrounded by rabbis—his father, grandfather, great-grandfather, and great-great-grandfather were all rabbis, as are his three brothers. He rose to be one the hottest comics in America in the early 1960s and continues to entertain his many loyal long-time fans and the legions of new fans he earns each year.

"Everyone knows by now that no one can kill our spirit."

To be a Jew is to watch with good humor how this planet has treated its Jews, and to remain humorous.

Among the most often thought-of peoples are the Jews, existing by a code of living given to the world and accepted thousands of years ago. In return, those inspired by the Jews reduced our numbers by torture, mass murder, forced conversion or dispersion, assimilation, or intermarriage, to the least number of people—barely thirteen million throughout the planet. Our divine birthright, the continuously embattled nation of Israel, is also among the tiniest nations on the globe, yet she manages to survive. Everyone knows by now that no one can kill our spirit, yet some are still trying.

I told you, it takes a Jew to read this script and stay humorous.

MAURICE LÉVY is chairman and CEO of Publicis Groupe S.A (the fourth-largest communication group in the world). He is an officer of the French Légion d'Honneur and commander of the French National Order of Merit.

"A sense of belonging, a deeply ingrained attachment to traditions, and, above all, a set of values that guide my actions."

Jew I am. It is not a source of pride or of embarrassment. It is just a fact. Born in a traditional family, I never had any question about my religion, my origins, or my belonging. I live my Jewishness as I live my "Frenchness," in a simple way. As a child it happened that I was insulted and assaulted. Things changed later, but not always in people's eyes. And then there were anecdotes that I prefer to definitely consider just anecdotes.

I'm in the habit of saying that the strength of a company, what makes it stand upright, lies as much in the strength of its values as in the strength of its balance sheet. Those values are the backbone of a company. They guide the actions of its management. They are the benchmark for any decision-making process.

I think the same applies to human beings. I grew up on a staple diet of text wisdom, of respect for others, of old-fashioned honesty to the point of being sometimes stupid, and of continuous references by my grandfather to the Talmud or the Kabbalah. What did I get out of it? A sense of belonging, a deeply ingrained attachment to traditions, and, above all, a set of values that guide my actions.

And finally, the happiness to see that in this environment of globalization, big business, and financial cynicism, it is possible to stay true to oneself and to succeed (more or less).

I do not feel that there are any contradictions in my life as a Jew and my life as a somewhat successful business leader.

I never worked on Yom Kippur, and it never was a problem. I've always respected the principles that I was taught (never feeling the need to ask myself questions about them), and I think it did me good.

I am a Jew: I know it, I feel it, and I live my Jewishness without feeling any contradiction with the other aspects of my personality.

 RABBI RACHEL B. COWAN is the director of the Jewish Life and Values Program at the Nathan Cummings Foundation in New York City. After sixteen years of marriage to the late writer Paul Cowan, she converted to Judaism, and was ordained at Hebrew Union College–Jewish Institute of Religion in New York City in 1989.

"The journey itself is not only the means, but also the end. I am blessed to be a voyager on an ancient pathway."

My mother claims that I fell in love with Judaism for purely gastro-nomic reasons. Our ninth-grade Sunday school class made a field trip from the Wellesley Hills Unitarian Church to a synagogue in neighboring Newton (Wellesley real estate agents in the fifties were bound by a covenant not to sell houses to Jews) to experience a Bar Mitzvah. The refreshments served after services (I did not then know the word *"Kiddush"*) were a banquet compared to the cup of watery coffee and two cookies we were served after services in our church.

I would say that I was first drawn to Jews and Judaism when I read the *Diary of Anne Frank*. Living in a town without Jewish friends, I made her my Jewish companion. As an outsider myself, I was nourished by the private joys, sorrows, judgments, and insight she shared so generously. And as her friend, I came to know something of the reality of evil and suffering. That initial perception of the combination of joy, pain, and deep humanity that underlies so much of Jewish life continues to move me.

But my actual entry into the Jewish community began when I fell in love with Paul Cowan. We met as coworkers in the civil rights movement in a small town on the eastern shore of Maryland. I was impressed when he told me that he was there because he was Jewish.

I did not identify myself as a Christian, just as a person with good values, learned from my parents, and I admired his sense of history and community. As it turned out, his journey to a fully-lived Jewish life, chronicled in *An Orphan in History*, was as long as my journey to conversion.

Paul offered a wonderful entry. When he opened the door, I had no idea how long, winding, hilly, and thrilling the journey would be. Today, twenty-three years after I converted, fifteen years after Paul died, fourteen years after I was ordained as a rabbi by Hebrew Union College, and two years after the birth of my grandson, Jacob Pablo, I see clearly not only why I became a Jew but also why I am a Jew. And as I keep learning and growing in my understanding of Judaism, I see that the journey itself is not only the means, but also the end.

I am blessed to be a voyager on an ancient pathway that continues to offer new insights and responses to new questions of meaning, ethics, and responsibility. It is rich with texts, teachers, and practices that help me cultivate the qualities of soul and character I need to live with greater humility, more courage, and deeper wisdom. It teaches me to choose life, to bring joy and gratitude into my world, even as I face tremendous personal and communal challenges. It gave me rituals and traditions that shaped the life of my family, and that will help nurture Jacob Pablo as he grows up in this complicated world. And finally, the Jewish communities in which I have been lucky enough to live have always held me when I grieved and danced with me when I rejoiced. And also—though not best of all—invited me to fabulous meals.

I am Jewish because the religion, the tradition, and the community inspire me and support me to follow the path that the Prophet Micah challenges us all to walk:

> To do justice
> > To love goodness
> > And to walk humbly with your God.
> > —**Micah 6:8**

MILTON FRIEDMAN is currently a senior research fellow at the Hoover Institution at Stanford University and a professor emeritus of economics at the University of Chicago. He received the Nobel Memorial Prize for Economic Sciences in 1976. His most recent book (with Rose D. Friedman) is *Two Lucky People.*

"A deep and brilliant stream of culture and intellectual activity."

My Jewish origin has always been a source of pride. I share in and benefit from a deep and brilliant stream of culture and intellectual activity that has flowed for thousands of years and is flowing strongly still.

LIZ LERMAN is founding artistic director of Liz Lerman Dance Exchange and a recent recipient of a MacArthur Foundation "Genius Grant" Fellowship.

"Sometimes I unroll my Jewish self in places where people expect a secular artist, which of course I am, but they also discover a Jew."

I am Jewish because my mother was Jewish. I inherited her restlessness about God, women, and empty prayers. But my father was an ecstatic Jew whose every step—whether organizing against segregation or teaching Hebrew school kids about the evils of real estate speculation—declared his commitment to making the world a better place. "This is the way to be Jewish," he told me over and over.

I try to unite their dual paths. Sometimes I bring my Jewish body, and its drive to make dances, to synagogues and other places Jews gather. People are surprised to find postmodernism creeping into the sanctuary or to have their Jewish minds reintroduced to their muscles. Sometimes I unroll my Jewish self in places where people expect a secular artist, which of course I am, but they also discover a Jew.

Now I have the joy of observing my daughter find her Jewish self. I watched with pride as she challenged everyone at her Bat Mitzvah with her struggle to believe in a God who needs so much praise. She is restless. After all, she is Jewish because I am Jewish.

 **DANIEL GILL,** a childhood and lifelong friend of Daniel Pearl, lives in Topanga, California, with his faithful dog.

"Being a 'survivor' is not what I think when I say 'I am a Jew.' I think about how we're different."

Years ago, while traveling across Uganda, in a world so green that the landscape assumed a monochromatic, black-and-white quality, I found myself surrounded by a train car full of people who had never before met a Jew. Black and white, we sat there, I as different as night from day. For more than an hour we discussed God, faith, Jesus and the prophets, the Hebrew Bible and the Christian texts. These kind people wanted to know from me what it meant to be a Jew. I was unable to adequately answer their questions then, and I am torn by doubts I can do so now. The question so resists reduction to black and white.

Was being Jewish what killed Danny Pearl? Was it what made him live? Surely I can be forgiven if some of my Jewish identity is constructed from enmity, from a steady diet of "us versus them." Pogroms, inquisitions, exile, genocide, hate in thousands of expressions over thousands of years—these burnt the ashes from which we've grown, again and again.

Nevertheless, being a "survivor" is not what I think when I say "I am a Jew." I think about how we're different.

For reasons that cannot be based on logic, considering the historical results, we are driven to be different. We are a people of the book, of law, but with challenge and debate of those laws, not blind observance. The Talmud is a treatise of argument more than answer. We question, challenge, debate, extrapolate, construct and deconstruct.

And we aspire to something more. We focus on this life, not what comes after. Being Jewish means striving for *tikkun olam*, a repairing of the world, of *hesed* and *rachamim* and *tzedakah*. We built nations, changed the histories of music, arts, science, law and jurisprudence, politics, academia, philosophy, finance, agriculture—every field imaginable. We marched with Martin Luther King Jr. and made *Duck Soup* and *E.T.*

The distinctions are never just black and white, but we *are* different. *Baruch Hashem:* Thank God!

David Suissa is the founder and CEO of Suissa Miller Advertising, and founder and editor of *OLAM* magazine and Meals4Israel.com.

"'We've been praying, learning, suffering, debating, and asking for two thousand years for what you have right now: the chance to take that final step back to our homeland.'"

When I think of being Jewish, I think of eighty generations of grandfathers and grandmothers, all holding hands. They're now looking at me, and with their eyes they whisper: "We've been praying, learning, suffering, debating, and asking for two thousand years for what you have right now: the chance to take that final step back to our homeland. Please be grateful for that chance, please hold our hands, and please make sure it's not the final step, but rather the first of many beautiful and holy steps that will continue our eternal mission of lighting up the world."

Yefim Bronfman, a Grammy Award–winning pianist, has recorded works by Prokofiev, Bartók, Mozart, Tchaikovsky, and others, and has performed with the world's top orchestras and conductors.

"Being a musician and being Jewish have something in common: constant wandering, and never-ending struggle."

Having grown up in Tashkent, music has become an "escape" from the reality of everyday life and from constant reminders of my Jewish background. In search of my roots and of that "escape," I realized that being a musician and being Jewish have something in common: constant wandering, and never-ending struggle.

Shelley R. Deutch Tayar was born in Jerusalem (at the time Palestine), worked as a writer and correspondent in Europe for nearly thirty years, and has always been active in both Jewish and non-Jewish communities. A model of and for the wandering Jew, she now lives in Malta.

"I believe that Judaism is not only heritage, tradition, ethics, and faith but also a whole encompassing spirit."

Centuries before the Christian Era, one of the Jewish sages defined Judaism in six seconds. He said, "Love thy Lord thy God with all thy heart, with all thy might and with all thy being, and don't do unto others what you don't want done to yourself." That was the core in the budding bulb of my Jewish being, and this sprouted more and more layers and flowered to the present bloom. I received my identity through my heritage. My family, refugees from the 1492 Spanish Inquisition, arrived many generations ago in old Palestine and settled in the Old City of Jerusalem. I was gened to recover whatever spark from every catastrophe. My learning through parental guidance adamantly rejected the "I, I" school of Sigmund Freud in favor of the biblical "You (plural and individual) and I" and its halakhic interpretation that places the general good ahead of the individual good.

Neither my parents nor I ever experienced anti-Semitism—that came through a third party when we children assisted Holocaust refugees from illegal boats onto Palestine (now Israel). Once the refugees were supplied with forged identity papers, we children were instructed to tell the searching British troops that all people in our house were immediate family and were visiting from Tel Aviv.

The social and learning layers on my Jewish core grew through impressions, traditions, and people I was introduced to.

My father often smoked a narghile with the Emir Abdallah (King Hussein's grandfather), and the bishop of Jerusalem brought us a Dalmatian puppy as a gift. I especially loved the pomp and glamor of Jewish tradition. As a small child, I attended the coronation of Rabbi Ouziel Rishon LeZion, chief rabbi of Jerusalem, which was held in the ancient synagogue Horvat Yehuda (destroyed in 1948 by the Jordanians). I was overwhelmed by the golden crown placed on the rabbi's head and his purple, gold, and silver vestments and the pageantry. The same night of the coronation a neighbor, Professor Joseph Klausner (author and famous history professor at the Hebrew University), came to the house with a stack of Jewish children's novels, and I started on my Jewish voyage of passion for knowledge.

S. Y. Agnon, a tiny giant and recipient of the 1966 Nobel Prize for Literature, was another neighbor. He used to sit for hours with my father and listen to tales of old Jerusalem. Itamar Ben Avi, the son of Eliezer Ben Yehuda (compiler of the first Hebrew dictionary), also lived in our suburb, Talpiot. I remember my father banging on the table and passionately (he always spoke passionately and loudly) telling him: "There is no nature preservation program better than that of the Bible. Do you know that a Jew is forbidden from living in a city without green? That any fruit windblown to earth belongs to God the custodian and therefore only the poor can pick it? Do you know anything of the biblical laws of 'do not destroy' *[lo tash-*

hit]? I spent four years up the Brazilian Amazon [on a research expedition from the Sorbonne around 1910] and learned firsthand that if you cut those trees down then you cut a treasure of undiscovered medicines!"

My father continued, "Do you know that the Bible contains the most compassionate protective laws for animals? One is commanded to give all working animals one day off a week, and a Jew is not allowed to harness an ox and a donkey to plough together. Why? Because it's not fair on the donkey! Surely, we need your modern way of life and your new Hebrew vocabulary, but we also need religion. Can you imagine a world without a Sabbath? The Torah gave humanity a day off a week; what a priceless eternal gift." My father died sixty years ago, but living with my parents left an indelible mark on me—I inherited his photographic memory for happenings, and I absorbed all this emotional exchange into my being.

More recent layers on my inner self have been spiritual and political dreams. I learned of the Jewish command, "Enjoy life," despite agonizing pain in life (I am handicapped). I learned that we Jews have to salvage what we can and beam out positive currents—it helps others and it helps us. I believe that Judaism is not only heritage, tradition, ethics, and faith but also a whole encompassing spirit—the vibrating immortal spirit of the Jewish people. Take Daniel Pearl: He may have been murdered, but his spirit is pyramiding. I can hear him say, "We Jews say 'Shalom' or 'peace,' the Arabs say 'Salaam Aleichum' or 'peace be with you'; let's work to unite these pieces through music, science, knowledge, and discovery. After all, the only way to completely destroy your enemy is to make him into a friend."

 **Douglas Rushkoff,** author of *Nothing Sacred: The Truth about Judaism,* is a professor of communications at New York University's Interactive Telecommunications Program and a commentator for National Public Radio's *All Things Considered.*

"Judaism is not a boundary; it is the force that breaks boundaries."

Jews are not a tribe but an amalgamation of tribes around a single premise: that human beings have a role. Judaism dared to make human beings responsible for this realm. Instead of depending upon the gods for food and protection, we decided to enact God, ourselves, and to depend on one another.

So, out of the death cults of Mitzrayim came a repudiation of idolatry, and a way of living that celebrated life itself. To say *"l'chaim"* was new, revolutionary, even naughty. It overturned sacred truths in favor of sacred living.

We are not passive recipients of law and truth, but active creators of ethical systems and models for the Divine. We are not believers, or even doubters, but wrestlers. Israel, more than a nation-state, is this very confrontation with the Divine. The wrestling is our continuity.

It's important to me that those who, throughout history, have attacked the Jews on the basis of blood not be allowed to redefine our indescribable process or our eternally evolving civilization. We are attacked for our refusal to accept the boundaries, yet sometimes we incorporate these very attacks into our thinking and beliefs.

It was Pharaoh who first used the term *Am Yisrael* in Torah, fearing a people who might replicate like bugs and not support him in a war. It was the Spanish of the Inquisition who invented the notion of Jewish blood, looking for a new reason to murder those who had converted to Catholicism. It was Hitler, via Jung, who spread the idea of a Jewish "genetic memory," capable of instilling an uncooperative nature in even those with partial Jewish ancestry. And it was Danny Pearl's killers who defined his Judaism as a sin of birth.

I refuse these definitions.

Yes, our parents pass our Judaism on to us, but not through their race, blood, or genes—it is through their teaching, their love, and their spirit. Judaism is not bestowed; it is enacted. Judaism is not a boundary; it is the force that breaks boundaries.

And Judaism is the refusal to let anyone tell us otherwise.

GLORIA GOLDREICH is a novelist who won the National Jewish Book Award for her work *Leah's Journey*. Her last published work was *That Year of Our War* and her novel *Walking Home* will be published in 2004.

"An intellectual and spiritual home."

I am Jewish because I was born into a tradition that engages my mind and delights my heart. My religion, my blessed sense of peoplehood, has added a wondrous dimension to my life and to my work as a writer. It has endowed me with a love of Zion, a deep and enduring involvement in the life of the State of Israel, and the beautiful and lilting language of that state. It has gifted me with the ability to dream in two languages and to take those bilingual dreams and translate them into stories that are enmeshed in the courageous and tragic history of my people. It has endowed me with a legacy to offer my children and grandchildren, a legacy of ethics and morality, of custom and celebration, of song and dance and prayer. I am Jewish because I have found an intellectual and spiritual home in my faith, and never, ever, would I want to wander from that safe yet challenging refuge.

 DANIEL JONAH GOLDHAGEN is the author of *Hitler's Willing Executioners: Ordinary Germans and the Holocaust* and *A Moral Reckoning: The Role of the Catholic Church in the Holocaust and Its Unfulfilled Duty of Repair.* In 1997, Goldhagen was awarded Germany's triennial Democracy Prize.

"The disquieting questions lurk in the background of one's mind and at times intrude into the foreground."

I suspect that many Jews who by dint of their work make themselves into potential targets for those who hate Jews have thought about the many aspects of their choice to do such work, including its possible violent consequences. Do the dangers to me outweigh the good that I can do? What precautions can I take? What would I do if I were ever abducted or confronted by those who would use my Jewishness as a cause for violent attack on me? Would I feign to reject my Jewishness or speak words of betrayal if through either I might survive or escape injury? If the final moments were upon me, would I decide that it had all been worth it, or at least that my calling had left me no alternative, regardless of how disastrous and frightening the end might be?

I suspect that those who choose such work ultimately convince themselves that the likelihood that the worst will happen is remote enough. Or given the anxiety, or the futility of assessing the probabilities accurately, that many simply choose to banish such thoughts. Still, the disquieting questions lurk in the background of one's mind and at times intrude into the foreground, especially during moments when one's Jewishness is actually or manifestly potentially of perilous issue. And given the binary outcome—live or die—even the most remote possibility of such danger can assume an overwhelming psychological presence. After all, it takes only one hate-filled fanatic or lunatic. When I go to Germany—where there is a small minority (but still a large number) of such people among an otherwise unthreatening and, in large measure, welcoming majority—full-time security is necessary, and reassuring.

Having been the object of intense antipathy for doing my work, these things have reverberated in my head more than once. I don't know the answers to all the questions and the tentative answers that I have given at different times have not always been the same. Yet do my work I must. It is a choice, but it doesn't feel like a choice.

EPHRAIM KISHON is one of the most widely read contemporary satirical authors. In 2001 he was nominated for the Nobel Prize in Literature.

"As a Jew, the message of Daniel is very clear to me: Our only safe shelter is Israel."

To plan the murder of a human being by virtue of his Jewishness defies my understanding. I am Jewish for no other reason but that of being born Jewish. I am a Holocaust survivor who was almost persecuted to death, and I still do not understand why. Those worthless people in Pakistan have murdered me as well, they murdered Jesus too, as well as Moses, who established the basic platform of their religion. Thus, without realizing it, what they in fact committed was a crime of patricide—father killing.

Unfortunately, the world has gotten used to this heinous custom of slaughtering Jews, and rarely does it stop to ask itself: "Seriously! Why?" In the course of two thousand years, many have managed to convert from perpetrators to spectators, but their responsibility nevertheless remains undiminished.

As a Jew, the message of Daniel is very clear to me: Our only safe shelter is Israel.

Menachem Z. Rosensaft, an attorney in New York City, was born in the displaced persons camp of Bergen-Belsen, Germany, in 1948. He is the founding chairman of the International Network of Children of Jewish Holocaust Survivors and the president of Park Avenue Synagogue in Manhattan.

"We believe, pray, and are because our parents and grandparents, and their parents and grandparents, believed, prayed, and were."

Judaism is far more than a religion. It is a living, vibrant culture, as well as an ethical, spiritual, and intellectual identity. We believe, pray, and are because our parents and grandparents, and their parents and grandparents, believed, prayed, and were. To be a Jew is not a function of suffering, destruction, and death. And yet, when the world learned that Daniel Pearl was murdered in Pakistan because he was a Jew, I instinctively thought of my five-and-a-half-year-old brother, who was murdered in a gas chamber at Auschwitz-Birkenau because he was a Jew. Their killers shared the same hatred. Which is why Daniel Pearl's last words, the dignity of his life, and the tragedy of his death so inexorably define us all.

Poland
I am the Jew
who would have prayed
three times a day
had black flames
not spewed me
into the August sky

without a grave
without a stone
my ashes
screams
burning blood

have penetrated
Carthage-like
this earth
that did not quake
to shatter crematory walls
that did not swallow
railroad tracks
whose grass refused
to become crimson

I know
of course I know
that all earth
is innocent
only the killers
killed

I know
of course I know
that Germans
not Poles
murdered the I
I would have been

but covered by the dust
of that other I
and of all the millions
of other I's
even fields
where flowers never withered
have become desolation
devastation

they stood there watching
Stashek and Leshek
as I was shoved
into the cattle car

good riddance to the bloody Jews
they thought
we'll get their houses now
they thought

they stood there smiling
Hans and Fritz
as they shoved me
into the gas
good riddance to the bloody Jews
they thought
it's almost time to eat
they thought

I am the last Jew to die
there
the last Jew to die
the last Jew
I am

ROBERT RABINOVITCH has been president and CEO of CBC/Radio-Canada, Canada's national public broadcaster, since 1999. He has held several positions in the federal government of Canada, including under secretary of state and deputy minister of communications.

"Being Jewish runs deeper than superficial identification and is, in fact, an essential element driving other values."

After completing my Ph.D. studies at the University of Pennsylvania, sometime during my first year working back in Canada, in Ottawa, the capital, for a minister of the government in Canada, a colleague took me aside and advised me that to get ahead I should not wear my Jewishness on my sleeve. The remark confused me, as I saw myself as a secular citizen of the world and could not conceive of what he meant. I was convinced that it was not meant as an anti-Semitic remark, but it was also as clear a statement as could be made that I was, in his eyes, different. I would like to think that it was my social values that I was wearing on my sleeve, and if that were the case, so be it.

On reflection, I concluded that being Jewish runs deeper than superficial identification and is, in fact, an essential element driving other values. To deny this would be to deny my history. To accept and embrace this is to accept that I have a moral compass that may differ from that of my friends. But it is my way of evaluating critical policy issues and directing my decision-making.

To accept being Jewish, to be proud of one's Jewish heritage, is the critical step in understanding oneself and in focusing a role in public life. I am Jewish, and I live in a world of Jews, Christians, and Muslims. My responsibility is to serve all Canadians. My Jewish roots give me the core values necessary to respect, and work for, all Canadians.

NAIM DANGOOR, eighty-eight years old, is the leader of Iraqi Jews outside Israel, and has edited and published *The Scribe: Journal of Babylonian Jewry* since 1971. Through his Exilarch's Foundation he intends to revive Jewish life in Iraq.

"A birthright, a glorious gift from one's forefathers of faith, culture, and heritage."

When I was a young boy a teacher at school asked me, "Why are you a Jew?" I, with all the practicality of youth, replied, "Because I was born one!"

There is, however, something in this sentiment that rings truer than one might think. Judaism is a birthright, a glorious gift from one's forefathers of faith, culture, and heritage.

For me, it is this: my strong Babylonian heritage, the heritage that Daniel Pearl also shared, his mother having been born in Baghdad, that makes me so proud to be a Jew.

Babylonia was one of the main birthplaces of the Jewish people, from where Abraham emerged as founder, and later from where the Babylonian Talmud, forming the framework for Rabbinic Judaism, was created. Its glorious Jewish intellectual eminence fanned out across the known world for more than a thousand years. Currently, the descendents of this tradition are spread throughout the globe, and it is for this reason that I have revived the position of the Exilarch and have published *The Scribe: Journal of Babylonian Jewry* for more than thirty years, in order to maintain and strengthen the legacy of our ancestors.

KERRI STRUG is an Olympic gold medalist in gymnastics.

"'You're Jewish?'"

I have heard the same question over and over since I received my gold medal in gymnastics on the Olympic podium. "You're Jewish?" people ask in a surprised tone. Perhaps it is my appearance or the stereotype that Jews and sports don't mix that makes my Jewish heritage so unexpected. I think about the attributes that helped me reach that podium: perseverance when faced with pain, years of patience and hope in an uncertain future, and a belief and devotion to something greater than myself. It makes it hard for me to believe that I did not look Jewish up there on the podium. In my mind, those are attributes that have defined Jews throughout history.

 SIR MARTIN GILBERT is one of Britain's most distinguished historians. Since 1968 he has published six volumes of the Churchill biography and a further eleven volumes of Churchill documents, as well as a one-volume biography, *Churchill: A Life*. Among his seventy-two books are nineteen on Jewish history. He was knighted in 1995.

"The themes from Jewish history combine the wide-ranging facts of creativity and courage, and of resistance and renewal, with a deep spiritual continuity."

For me, being Jewish goes back to my first childhood memories of Shabbat supper and Passover, at an uncle's home in London, and then, as a wartime evacuee, with the family that took me in when I was three and a half years old, having been sent by sea from London to Canada in 1940. Returning to Britain in the early summer of 1944, from my early years as a schoolboy I found Jewish history (which was never taught at school) both fascinating and inspiring. I read everything I could lay my hands on, and when I graduated from Oxford University in 1960, I decided to explore Jewish history in depth even though I had to devote so much time to working on the Churchill biography. Today, in my writing and lecturing, I find that the themes from Jewish history combine the wide-ranging facts of creativity and courage, and of resistance and renewal, with a deep spiritual continuity. To be Jewish is to be part of a remarkable, vibrant, and life-enhancing tradition that goes back to biblical times, and has never faded or failed.

Deborah E. Lipstadt is Dorot Professor of Modern Jewish and Holocaust Studies at Emory University in Atlanta. In 2000, she won a decisive victory in the British courts over David Irving, who sued her for libel for calling him a Holocaust denier and an anti-Semite.

"'Who knows if not for this very purpose' I had long been preparing."

I can no more answer why I am a Jew than I can answer why I am a woman or an American. So I was born. I do, however, know that my Jewish identity has sustained me at pivotal moments. Such was the case when I was sued by David Irving, one of the world's leading Holocaust deniers, for calling him a Holocaust denier. Forced to defend myself in a British court, I was terribly frightened.

On the first morning of the trial, as I gathered with my lawyers before court, I thought of the Twenty-Third Psalm. Would this be a "valley of the shadow of darkness"? Did I need to "fear the evil" confronting me? My reliance on this psalm as a lens to contemplate this moment was not random. My friend Debbie Friedman, a uniquely gifted composer, has set many classical Jewish texts to music. The gentle pathos of her setting for this psalm has long moved me. Debbie's voice was still wafting through my mind when the clock struck ten and my barrister declared: "It's time."

The trial ended right before the festival of Purim. The Book of Esther tells how the wicked Haman wanted to destroy the Jews. Mordecai, the Jew, urges his niece, Queen Esther, to go to the king. Frightened, she refuses. He challenges her: "Who knows if not for this very purpose you became Queen?" This is one of my favorite verses because it seems to call for people to prepare to rise to major challenges. Although I hardly equated a legal battle against David Irving with becoming royalty, I wondered, "Who knows if not for this very purpose" I had long been preparing.

On the night before the verdict I learned that the next morning the *minyan* at my synagogue would recite Psalm 51—"God, You are right in Your sentence and just in Your judgment." A cousin called from Poland, where she was accompanying a group of two hundred teenagers on a tour of Jewish sites. "Deborah, the young people are praying on your behalf."

A Warsaw-ghetto survivor called: "Deborah, tonight you can sleep soundly because none of us is sleeping." The first night of Passover is called the "Night of Watching," because Jewish tradition posits God watched over the Israelites as they fled Egypt. That night I imagined myself watched over by a band of resolute angels—survivors of the Holocaust.

The judge dealt Irving a devastating blow. The *Daily Telegraph* described the judgment as having "done for the new century what the Nuremberg tribunals or the Eichmann trial did for earlier generations." The judge described Irving as a denier, anti-Semite, and racist. Once again, Debbie's setting for the Twenty-Third Psalm came to mind. The "goodness and mercy" of countless friends and supporters had brought me to this moment.

Jewish tradition highly values taking care of the dead, because—in contrast to other acts of loving-kindness, including visiting the sick, feeding the hungry, and welcoming the stranger—it cannot be reciprocated. Taking care of the dead is called *hesed shel emet,* the most genuine act of loving-kindness, because it is then that we most closely emulate God's kindness to humans.

For five years I had the privilege to do *hesed shel emet,* to stand up for those who did not survive or who, had the Nazis succeeded, were not intended to survive. I did not choose this fight. It was an arduous road with many frightening moments, but throughout, I had been sustained by Jewish tradition. Truly, my cup runneth over.

 **BERNARD LEWIS**, Cleveland E. Dodge Professor of Near Eastern Studies Emeritus, Princeton University, holds thirteen honorary doctorates and is a fellow of the British Academy, a member of the American Academy of Arts and Sciences and of the American Philosophical Society, and a corresponding member of the Institut de France. Author of more than twenty books and two hundred articles, his most recent book is *The Crisis of Islam: Holy War and Unholy Terror.*

"A heritage, preserved through millennia by courage, achievement, and loyalty, and for all these reasons, a source of legitimate pride, to be cherished and passed on to those who come after us."

It was more than sixty years ago, but I still vividly remember the occasion and the conversation. It was in the middle of the night, and apart from the routine rumble of shells and bombs, things were relatively quiet. I was on night watch. In the branch of His Majesty's service in which I served, we took turns staying awake, two at a time, all night long, to deal with any emergency that might arise. It so happened that this was a quiet night, and we whiled away the time chatting about nothing in particular and, of course, about our work. My colleague was from another department, so even our shoptalk was limited by the "need-to-know" restriction, and therefore not very interesting.

Suddenly, my colleague George started a new and very different conversation. "Forgive me," he said, "I don't want to intrude, but am I right in thinking that you are Jewish?"

"You are right," I replied, "I am Jewish, and there is nothing to forgive."

"Forgive me," he said again, "but I have the impression that you are not a devout and observant Jew."

"You are right again," I said.

"Then I don't understand," he said. "Why do you bother?"

"Now I don't understand," I said. "What do you mean by that?"

"Let me try to explain," said George. "You must agree that being Jewish is often difficult and sometimes dangerous."

"Yes indeed," I said. One could hardly deny this statement in a branch of the intelligence service in 1942.

"Then I don't understand," said George yet again. "I can see that you may be ready to face persecution or death for your religious beliefs. But if you don't hold or live by those beliefs, then why bother?"

This time I began to understand George's question, even his incomprehension. George obviously thought of Judaism as a kind of sect or cult, like so many others. Membership in such a group was meaningful if one was a devout and practicing member, meaningless if one was not. In such a case there would be no good reason to remain a member, particularly if membership involved inconvenience or worse.

I set to work to try and explain to George—and to myself—why being Jewish meant not only belonging to a community defined by religion, though that was obviously a primary part of it. There were other elements besides belief and worship that mattered, and could somehow survive even the loss of these. Jewishness—I prefer this word to Judaism, which sounds rather theological—is a shared memory and experience of life. It is a many-faceted culture—distinctive, yet compatible and combinable with other cultures. It is an identity—not a whole or exclusive identity, but an important part of the multiple identities that all civilized people bear. Finally, it is a heritage, preserved through millennia by courage, achievement, and loyalty, and for all these reasons, a source of legitimate pride, to be cherished and passed on to those who come after us.

There have always been some who indeed did "not bother," finding the retention dangerous, difficult, or merely burdensome. For many centuries, hostility against Jews was theologically defined. This gave a Jew freedom of choice. By a simple act of conversion he could escape persecution and even, if he wished, join the persecutors. The racially defined hostility of the nineteenth and twentieth centuries removed this option and forced even the most vestigial of Jews to remain what he was, if only in name. In our own day, events in the Middle East have provided, for those who need it, a new rationale for Jew-baiting; this in turn has restored, for Jews who want it, the lost option of changing sides.

But for most, even for those whose religious faith is at best tenuous and whose Jewish identity is overshadowed by other, larger identities, denying that Jewish identity would be an act of falsehood, if not to others, then to oneself.

PART III:

COVENANT, CHOSENNESS, AND FAITH

 **SENATOR JOE LIEBERMAN** has been representing the people of Connecticut in the United States Senate since 1988. In 2000, he was the Democratic candidate for vice president, becoming the first Jewish American to be nominated for national office. He is a candidate for the Democratic nomination for president in 2004.

"Joyful gratitude that there is a God who created the universe."

What does being Jewish mean to me? To me, being Jewish means having help in answering life's most fundamental questions. How did I come to this place? And, now that I am here, how should I live?

My faith, which has anchored my life, begins with a joyful gratitude that there is a God who created the universe and then, because He continued to care for what He created, gave us laws and values to order and improve our lives. God also gave us a purpose and a destiny—to do justice and to protect, indeed to perfect, the human community and natural environment.

Being Jewish in America also means feeling a special love for this country, which has provided such unprecedented freedom and opportunity to the millions who have come and lived here. My parents raised me to believe that I did not have to mute my religious faith or ethnic identity to be a good American, that, on the contrary, America invites all its people to be what they are and believe what they wish. In truth, it is from our individual diversity and shared faith in God that we Americans draw our greatest strength and hope.

Daniel Pearl was a journalist—and a humanist, an American, and a Jew. He did not simply see the world and take notes on its condition. He lived in it. He loved it. He nurtured it and tried to make it better. He asked the most important questions, as Judaism asks us to, and strove to find the truth.

In her foreword to *At Home in the World,* the collection of Daniel's writings, his wife, Mariane, wrote that those "who killed Danny stood at the other extreme of what Danny represents. They could only wield their knife and cowardice against Danny's intellectual courage and bold spirit. Danny died holding only a pen. They stole his life but were unable to seize his soul."

Jews around the world and all who love freedom—the freedom to think, to speak, to write, to question, to pray—will hold Daniel near to our hearts, and from his courage we will draw eternal light and strength.

ROBYN J. FRIEDMAN, 10, Boca Raton, Florida

When I say I'm Jewish I think of three things. Lighting a menorah on Hanukkah or just having a tradition with your family. But the thing I think about more is being someone special and different than other people; it's just like having a birthday but better.

DR. DAVID HARTMAN is one of the most respected Jewish theologians in the world today. He is the founder and director of the Shalom Hartman Institute in Jerusalem, a frequent lecturer in the United States, and author of several widely acclaimed books, including two winners of the National Jewish Book Award.

"God has burdened human beings with the task of being the carriers of God's vision for human history. The law and the commandments express not only God's legislative authority but also, and above all, God's need for human beings."

Despite the varieties of lifestyles and outlooks among Jews today, there are certain organizing principles that cut across many of these differences and underlie the sense of common destiny and interdependence that so many Jews feel. From my own experience, the concepts of relationship and memory are two such fundamental categories.

The Jewish concepts of God and of *mitzvah* (commandment) and the biblical narratives of creation and of history are interwoven into Jewish practice, producing a distinctive outlook that shapes Jewish identity.

RELATIONAL THEOLOGY AND COVENANTAL CONSCIOUSNESS

In contrast to the self-sufficient God of Aristotle, the biblical God was considered philosophically "scandalous" because of the notion of a God who was vulnerable and affected by human history. Aristotle's God was totally unmoved and oblivious to human beings, whereas the biblical God was, as A. J. Heschel wrote, "in search of man" or, as Professor Lieberman remarked, "the most tragic figure in the Bible."

The idea that divine perfection is a relational category involving interdependence begins in the biblical story of creation. The idyllic description of an omnipotent God, whose unbounded will is automatically realized in the material world ("Let there be ... and there was ..."), abruptly changes with the creation of human beings, who challenge and oppose the divine will. In the Bible, the development of the notion of covenantal history is related to the transition in the character of God from an independent, unilateral actor to a God who recognizes that only through human cooperation can the divine plan for history be realized.

Abraham is the first covenantal figure because of the presence of mutuality in his relationship with God. Abraham's appeal to principles of morality—"Far be it from You ... to bring death upon the innocent as well as the guilty.... Shall not the Judge of all the earth deal justly?" (Gen. 18:23–25)—reflects his unqualified belief in his intuitive sense of justice and love. His ability to judge God's intended actions without having to "quote Scripture" reflects the dignity and self-assurance of being in a covenantal relationship with God.

The covenants with Abraham and later with the people of Israel at Sinai express the principle of divine self-limitation that makes room for human involvement in determining history.

RELATIONAL THEOLOGY AND INTIMACY

The God I meet in history is not an omnipotent, perfect, overwhelming presence that crushes my sense of worth and empowerment. Covenantal consciousness begins with the awareness that God has burdened human beings with the task of being the carriers of God's vision for human history. The law and the commandments express not only God's legislative authority but also, and above all, God's need for human beings. In addition to the normative moral content of religious life—the pursuit of justice, love, and compassion in our personal and collective lives—the covenant at Sinai expresses the interpersonal intimacy of God's relationship with Israel.

THE JEWISH YEAR: JEWISH IDENTITY AND
COLLECTIVE MEMORIES

The notions of relationship and interdependence expressed in the Jew's theological universe of discourse play an important role in defining the meaning of being a Jew and living a Jewish way of life. Being a Jew is first and foremost being part of the collective history of the Jewish people. In Judaism, you meet God within the framework of the collective history and practices of the Jewish people.

The individual's journey of discovering the meaning of being a Jew begins with the collective memories of the foundational events of the Jewish people. By appropriating these memories, the individual becomes part of a Jewish "we" that precedes and shapes the emergence of his or her Jewish "I." How you understand these foundational events determines the meaning of your individual Jewish identity within the collective life of the community. The Pilgrimage Festivals, Pesach, Shavuot and Sukkot, filter how a Jew understands the everyday meaning of being Jewish.

Pesach (Passover) negates the idea that the ultimate purpose of being Jewish can be realized by an individual's "leap of faith" or by fulfilling the commandments at Sinai. The conventional notion of religion as private faith and good works is incompatible with the message of Passover, which reminds me that I must first identify with my people's struggle for freedom and security before I can pledge covenantal allegiance to God at Sinai. We begin the annual pilgrimage of Jewish self-understanding by recollecting and identifying with the enslavement of the Jewish people in Egypt. We begin by retelling the story of our struggle for liberation: "We were slaves to Pharaoh in Egypt"—with the emphasis on the fact that *we* were slaves to Pharaoh in Egypt.

Empathy and solidarity with the political, social, and economic conditions of the Jewish people are necessary conditions for any "leap of faith" or spiritual journey within Judaism. We do not approach the sacred moment of the Sinai revelation as individuals. We hear the word of God and receive the Ten Commandments as "we." Heresy in Judaism is separating oneself from the collective experience of the Jewish people. The "wicked son" of the Passover

Haggadah is he who addresses other Jews as "you" ("you and not him"). Jewish heresy is an existential state of excluding oneself from the destiny of the Jewish people.

Passover thus begins the yearly celebration of our collective memory by situating the individual within the historic drama of the Jewish people. Passover leads into Shavuot, the time of receiving the Ten Commandments, the normative way of life known as Torah and *mitzvot*. This festival is essentially a holiday of freedom, the freedom of living a disciplined, normative way of life.

While identification with the suffering in Egypt is necessary for developing a collective consciousness, the memory of suffering is not in itself constitutive of Jewish identity. Although our oppression in Egypt could have become the predominant motif of our collective identity, the tradition took the experience of victimization and transformed it into a moral impulse. At Sinai, the memory of Egypt becomes a compelling reason for aspiring to the collective ideals of justice and love and becoming a holy people. "And you shall love the stranger, *for you were strangers in the land of Egypt*" (Deut. 10:19; see Exod. 23:9, Lev. 19:34, Lev. 24:17). At Sinai, we are challenged by God to take responsibility for our daily lives and to aspire to the freedom of being claimed by a normative vision of life.

Freedom involves the capacity for self-transcendence, for being claimed by what is other than myself. For Jews, the law is not a source of guilt, as the Christian apostle Paul claimed. We are not paralyzed by the elaborate structure of Halakhah and *mitzvot*. On the contrary, the Law (our Torah) gave us a sense of personal dignity— the dignity of beings accountable before God. At Sinai, we heard a God address us as responsible moral agents in spite of our human vulnerabilities and weaknesses. It is for this reason that Yom Kippur, the Day of Atonement, is so central to Jewish life. Yom Kippur provides us with hope and renewed conviction to begin anew and not to revel in the failures of the past.

After Shavuot, the next Pilgrimage Festival, Sukkot, evokes the desert experience and the yearning to reach the Promised Land. The land adds the dimension of the realization of our values and ideals within the total life of community. God desires that the material conditions of history, the social, economic, and political realities in which we live, mediate the divine presence. God's command to pursue justice and compassion cannot be fulfilled unless the public frameworks of communal life reflect these normative ideals. The land takes holiness, *k'dushah,* beyond the private realm of the individual, or even of the enclave, into the public marketplace, the factories, the hospitals, the welfare system, the military—the vast array of living frameworks that make up human society. Without the land, we are a family. With the land, we are a people in the fullest sense of the term. Our family circle of values, ideals, and responsibilities expands to embrace the total Jewish people.

By appropriating the memory of Passover, I learn that I can never forget Auschwitz or be indifferent to any manifestation of anti-Semitism in the world. Yet, no matter how powerful and compelling the experience of the Holocaust is for Jews today, we must not define ourselves as victims but must move from Auschwitz to Jerusalem. Like the movement from Egypt to Sinai, we must learn to celebrate our people's yearning to build a new future by taking responsibility for our lives as individuals, as a people, and as a country.

Our return to Israel as a sovereign nation can be understood figuratively as a reenactment of the drama of Sinai, where we learned not to define ourselves as victims but to take responsibility for how we lived. In the Land of Israel, the voice of Sinai speaks to Jews, holding them accountable for all aspects of their lives.

THE CREATION NARRATIVE AND JEWISH IDENTITY

While the festivals indicate the importance of the historical narrative in organizing Jewish identity, there is another type of narrative, the narrative of creation, that informs Jewish consciousness every week through the observance of the Sabbath. The Jew's perspective on life is nurtured not only by the collective memories of the Jewish people but also by awareness of the shared condition of all human beings.

The creation story is about the common source and condition of all humankind. The biblical description of the first human being as a creature is a graphic representation of the normative rabbinic principle "beloved is every human being who has been created in the image of God."

The historical narrative develops a sense of intimacy with the Jewish people. Through it we become a family and embrace our particular identity with joy and love. But the family narrative is not our only living framework. Every seventh day we interrupt the flow of our tasks and ambitions and stand quietly before God the creator. The dialectic between our particular and universal identities, between the God of Israel and the God of creation, is the fate and challenge of being a Jew.

ERIC H. YOFFIE is a rabbi and the president of the Union for Reform Judaism.

"The concept of the Jews being one people is a *religious* idea and not an ethnic, political, or cultural one."

I am Jewish. This means, above all else, that I was present at Sinai, and that when the Torah was given on that mountain, my DNA was to be found in the crowd.

I have devoted much of my life to understanding the process of revelation that began on that day. Torah, I know, was transmitted first to Moses and then to his spiritual descendants—the prophets and rabbis who fashioned our tradition and passed it on to subsequent generations. Studying Torah and tradition is my first priority and greatest joy, just as it has been the central, incandescent passion of Jews throughout all of Jewish history. There is, however, nothing easy about it. Those who recorded Torah were fallible human beings, products of the unique conditions of their time, and Torah is therefore a record of both divine command and human response. As a liberal Jew and a modern person, I must struggle to determine what in Torah is divine revelation and what is human interpretation—that is, what is eternally binding and what is merely of historical interest. Yet I am continually amazed and delighted by the wisdom and relevance of our sacred texts, by how much of Torah speaks to me directly, and by the power of Torah to shape my life. Whenever I perform a *mitz-*

vah, I feel awe and humility in the face of mystery, and I yearn to share this experience with my fellow Jews.

I am Jewish. This means that I am part of the People Israel. The Jewish people are a contentious lot, and my fellow Jews infuriate me more often than not, but I am bound to them nonetheless. Just as I do not like all the members of my family but I am obligated to love them, so too do I love the Jewish people even when I am profoundly unhappy with the actions of individual Jews.

A people is usually defined by race, origin, language, territory, or statehood, and none of these categories is an obvious common denominator for the worldwide Jewish people. Peoplehood is a puzzling concept for modern Jews, particularly younger ones, who often cannot understand what connects them to other Jews in Moscow, Buenos Aries, and Tel Aviv. But I am convinced, to the depth of my being, that Jewish destiny is a collective destiny. And I believe as well that the concept of the Jews being one people is a *religious* idea and not an ethnic, political, or cultural one. The foundations of peoplehood are not to be found in nostalgia, gastronomy, or a shared sense of vulnerability, but in the covenantal relationship between God and the Jewish people. It is the covenant at Sinai that links all Jews, including nonobservant ones, in a bond of shared responsibility. And if we hope to strengthen the unity and interdependence of the Jewish people, we will have to revive the religious ideas on which these notions are based.

I am Jewish. This means that the State of Israel has a special hold on my soul. Jewish life, I believe, cannot be sustained without Israel at its core. The Torah that spells out for us a way of life and a religious destiny also binds us to a land. And in a world capable of infinite evil, the establishment of Israel restores to a segment of the Jewish people control over its own destiny. With the memory of the Holocaust fresh in our minds, the absence of power is a curse, and the State of Israel has removed that curse by returning power to Jewish hands.

The religious significance of the Jewish state lies in the fact that it provides a framework in which Torah is to be observed and a holy community is to be created. But barely half a century old and located in a hostile neighborhood, Israel until now has focused its attention on saving Jews and ensuring the security of its citizens. Yet the day will come, I know, when Israel will not only save Jews but will also save Judaism. The day will come when the State of Israel will become the classroom of the diaspora, providing ongoing seminars in Jewish identity and restoring to Jewish life its public dimension and collective pulse. And to be Jewish means not only to support Israel's security concerns but also to join in partnership with Israelis in strengthening Jewish religious civilization wherever Jews are found.

I am Jewish. This means that I am obligated to bring repair, wholeness, and sanctity to all of humankind. The God who has commanded us to study Torah, engage in prayer, and observe the rituals of our tradition also requires us to be aware of each and every instance of human suffering and to resuscitate throughout the world the fundamental values of Torah—that human life is sacred, that justice is a supreme value, and that freedom is the touchstone of civilization.

I am not unaware of the dangers Jews face. Anti-semitism has reared its ugly head in Europe, and a virulent brand of Islamic Jew-hatred targets Jews in Israel and elsewhere. But I have no patience for those who wish to respond to these dangers by retreating into a Jewish ghetto. We still have allies in the world and we still have neighbors who will listen to our concerns. And those of us who live in America are more influential and secure than Jews have ever been. Under any circumstances, if we wish to remain Jews, we have no choice but to commit ourselves to the welfare of the general society— first, because escape from the world is impossible in an age of globalization and, second, because our tradition could not be more clear on our responsibilities. The Jewish voice is a moral voice, and the Jew is someone who is touched by other people's pain. And a central message of Judaism is that redemption is of this world, and that every time we help the poor escape from poverty or cause the unheeded to be heard, we bring God's kingdom one step closer.

Finally, I am Jewish, and this means that I am filled with hope. I know that from the earliest days of our history, we Jews have been a future-oriented people and that our golden age—and the golden age of humankind—is not in the past but in the future. I know that humanity, though capable of terrible deeds, is nonetheless redeemable. I know that Jews respond to crisis not with despair but with renewal, and with stunning bursts of creativity. I know that we Jews have recreated the past in every generation and we will do so in my generation as well. I know that when the collective Jewish will is mobilized, it has astonishing power to change the world for good. And above all, I know that being Jewish is a privilege that every day enriches and ennobles my life.

SARAH LEVIN, Anchorage, Alaska

I think that being Jewish is not just the religion I practice, but the life I live. I think that it takes a special person to believe in a religion when you are surrounded by people who believe differently. I believe that you are born into a religion, chosen by a higher power, and it is up to you to do what you can to keep it alive; I feel really blessed to be Jewish.

ALAN DERSHOWITZ is a professor of law at Harvard. His latest book is *The Case for Israel*.

"Being part of this people, I am part of the unfolding mystery."

I am a Jew. I was born a Jew. I have lived my life as a Jew. And I will die a Jew. This I know for certain. The rest is shrouded in mystery, doubt, and metaphor.

I regard myself as fortunate to have been born a Jew, though I attach no cosmic or even religious significance to the happenstance of my birth. I do not believe in destiny or chosenness. But having been born into the Jewish tradition, I feel an enormous responsibility to help preserve it and make it thrive.

The Jewish people have played an important, and in some ways a unique, role in human history. In part they have chosen this role. In part it was thrust upon them by their persecutors. They have challenged the conventional wisdom, thereby provoking the antagonism of governments, churches, universities, and other established institutions. They have been restless wanderers, moving—sometimes by force or threat—from place to place, without a singular home. They have been stiff-necked in refusing to bow to tyrants or to change their ways in the face of physical threats. The very survival, not to speak of the disproportionate influence, of this tiny group of people is a remarkable mystery.

By being part of this people, I am part of the unfolding mystery. Were I a Jew who literally believed in the biblical narrative of chosenness or the theological notion of predetermination, the mystery would be less interesting. But I believe that we make our own destiny and history—that we are responsible for our choices. I love the Jewish Bible, Talmud, and other sacred texts, but I study them as metaphor—*midrash*—on the Jewish experience, written by fallible human beings, for other fallible human beings. It is their very human quality that has inspired, fascinated, and educated me over so many years. It has been these books that have encouraged me to challenge everything, even their status as sacred and their authorship by God. They have also encouraged me to challenge all secular truths and accepted wisdom. Judaism is a tradition of challenge—of questioning, of doubting, of debating, and of living with uncertainty. Being a Jew means always living with uncertainty—never letting one's guard completely down. History is too powerful to ignore or deny. Being a Jew means facing constant challenge. Challenge for me is not only a means toward finding enduring truths. It is also the end state. Constant challenge is the only truth. The hardest moral questions have no singular answer. If the Torah has one hundred faces, it is because it reflects the complexity of life.

Over the years, some Jews have chosen or been compelled to abandon their tradition and join the mainstream. That is their right, and perhaps their need, but for those of us who have chosen to remain Jewish—in whatever way we have defined that choice—a special responsibility accrues. We have chosen to remain part of a wonderful civilization—an ever-changing yet enduring civilization. Although originally based on a distinct theology, the Jewish civilization has diversified to include many components beyond religion. We are a culture, a heterogeneous culture to be sure, but a culture nonetheless. Aspects of that culture—such as the Yiddish language, literature, and lifestyle of eastern Europe—have been destroyed, while other aspects—such as largely secular, Hebrew-speaking Israel—have emerged. We are a living history, an often quite tragic history, but one with a remarkable and enduring record of accomplishment. We are a religion, though not practiced nor even believed by many who proudly identify as Jews, and yet we have influenced the two dominant religions of the world beyond calculation. We have helped change science, create new genres of literature, cure illnesses, and promote human rights, and we have left tracks everywhere we have wandered.

Despite our collective accomplishments as a people—indeed, perhaps because of them—we have been despised and persecuted, but never ignored. *Why* we have so often been persecuted is part of the mystery. *That* our persecution persists even now in some parts of the world is the reality.

Today, Jews are hated because there is finally a Jewish state, with a fallible Jewish army and fallible Jewish political leaders. Although this imperfect Jewish state has behaved better than any state in history facing comparable dangers, more is demanded of it. Because the Jews of Israel have become "normalized"—with their own country and their own ability to defend themselves—they have become a pariah to many. The bigotry persists, but this time it is called anti-Zionism, rather than anti-Semitism. The Jew among nations has replaced the Jew within nations as an object of double-standard criticism and persecution. Among the worst offenders are the United Nations, the European community, and many in academia. Some churches, too, must be included in this list of infamy. The world will once again stand judged—as it has throughout history—by the manner in which it treats the Jew, whether as an individual or as a nation. Will Israel's legitimate efforts to defend itself from those who would destroy it and terrorize its citizens become the new justification—excuse—for the oldest of prejudices? That is among the most daunting of moral questions confronting the world in this millennium. The Jewish community faces internal challenges as well, but none as serious as the external threats directed at vulnerable Jewish communities and individuals. We are responsible for resolving the internal demographic threats, but others bear much of the responsibility for the external physical threats that are largely beyond our control.

Will our influence continue? Will so many of us choose to assimilate or turn inward that we become a historical curiosity? Will we be destroyed by our current or future enemies, who will soon have the weapons of mass destruction denied to our past enemies? No one can know the answers to these haunting questions. The mystery continues.

Each of us who regards himself or herself as a Jew has a responsibility to do something to maximize the chance that our civilization will not only endure but also thrive. Our survival and continuing influence is a moral imperative for at least two reasons—one positive, the other negative. The positive reason is that Judaism has so much to offer—both to Jews and non-Jews alike. If diversity means anything, it must include a significant Jewish presence and influence. The negative reason is that if the forces of evil that would destroy us are allowed to succeed, it would set a terrible precedent for other vulnerable minorities. We have always been the "miners' canary"—the litmus test for tolerance in the world. Some see enhancing the positive as their primary role. Others see preventing the negative as their mandate. I see my own role, as a human rights advocate, as including helping to ensure that never again will any Jew be murdered—as Daniel Pearl was—because he was a Jew.

Rabbi Lawrence Kushner, spiritual leader of Congregation Beth El in Sudbury, Massachusetts, for more than twenty-five years, is an author of many books. He is currently the Emanu-El scholar at Congregation Emanu-El in San Francisco and an adjunct professor at Hebrew Union College–Jewish Institute of Religion.

"Life in all its forms is sacred; in the face of each creature I see my Creator."

When I say that I am a Jew, I affirm the following:

1. The only sound my God utters is *alef*—the first letter of the Hebrew alphabet, which has no sound, the sound of Nothing. The Hebrew word for "I," *Anochi,* begins with *alef.*

2. My God is not visible; my God is not invisible. My God looks like Nothing. There is Nothing to see.

3. The Name of my God is made from the root letters of the Hebrew verb *to be,* which are themselves vowels. It probably meant something like *The One who brings into being all that is.* It is the sound of Nothing—only breathing.

4. One day each week I try to pretend that the universe is done, finished, that it (and I) need nothing more to be complete.

5. My parents are the instruments God used to bring me into being. Through trying to understand and listen to them, I begin to comprehend myself.

6. Life in all its forms is sacred; in the face of each creature I see my Creator.

7. The relationship I share with my life-partner is sacred and ultimate. She is my Only One.

8. You are other than me and your things are extensions of who you are. I may not appropriate your things for myself; they are yours.

9. I respect society's mechanisms for resolving disputes: I renounce perjury.

10. To the extent that I can rejoice in and want nothing more than what I already have, I begin to resemble my God who has, wants, and is Nothing.

Ich bin a Yid. I am a Jew.

FELICIA LILIEN, 14, Naples, Florida

Being Jewish is not keeping kosher, it's not going to services every week, and it's not reading from the Torah daily. Judaism is a decision only you can make. There's no right or wrong way to be Jewish because no one can tell you how to connect with God. I am a giver, I am a receiver, I am a believer, I am strong, I am proud, and, most important, I am Jewish.

 **Arno Penzias,** a refugee from Nazi Germany, grew up in New York City, worked at Bell Labs for most of his life, and now coaches small technology companies. In 1978 he was awarded the Nobel Prize in Physics for a discovery related to the origin of the universe.

"The all-encompassing perfection of the world's physical laws reflects the power of the creative force that brought them into being."

For me, being Jewish means seeing the creation of the world in terms of the creation of laws—with its creator as the law-giver. I hadn't planned it that way when I chose physics as my vocation, but that choice has led me to frame the question, "What does it mean to me to be a Jew?" in the light of my own scientific discoveries about the origin of the universe. As a Jew who is also a scientist, I'm happy that the weight of scientific evidence has compelled the scientific community to accept the so-called big bang (creation as an instantaneous event) picture as the only viable model upon which to base our study of the universe. Nonetheless, had the steady state (the world has been around forever) alternative been supported by observational tests, I would still be a Jew. I would still give charity and go to synagogue.

Like most scientists, I see the entire physical world—all of it, down to its smallest detail—to be governed by a powerfully precise, and all-encompassing, set of laws. Unlike many scientists, however, I don't agree with Stephen Weinberg's assertion, "The more I study the universe, the more meaningless it becomes." Looking at the ever-richer variety of phenomena that modern instruments allow us to probe, both Steve and I find ourselves able to interpret everything we can see, or infer, in terms of a small handful of physical laws. These laws underlie all we see around us, including human beings capable of love, learning, and free will. No physical phenomenon—from the merest instant after the big bang, to the present day—requires a supernatural explanation. The laws, in other words, govern all the world, and everything in it.

Summarized in less than a single page of dense mathematics, a half dozen or so equations provide accurate descriptions of phenomena as diverse as the creation of iron in the envelopes of supernovae, the structure of snowflakes, and the protein generators that imprint significant events in our long-term memories. With *everything,* as far as we can see, following the same blueprint, small wonder that Weinberg—and many others—see no room left for a Supreme Being.

For me, on the other hand, the all-encompassing perfection of the world's physical laws reflects the power of the creative force that brought them into being. Being Jewish encourages me to seek physical explanations, rather than look for miracles to sustain my belief. To me, the miracle of creation obviates any need for smaller-scale miracles to keep the world going. In that regard, I find support in the writings of Moses Ben Maimon. A biblical scholar, revered as the Rambam by all who study the Talmud, he was also a physician and philosopher. Commenting on the biblical story of how Jacob wrestled with an angel and emerged with a lifelong limp, Maimonides offers a physical—rather than miraculous—explanation, linking it to his experience with psychosomatic symptoms among his patients. At the same time, he remains steadfast in his belief in the overarching miracle of creation, as well as in its creator. When dealing with the creation, therefore, those of us who see an underlying meaning in the world part company with those who see everything as meaningless.

In concert with this latter view, the steady-state theory referred to above posited a framework in which creation didn't happen. Confronted with compelling observational data that showed our universe to have begun in a discrete event, theorists have now responded with a new scenario. Instead of maintaining that creation didn't happen, their new theories postulate a meaningless creation, just one of an infinite number of similar events happening at random. In a current version of this line of thinking, our four-dimensional universe emerged from a random ripple in an eleven-dimensional "false vacuum." As higher-dimensional objects collide with one another, this theory maintains, they sometimes produce nascent bubbles of time and space, each with its own randomly produced set of physical laws.

Meaninglessness, in other words, requires a theory so complex that most scientists can't even understand the mathematics that underlies it. Small wonder, then, that science writers can offer general readers little more than respectful descriptions of this new version of an old orthodoxy. In addition to "science," everything from Greek philosophy (Aristotle's eternity of matter) to everyday common sense ("there had to be something before the big bang") reflects human rationality's longstanding antipathy to creation.

What then does it mean to be a Jew? The Rambam gives us an answer. In his *Guide to the Perplexed* he writes, "In these matters, take no notice of any man, for it is the foundation of our father that the Holy One created the world from nothing, that time did not exist before, because it depends upon the motion of the Sphere, and that too was created."

 RABBI PATRICIA KARLIN-NEUMANN is the senior associate dean for religious life at Stanford University. She teaches and lectures widely on Jewish feminism, rabbinical ethics, and social justice.

"To discover a frame through which to understand experience."

I am Jewish, deeply rooted in a culture and tradition whose streams have watered me throughout many seasons. Through adversity, celebration, uncertainty, and change, Jewish tradition has offered words, symbols, rituals, comfort, challenge, and hope. It has become my language and my guide. And in turn, I try to provide those to others. But it was not my first language.

As a teen, I attended Mitzvah Corps, a summer program where high school students lived and worked together in the inner city, pondering questions of poverty and fairness. I asked my parents why the discussions flourishing among my peers about life, social responsibility, and justice had been missing from our dinner table. My father answered that he was busy trying to make a living, wanting to provide my siblings and me with what he had lacked in his youth.

What my parents did provide was a model for loving human beings, whatever their education or accomplishments, whatever their race or background. My father hired former convicts in his small business, willing to trust those who had been identified as untrustworthy. My mother, a tentative driver, regularly chauffeured women who didn't drive when she went on her daily errands.

Pirkei Avot (Ethics of the Ancestors) teaches, *"Ohev et ha briot, u'mekarvan l'Torah."* "Love human beings and draw them close to Torah." Upon learning this teaching, I grasped that Judaism offered a language of intention and eternality. It was as if loving human beings were the letters, the building blocks of a Jewish vocabulary, and drawing close to Torah shaped that love into words, standing in relationship, spelling out meaning.[1] I sought out and found teachers who were willing to share the language of Jewish life, to explore the world of ideas, and to discover a frame through which to understand experience. By drawing close to Torah, I came to name my father's faith in others as *teshuvah*—repentance and trusting the possibility for change; I came to know my mother's generosity as *gemilut chasadim*—acts of loving-kindness that foster relatedness and community. Through study and practice, I learned that drawing close to Torah means being engaged in living an examined life, in delving into the texts and traditions of Judaism to inform and shape that life, in attempting to discover how to live in a way that engenders gratitude, justice, and compassion in the world.

I try to incorporate *Pirkei Avot*'s teaching into my family, community, and work. I want my children to grow up in a home where the aroma of *challah* baking pervades the air on Friday, anticipating the taste of time for family and community that Shabbat bestows. There is love for them and for tradition baking in the oven. For nearly two decades, I have worked as a rabbi in colleges and universities, speaking the language of Jewish life to help make meaning, invigorated by learning with, caring for, and drawing students close as they discern who they are and what is worth doing with their gifts and their lives.

I am Jewish, joining with other beloved human beings to deepen our humanity; to create lives of purpose; and to study, interpret, and live out the Torah we have received. And together may we live our lives so as to shape the Torah, the teachings, and the wisdom that is yet to unfold.

1. Rabbi Edward Feld, private correspondence.

SHIA LABEOUF appeared in 2003's *Dumb and Dumberer, Charlie's Angels: Full Throttle,* and *Holes.* He won a Daytime Emmy for his role in the Disney Channel series *Even Stevens.*

"Judaism to me is the name of the telephone in my heart that allows me to speak to God."

First off, let me make it clear that I am in no way a Jew who attends Shabbat every Friday or puts *t'fillin* on before I go to sleep.

I am what you would call a claimer Jew. See, I claim to be Jewish because it is beneficial to be Jewish. I benefit from saying I am Jewish. How?

I have a personal relationship with God that happens to work within the confines of Judaism.

Judaism to me is the name of the telephone in my heart that allows me to speak to God.

Really, I feel cocky when I say I am Jewish, not bad cocky, but good cocky. Because what I am really saying is that I am one of the few chosen ones out there. I made it; God chose me and I take pride in that.

 SANDY EISENBERG SASSO was the second woman to be ordained as a rabbi and the first rabbi to become a mother. She holds a doctorate in ministry, is active in the interfaith community, and is an award-winning author of many inspiring books for children.

"At the heart of what it means to be a Jew is to ask questions."

Visiting groups often come to the synagogue to learn about Judaism. They ask about ritual, history, practice, and symbol. But one day a young middle-school student posed a question I had never really considered before: "Does Judaism give you the answer to all your questions?" What appropriate response could I offer this young girl? Of course, in good Jewish style, I could have answered her question with another question! But I believed she deserved something more.

At the heart of what it means to be a Jew is to ask questions. The Haggadah, which retells the core story of the Jewish people from slavery to freedom, begins with questions. And what follows are not definitive answers but a story. As I reflect back on that young girl's challenge, I realize that our most cherished sacred texts are based on questions. Not only is the Talmud known for its interrogative and argumentative style, but even the Bible is at heart a questioning text, exploring life's meaning and mystery.

Daniel Pearl, to whose memory this anthology is dedicated, was a journalist whose art was in asking the often difficult questions that uncover a story. The story of Judaism is, from the beginning, grounded in the hard questions with which every generation has to struggle.

Four biblical questions offer us a framework for understanding the story of Jewish identity. In the first two questions God addresses us; in the other two, we address God.

- Where are you? (Gen. 3:9)
- Where is your brother? (Gen. 4:9)

- Shall not the Judge of all the earth do justly? (Gen. 18:25)
- I lift up my eyes to the mountains, from where will my help come? (Pss. 121:1)

"Where are you? (Gen. 3:9) and "Where is your brother?" (Gen. 4:9). God speaks first to Adam in the Garden of Eden, and then to Cain following his act of fratricide. God is not asking for information. There is no simple answer: "I am here in the Garden, God." "My brother is over there, lying dead in the field." Rather, the divine address probes issues of spiritual location and relationship, of self and other.

What does it mean to be a human being? Judaism tells us that we are but dust and ashes, like the grass that withers and the flower that fades, and yet, we are created in the image of God, little lower than the angels. Caught somewhere between heavenly grandeur and earthly mortality, we are to figure out our place in the universe, our accountability to self and to that which transcends us.

The second question reminds us that Judaism is not just a matter of individual identity. I cannot be a Jew alone. We are connected and responsible for one another. Study is not meant to be a solitary act. It is done in *hevruta,* with others. Prayer is not intended to be a lonely meditative exercise. It is done in a *minyan,* with a community. We are linked to a long history; we are descendents of Abraham and Sarah and ancestors of future generations.

There is a story told of a young boy who likes to wander in the forest. The boy's father is concerned that the forest is a dangerous place. He asks his son why he spends so much time there. The son answers, "I go there to find God." The father responds, "Don't you know that God is everywhere?" "Yes," answers the boy, "but I am not."

Another story tells of two people who meet in the forest. Both are lost and have been wandering for days. One says to the other, "The way either of us has been going is not the way. Come, let us find our way out together."

There is a place that is unique to me, that is my place alone, where I meet God; yet it is connected to other places and people. I cannot know my place in the world without knowing my brother and sister's place. I discover myself, and God, in my encounter with another.

Even as God asks questions of humanity, Judaism teaches us that humans also challenge God. When Abraham hears the divine decision to destroy the cities of Sodom and Gomorrah, he confronts God, "Shall not the Judge of all the earth do justly?" (Gen. 18:25). When the psalmist seeks meaning and solace, he writes, "I lift my eyes to the mountains, from where will my help come?" (Pss. 121:1).

Judaism struggles with questions of justice. With eyes open to the unfairness of life, to the suffering of the righteous, it does not offer simple solutions, excuses for God. Even as our faith asks God to exercise justice in the world, it also requires it of humanity. Tradition teaches that while we may hope for miracles, we may not depend on them.

As Moses stood before the Sea of Reeds with the Egyptians fast approaching, he prayed. But the Midrash teaches that God interrupted him, saying, "There is a time for prayer and a time for action, now is the time to act, to go forward."

To be Jewish means to go forward, to bring order where there is chaos. It means both to cry out against injustice and to act against it. Ultimately, Judaism realizes that injustice and suffering are not divine problems but human responsibilities, that human acts of goodness bring God's presence into the world. Judaism recognizes God in small acts of heroism, in deeds of compassion and courage, in the hands and hearts and voices of those who work to bring healing and justice to the world.

Just as Judaism confronts God, so it comforts us with the awareness that God is always present. Even when our best acts fail, our finest intentions fall short, we yet affirm the words of the psalm: "I lift up my eyes to the mountains, from where will my help come? My help comes from the Eternal who makes the heavens and the earth."

To be a Jew means never to despair, to be able to see beyond loss and fear to hope and faith. The Rabbis teach us that when Adam experienced the first setting of the sun, he was afraid. He was certain that once the sun went down it would not rise again. The world would be forever dark and cold. Life as he knew it would cease. Adam wept at the disappearance of the sun; he mourned the loss of warmth and light. Then God taught him to make fire to get through the night. And after that long and frightful night, morning came and the sun rose again.

Our Jewish faith is what enables us, despite sunset and darkness, despite terror and war, despite uncertainty and difficulty, despite all our questions, to go on with life and redeem it. It is what enables us to live with mystery and say a blessing over it. Judaism teaches us through words and rituals to kindle the fires that will get us through the night, and to celebrate and rejoice in the new day.

The Rabbis tell us that the fire that God taught Adam to light is the same fire we make at the close of every Shabbat when we kindle the *Havdalah* candle. Every week we remind ourselves that we can get through the night, that we can live with the questions to which there are no answers, and that morning will come again.

And so, we hold in tension our two questions to God—"Will not the Judge of all the earth do justly?" and "I lift up my eyes to the mountains, from where will my help come?" With one hand we shake a fist, demanding a world that is kinder and more just. We cry out to God, outraged at a world unredeemed, torn by war, pained by natural disasters, and devastated by human failings. With the other hand, we reach out to find compassion in the knowledge of God's eternal embrace. We find refuge in the shelter of God, in the belief that we are not alone in the universe and that we can reshape tomorrow.

In a world that seeks single solutions, the Jew asks questions. In a world where people are dangerously preoccupied with finding divine answers, the Jew is more concerned about struggling with the hard questions about life and death, about good and evil, about God and humanity. And so to the young student who wondered whether Judaism gave me the answers to all my questions, I responded, "No, Judaism does not give me the answers to all my questions, but it helps me ask the right questions and enables me to live with those to which there are no answers."

Amos Oz is the internationally acclaimed author of numerous novels and essay collections that have been translated into thirty languages. He lectures in literature at the Ben Gurion University of the Negev and lives in Arad.

"A Jew, in my unhalakhic opinion, is someone who *chooses* to share the fate of other Jews, or who is *condemned* to do so."

I wrote these sentences in 1967. Three and a half decades later as I reread them, I find that I still agree with myself. That does not often happen to me. May I dedicate this quote to the memory of Daniel Pearl, who not only died for being a Jew but also died as a Jew.

I am a Jew and a Zionist. In saying this, I am not basing myself on religion. I have never learned to resort to verbal compromises like "the spirit of our Jewish past" or the "the values of Jewish tradition," because values and tradition alike derive directly from religious tenets in which I cannot believe. It is impossible to sever Jewish values and Jewish tradition from their source, which is revelation, faith and commandments. Consequently nouns like "mission," "destiny" and "election," when used with the adjective "Jewish," only cause me embarrassment or worse.

A Jew, in my vocabulary, is someone who regards himself as a Jew, or someone who is forced to be a Jew. A Jew is someone who acknowledges his Jewishness. If he acknowledges it publicly, he is a Jew by choice. If he acknowledges it only to his inner self, he is a Jew by the force of his destiny. If he does not acknowledge any connection with the Jewish people either in public or in his tormented inner being he is not a Jew, even if religious law defines him as such because his mother is Jewish. A Jew, in my unhalakhic opinion, is someone who *chooses* to share the fate of other Jews, or who is *condemned* to do so.

Moreover: to be a Jew almost always means to relate mentally to the Jewish past, whether the relation is one of pride or gloom or both together, whether it consists of shame or rebellion or pride or nostalgia.

Moreover: to be a Jew almost always means to relate to the Jewish present, whether the relation is one of fear or confidence, pride in the achievement of Jews or shame for their actions, an urge to deflect them from their path or a compulsion to join them.

And finally: to be a Jew means to feel that wherever a Jew is persecuted for being a Jew—that means you.

Samantha Schram, 10, West Palm Beach, Florida

When I say I'm Jewish I think of my uniqueness and how lucky I am to be a Jew. I am one of the chosen people and that makes me feel as special as a movie star. Every Saturday I go to temple to pray to G-d and every single night I say the *Sh'ma.*

Rabbi Israel Meir Lau was born in Poland in 1937 and saved from Buchenwald in 1945. He served as chief rabbi of Israel for ten years.

"'I am Jewish, and I fear Hashem, the G-d of the Heavens, who made the sea and the dry land.'"

The ship was on a journey from Jaffa to Tarshish when a storm suddenly descended upon it, threatening to destroy it. With the fear of death gripping their hearts, the sailors turned to their pagan gods and prayed for a miracle.

The ship's captain descended into the hold and found Jonah the Prophet fast asleep in his bunk despite the chaos and the panic. "How can you sleep so soundly? Arise, call out to your G-d!" he said to Jonah.

The sailors cast lots to see whose sins were responsible for the storm, and it turned out to be Jonah. "What is your trade?" they asked him. "From where do you come? What is your land? And what nation do you belong to?"

This is when Jonah pronounced his historic declaration: "I am Jewish, and I fear Hashem, the G-d of the Heavens, who made the sea and the dry land."

Jonah the Prophet's proud declaration of Jewish identity, which he courageously declared to the world in spite of the dangers surrounding him, became a symbol of Jewish affiliation and belief that would be uttered time and again throughout the millennia of Jewish suffering. With these code words "I am Jewish," Jonah set an example of Jewish pride for all generations. And it was he who caused the people of Nineveh to repent for their sins.

Before Jonah the Prophet, a historical precedent had already been set by Joseph, when he was imprisoned under harsh and life-threatening conditions in Egypt. Alone, separated from his family, incarcerated in a foreign land for a crime he did not commit, he declared to Pharaoh's butler, "I was kidnapped from the land of the Jews." He made no attempt to hide his nationality or to assimilate among the Egyptians. He proudly declared he was a Jew.

Our sages, never ones to hide from the truth when it comes to teaching us object lessons, point out a sharp distinction between Joseph and Moses when confronted with similar circumstances. Joseph, who readily admitted his nationality, merited burial in the Land of Israel. Moses, on the other hand, did not. Why was this?

The Midrash tells us that when Moses fled from Egypt and rescued the daughters of Jethro from the Midianite shepherds who were accosting them, the girls told their father, "An Egyptian man saved us." Moses remained silent and did not reveal his correct identity.

Moses could have been excused for this. In contrast to Joseph, who was born in Israel, Moses was born and raised in Egypt, and the description of Jethro's daughters was accurate. Yet our sages tell us that Moses should have spoken up. Because he did not, he was punished and was buried outside of Israel.

Since the epoch of our forefathers and prophets, the list has grown long of those who have given their lives for the public sanctification of G-d's name. Prominent among them were Rabbi Akiva and his colleagues, known as the ten martyrs. Our sages tell us no mortal man will ever come close to the lofty levels these martyrs attained in the eternal world for the sacrifices they made. In the *Sh'ma Yisrael,* we are commanded, "And you shall love G-d with all of your heart, all of your soul, and all of your means." Our sages say all of your soul includes giving one's very life for sake of G-d's name.

Daniel Pearl sanctified G-d's name. His ancestors, who planted deep roots in Israel, paved the way for his sacrifice. His grandfather was a founder of Bnei Brak, where a street was named for him. The soul of Daniel Pearl is hewn from this source of self-sacrifice for the values and ideals implanted in him by those who preceded him. These same values and ideals are what have enabled the remnants of our nation to survive and reestablish itself, and they are worthy of continued sacrifice.

 LEON WIESELTIER is the author of *Kaddish* and the literary editor of *The New Republic.*

"When I say that I am a Jew, I mean to say that a Jew is what I desire to become."

I prefer to declare not that I am Jewish but that I am a Jew. There is nothing adjectival about this dimension of my being. It is not a quality of anything else, not a modification of another essence; it is itself a noun, itself an essence; it is itself. When I say that I am a Jew, I do not mean to say that I am only a Jew—existence is never single or whole, except when it is debased; but the Jew that I am is primary, irreducible, a raw and rich fact of my fate. And yet I do not appeal to its facticity for its justification. Quite the contrary. Such an appeal would be repulsively tribal; and it is the first lesson of Jewish history that the Jews are considerably more than a tribe. No, the facticity of my identity, the accidental truth that it is what I have inherited, rather embarrasses me. I wish that I could have chosen it. I pray that I would have chosen it. Accident is not an adequate foundation for a life. I envy converts, once the sons and the daughters of their parents and now the sons and the daughters of Abraham and Sarah. They are Jews as a consequence of their own reflection and their own freedom. They became Jews out of inner necessity. But I must transform outer necessity into inner necessity.

Kierkegaard once remarked that it is easier for a non-Christian to become a Christian than for a Christian to become a Christian. When I say that I am a Jew, I mean to say that a Jew is what I desire to become. The sense in which I am already one—the biological and the sociological—does not affect my soul or reveal what it can accomplish, though it certainly affects my historical allegiances and my political actions. I am proud to be the heir of my ancestors, but I am too proud to be just an heir. I wish to be also one of my ancestors, an artificer of this tradition and thereby an artificer of myself. So I am a Jew who is becoming a Jew, if I am a serious Jew at all. I make myself known as much by my chosen destination as by my unchosen origin. (One of the many unfortunate consequences of the concept of the Chosen People is that it has relieved many Jews of the responsibility of choice, or so they think.)

I am a Jew: This is another way of saying that I am busy at work. But the study of Judaism, and of the civilization that it bred, makes the toil easy: The exposure to the words and the ideas of Judaism has always been, for me, an experience of seduction to which I keenly capitulate. Here is an example, a text to raise up (as the rabbis believed) the soul of the deceased, a *yahrzeit* text from the tradition of nineteenth-century Polish Hasidism, in sorrowful and respectful recollection of Daniel Pearl. Menahem Mendel of Kotzk reported an interpretation of a verse and a prayer in the name of his teacher, Jacob Isaac of Przysucha. In Numbers, after Aaron is instructed to light the lamps in the Tabernacle, it is recorded that "Aaron did so." Rashi glosses these otherwise superfluous words with the midrashic comment: "This is said in praise of Aaron, to indicate that he made no changes [in his fulfillment of the command]." The Kotzker produces a deep hermeneutical pun in Rashi's comment: The Hebrew words *shelo shina,* or "he made no changes," the Kotzker reads as *shelo na'asah yashan etzlo,* or "it did not become old for him." Or as he remarks in Yiddish, *ess iz nisht alt gevorn,* explaining that Aaron "would do his work every day as if for the first time, not out of habit, as if it had grown stale."

135

This power of refreshment the Kotzker takes to be the implication of a peculiar blessing at the start of the morning prayers. "Blessed art thou, O Lord our God, King of the Universe, who did not make me a gentile." *Shelo asani goy:* This formulation is uttered every morning, the Hasidic philosopher suggests, "because one must feel in one's soul every day as if one has gone from being a non-Jew to being a Jew." It is a startlingly modern ideal of self-creation. It is about as spiritually realistic as the other modern fantasies of a completely new beginning, of emptying oneself entirely of what one has found so as to fill oneself entirely with what one has made—but it is a very useful exaggeration. It demands that every Jew acknowledge the contingent nature of his Jewishness, and then correct it. For if I cannot imagine not being a Jew, I cannot glory in being a Jew, or at least I have not earned the right to this glory.

And may it always be said about the memory of Daniel Pearl that *ess iz nisht alt gevorn.*

NAOMI RAGEN, an American-born novelist, playwright, and columnist, has lived in Jerusalem for more than thirty years. Her books include *Jephte's Daughter, Sotah,* and *The Ghost of Hannah Mendes.*

"Keep loving, despite all the hatred."

To be a Jew is to keep building through all the destruction; to keep loving, despite all the hatred; to be charitable and kind and wise because this is what your God asks of you, and you would not want to disappoint Him.

 GERSHOM SIZOMU, leader of the *Abayudaya* (Jews) of Uganda, received his bachelor's degree at the Islamic University in Uganda and is currently studying at Ziegler School of Rabbinic Studies of the University of Judaism in Los Angeles.

"I do not look Jewish in the eyes of the international Jewish community and I am frequently asked, 'How did you become Jewish?' and 'Who converted you?'"

I am the spiritual leader of the *Abayudaya* (Jews) in Uganda, Africa. Our number is small, but we are a strong, spiritual, and deeply religious Jewish community. There are more than six hundred of us, although our numbers have dwindled from several thousand.

Born in 1969, I am thirty-four years old. My wife, Tzipporah, and I have brought our two young children with us on my five-year journey through rabbinical school here in Los Angeles, California. We are far from our home.

In 1919, eighty-four years ago, Shimei (Semei) Kakungulu, the founder of our community, was a military general. After reading the Bible, he abandoned his military service, broke away from the Imperial British East African Company, where he served as a local governor of the Eastern region, and rejected ongoing missionary efforts still prevalent in our country.

Shimei circumcised himself, his children, and the males of our tribe. He started strict observance of Shabbat every Saturday. More than three thousand of his followers—our previous generation—celebrated Jewish festivals, observed fasts, and began complete adherence to kashrut, as written in the Five Books of Moses.

When I was only two years old, Iddi Amin Dada, legendary for his cruelty and corruption, grabbed political power and the presidency at gunpoint. Between 1971 and 1979, when he was overthrown, Amin ordered us to stop our religious observance and warned us against calling ourselves Jews. He gave us three alternatives:

convert to Islam or Christianity, become unaffiliated, or face public execution.

While many of our people succumbed to the first alternative and converted, my family and several other families continued to observe Shabbat and the other *mitzvot* in secret. Most often, we held services in bedrooms, where we would worship in whispers to our God.

In 1989 at the age of twenty, I was arrested with three fellow Jews. We were caught mobilizing our youth to learn about Judaism and the Hebrew language, and we were also rebuilding the foundation of our main synagogue, which had been destroyed during Amin's regime. We suffered in the hands of local Christian and Muslim government administrators, who were not at all interested in the existence of a Jewish community.

To be Jewish in Uganda we must withstand many levels of intimidation, oppression, and abuse. We face restricted access to social services owned or managed by Christians and Muslims. But, Uganda is not our only challenge.

I do not look Jewish in the eyes of the international Jewish community and I am frequently asked, "How did you become Jewish?" and "Who converted you?"

A *beit din* (rabbinical court) of Conservative rabbis performed "mass conversions" for our community members to bring us officially into the Jewish world family in February of 2002.

When I'm weak from my Yom Kippur fast, I realize I am a fragile being, but my God lives forever and ever. I look forward to every Shabbat, which brings meaning, joy, comfort, and spiritual restoration into my life for twenty-six hours. Communal Pesach Seders and celebrations of every holiday from Shavuot and Sukkot to Bar and Bat Mitzvot connect me at once to the past, present, and future of the Jewish people.

I will forever walk in the path of Torah and identify with the holy traditions of Judaism passed down from one generation to another. I will work hard to ensure that Judaism continues for the sake of maintaining an even stronger bond between me and my God, who is most high. He is the creator of space and all its mysteries, world architect, the source of life, and a permanent force behind nature and cosmic order.

Although I have faced life-threatening dangers during my thirty-four years as a Jew in Uganda, I am also one of a special people—the Jewish people—who have resisted many centuries of hatred and oppression and continue to say *shalom* to the world.

 MICHAEL H. STEINHARDT was the managing partner of Steinhardt Partners. He retired in December 1995 and is now concentrating on projects in Israel and his newly formed Jewish Life Network.

"Today, we are all Jews by choice."

"I am Jewish"—one might think this is a simple, unambiguous, declarative statement. I believe a Jew is anyone who affirms his Jewishness by associating his/her future with the future of the Jewish people. The "lineality" that has historically characterized Judaism is no longer a central criterion for most Jews. Today, we are all Jews by choice. For most Jews, the Torah remains the profound source for inculcating the values of our people, but we will forever debate the applicability of some of its statements and dwell on the interpretation of some of its visions that seem less than timeless.

In the contemporary world, Jewish pride often comes from the secular achievements of individual Jews, i.e., the disproportionate number of Nobel Prize winners, successful businessmen, writers, scientists, etc. We speculate on issues of nature versus nurture. We consider social Darwinism. We confidently ascribe success to overwhelming emphasis on education, religious but also secular. In the end, we don't know why, but we do know that there is something special ... something "chosen."

Albert Einstein, a secular Jew, perhaps an atheist, once said that he was sorry to be born a Jew because he was thus denied the opportunity and personal satisfaction of independently choosing Judaism. Such would be an ennobled, voluntary act that could be recognized by most Jews. It was for Danny Pearl. I knew Danny Pearl only at the end of his life, and then only through the media. However, this has created an awesome, infinite vision. I have no knowledge of his Jewish learning or his involvement with Jewish community, his personal theology, etc., but I know he was a Jew. A Jew with pride following a great tradition of which he was proud. No more need be known.

DENNIS PRAGER is the author of four books, including the recently revised *Why the Jews? The Reason for Antisemitism* and the national bestseller *Happiness Is a Serious Problem.* He is a nationally syndicated radio talk-show host and columnist, and may be contacted through his website, www.dennisprager.com.

"A conscious decision to be a Jew and an ongoing commitment to leading a Jewish life."

I am a Jew. But more important, I am Jewish.

To be a Jew one needs only to be born or raised a Jew. To be Jewish involves a conscious decision to be a Jew and an ongoing commitment to leading a Jewish life.

I have made this decision because I believe that God wants Jews to be Jewish. For some inexplicable reason, God chose the Jews to be His emissaries to mankind, to spread ethical monotheism, to live exemplary lives of ethics and holiness. The Jews, whether consciously or not, have focused humanity's attention onto good and evil, just as the Jews' state does today in its battle against those who wish to destroy it. The Jews have suffered for thousands of years for giving humanity a morality-giving and morality-judging God and Bible.

If I did not believe in the Jews' God-given mission, I would not have raised three children as Jews, nor would I have devoted much of my life to influencing Jews to be Jewish and non-Jews to take seriously the God of the Jews. After Auschwitz, there are only religious (i.e., God-based) reasons to be a Jew.

Some time ago, after giving a lecture to the Jewish community of Phoenix, Arizona, on the plane back home, I coincidentally sat next to a woman who had attended my talk. She told me that she was a non-Jew married to a Jew. He, however, did not attend the talk because, as a Holocaust survivor, he had long ago decided to assimilate and to raise his children with no Jewish identity. After what he had seen, he concluded that being a Jew wasn't worth it. He would work to spare his children and grandchildren the horror of some future recurrence of anti-Semitic violence.

I have asked secular ("cultural," "ethnic") Jews what argument they would offer that man to remain a Jew and to raise his children as Jews. I have never received a convincing answer. There isn't one. Without God and the Torah at the center of a Jew's identity and as the basis of his values, being a Jew is just another ethnic identity, and raising one's children as Jews, as desirable as it is for the Jews' survival, is little more than an ethnocentric irrationality.

Contrary to what most Jews are led to believe in the secular cocoons in which they are educated and in which they live, it is not the Jew who believes in the divine mission and destiny of the Jews who is irrational. It is the Jew who does not.

Is there a rational secular explanation for the centrality of the Jews in human affairs? What is the secular explanation for why so few people have aroused such passion for thousands of years wherever they have lived (and even where they haven't lived)? Why do the most evil human beings in each generation focus their hatred on Jews? Why has the Jewish state alone been singled out for delegitimization by so much of the world (and for years by the world's parliament, the United Nations)?

For the Jewish Jew, the answer is clear. Both the joy of a Judaism-based life and the pain of an anti-Semitism-caused death are suffused with Jewish meaning.

Since 9/11, more Jews than ever before in the modern age are willing to challenge their secularism. Perhaps the love of death and the purity of the evil among Israel's and the Jews' enemies has made Jews more capable of realizing that the Jews are at the center of the world's battle for life and for good. Maybe the ritual killing of Daniel Pearl has made them aware of how clear the Jewish challenge is to today's most evil doctrine. Whatever the cause, the old secularism is failing to answer more and more Jews' questions.

You do not have to be an Orthodox Jew to answer these questions. In fact, you do not even have to be a Jew. You have to take God and the Torah seriously. This is why most religious Christians understand the Jews' role better than secular Jews do. They believe in the Jews' God, the Jews' Torah, and the Jews' chosenness.

It is time for Jews to.

KIRK DOUGLAS has acted in eighty-five movies and has been awarded a special Oscar for Lifetime Achievement from the Academy of Motion Pictures. His Douglas Foundation was responsible for the construction of playgrounds in Israel for both Israeli and Palestinian children.

"'Kirk, I think you like being Jewish 'cause it's so dramatic.'"

After a mid-air helicopter crash, I broke my back and two young people were killed. Then a pacemaker, to help my aching heart. This was followed by a stroke and I lost my speech.

I began to think maybe God was punishing me for abandoning my Judaism since my first Bar Mitzvah. I began to study Judaism. I worked with many rabbis; as a matter of fact, I knew more rabbis than Jews. One of them, Rabbi Braverman, said to me: "Kirk, I think you like being Jewish 'cause it's so dramatic." Maybe that's true. It led me to a second Bar Mitzvah when I was eighty-three years old. I'm still around, and I think my Judaism has helped me.

 **DR. RICHARD A. LERNER'S** thirty-year scientific career is particularly significant not only for the broad scope of his achievements in several diverse areas of biomedical research, but for his leadership and vision in concurrently directing the totality of scientific activities at The Scripps Research Institute, the country's largest private, nonprofit biomedical research organization.

"The past dictates the future."

To me, being Jewish means that one has an internal set of marching orders that are independent of the current surround. These "orders" mandate a responsibility of perpetuation and include incorporating the past into the future. We are "ordered" to obey the laws of scholarship in all endeavors. We are "ordered" to obey the seemingly conflicting positions of not being overly joyous with incremental gains while placing what we perceive to be new in its historical context. As we follow the principles of biological sciences we are like archeologists, except that instead of digging in the ruins of civilizations we dig in the "ruins" of evolution. Again the past dictates the future. We are "ordered" not to envy, not because we lack emotion, but because the work of others is rightly incorporated into the historical context of our own work. We are "ordered" to understand that generosity is necessary to the concert of scholarship. Our greatest joy is when a piece of the historical puzzle is moved into place. We are "ordered" to explain even when our view is unpopular and to march with the common view would be easier. We are "ordered" to be fair even when our enemies can transmute fairness into meanness. These are the "orders" that make some uncomfortable and even bring others to hate.

Julius Lester is the author of *Lovesong: Becoming a Jew* and a professor in the Judaic and Near Eastern Studies Department at the University of Massachusetts at Amherst.

"To suffuse history with holiness."

It is the particular responsibility of the Jew to suffuse history with holiness. This is not something that, done once, is done for all time. It must be done every day, for every day a Jew must choose anew the responsibility of holiness.

To be holy is to be apart from, the Torah teaches us. We must be apart to possess our unique identity as a people. We must be apart to offer the world those aspects of the holy which God put into our keeping.

There is the paradox: The world needs us to be apart as Jews, though it may be loathe to acknowledge it. It does not need us to be just another ethnic group. It does not need us to dissolve our particularity into an undifferentiated and colorless mass.

The world needs us to assume the difficult task of living as Jews and to do as Jews have sought to do through the ages—merge past and present and future into a Holy Now.

We do this by becoming a continuous *bracha*—a blessing of joy that refuses to be suppressed or destroyed despite what others have said and done, despite what others say and do. To be a Jew is to be a *bracha* of laughter expressing our surprise, delight, and wonder in creation and our place in it as Jews. We are called to be a *bracha* of unending love because to be a Jew is to be in love—with a God, a people, and a land. To be a Jew is to live that love—boldly, defiantly, joyously—to become that love and live with the fluidity of a melody understood in the silence of the soul.

To be a Jew is to be a love song—to the God of our people—and to the world.

 CHAIM KRAMER is founder and director of the Breslov Research Institute in Jerusalem, which is dedicated to the translation and dissemination of the teachings of Rebbe Nachman of Breslov (1772–1810).

"Chosenness means taking responsibility for making our world a better place."

For me, being a Jew means living the balance: between generations past and future, the time-honored and the modern; between justice and compassion, joy and sorrow; between body and spirit, man and God.

I received a Jewish day school education. My study of Torah and Jewish history taught me much about our rich and ancient heritage. To this day it amazes me how our traditions remain a bedrock of stability, a grounding force in a fast-changing, chaotic world. Perhaps the lessons that inspired me most—that most influenced my choices in life—were those that spoke of the Jewish people's gift for giving.

For me, being a Jew means being proud to be part of a people that has contributed much to the advancement of civilization; a people that has lived through the worst and yet embraces the future with *joie de vivre*.

My rebbe, the Hasidic master Rebbe Nachman of Breslov, spoke often of the special pride that God takes in His chosen nation and their achievements. For me, this chosenness means taking responsibility for making our world a better place—for my family, my community, my people, and all humanity. As Rebbe Nachman taught:

> If you believe that you can damage, then believe that you can fix. If you believe that you can harm, then believe that you can heal.

—Rebbe Nachman in *Likutey Moharan II:112*

JOSEF JOFFE is editor of the German weekly *Die Zeit*. Raised in postwar Berlin, he went to college and graduate school in the United States. He is chairman of the Board of Trustees of the Abraham Geiger College in Berlin, the first liberal rabbinical seminary in postwar Germany.

"The core of the relationship is freedom and equality, the two essential conditions of the moral life that, in turn, revolves around responsibility—to oneself and others."

Danny Pearl's last words were "I am Jewish." But what does "Jewish" mean? One classical feature of Jewishness is to tackle a tortuous question by way of anecdote or parable—in this case, two.

The first comes from the Torah (Num. 14:11–35). As was his wont, and always with good reason, the Lord once more was angry with His people, and this time, His patience had run out. So He spoke to Moses: "I shall strike them with pestilence and disown them." Now listen to Moses' response, one of the most brilliant pleas in the history of the bar. In so many words, he first soothes the Almighty: "I hear You, O Lord, I know where You're coming from." But then, he moves in with his rapier: "If You slay this people to a man, the nations … will say, 'It must be because the Lord was powerless to bring that people into the land He has promised them on oath that He slaughtered them in the wilderness.'"

God simmers down and relents. He commutes the punishment to forty years in the wilderness so that none of those who still remember Egypt will actually see the Promised Land.

What is the moral of this tale? It drives home an essential quality of the Jewish relationship with God. Jews don't commune with the Lord by way of prostration, as Muslims do, or with bent knees, which informs the Christian ritual. Made in His image, they are *au fond* His equal. Like Moses, they reason and argue with Him; they are a "stiff-necked" people.

Moses exacts a wondrous commutation of sentence by tapping into God's "human, all too human" vanity. In the contemporary vernacular, he appeals to the Lord thus: "I know that You are the most powerful entity in the universe, but think of the bad press You'll be getting back in Cairo. They'll be saying: 'This God of theirs may be strong enough to lead them out of Egypt with a mighty hand and an outstretched arm, inflicting plagues galore on us in the process. But He is not powerful enough to make them obey His law. And this is why He killed them. Some God.'"

It all started in the Garden of Eden when God gave Adam and Eve the power of autonomous choice in the matter of the apple—free will, as the philosophers call it. Man is not His slave, nor a programmed automaton. The core of the relationship is freedom and equality, the two essential conditions of the moral life that, in turn, revolves around responsibility—to oneself and others. Original sin or *kismet* plays little or no role in this relationship. Obedience to the law, yes, but to a law freely chosen.

This is why Moses, in Numbers and elsewhere in the Torah, goes *mano a mano* with God (verbally, that is). He is respectful, but fearless; he is a tenacious (and pretty deft) defense counsel for his people, not a Ph.D. in victimology. The moral autonomy of man was invented here (and perhaps also the Jewish penchant for lawyering).

The second story makes the same point in a different way. The Talmud (Bava Metzia, 59b) relates a famous debate among the Rabbis about a fine point of *pilpul*. So Rabbi Eliezer seeks to clinch the argument by invoking divine authority, executing a set of fancy miracles to buttress his case. The Rabbis are not impressed. So finally, Eliezer appeals directly to God: "If the law is as I say, let it be proved from heaven." Immediately, God rushes to his support: "Why do you dispute with Rabbi Eliezer, seeing that in all matters the law is as he says?" Unfazed, Rabbi Joshua retorts: "It is not in heaven!"

What did he mean by that? the Talmud asks. Rabbi Jeremiah replies: "That the Torah had already been given at Mount Sinai [and that] we pay no attention to a heavenly voice ..." And what did God do? "He laughed, saying: 'My sons have defeated Me.'"

This is Jewish, while schmaltz and herring are but heart-warming memories of a way of life long past. "Jewish" is the moral and intellectual autonomy of man, though that life comes with a heavy price, as the children of Israel were to learn endlessly ever since Moses pleaded their case before God in the wilderness.

Is it *only* Jewish? I think not. It is also some of the best of the West that was invented there: the distinction between faith and reason, the separation of God's and man's realms, the defiance of the supernatural, the skepticism toward received authority, the exhilarating burden of human responsibility, and, last but not least, the sheer joy of a good debate. Danny Pearl's murderers tried to annihilate these gifts. They must not prevail, and they will not prevail.

Rabbi Uri Regev is the executive director for the World Union for Progressive Judaism. As a rabbi and jurist, he is active in international and Israeli Jewish and civil rights organizations.

"A unique, private, and national identity rooted in a common mission and a responsibility for partnering with God in ever perfecting the work of creation."

Lord of the Universe! You have done much to have me abandon my religion. I want You to know clearly that, in spite of the forces of Heaven, I am a Jew and I will remain a Jew, and whatever You have brought or will yet bring against me will be to no avail!

—**Section X: The Staff of Judah (Shevet Yehuda), quoted from Solomon Ibn Verga (c. 1450–1520)**

While reading Daniel Pearl's words "I am a Jew," uttered shortly before his horrific execution by Muslim fundamentalists in Pakistan, I recalled the words above. Solomon Ibn Verga recorded them in his famous account of the aftermath of the Inquisition and the expulsion of the Jews from Spain. Daniel Pearl's tragic death inspires us to look beyond the devastating worldwide manifestations of human cruelty and religious fundamentalism. We are compelled to ask what his testimonial, whether uttered willfully or under coercion, means for Jews.

Seldom does one find among the large, secular Jewish majority in Israel a sense of mission about being Jewish. If individuals face this challenge, so much greater is that of Israel, a modern Jewish state struggling to define its Jewish identity. More than fifty years after its establishment as a state, no consensus as yet exists on this core issue. It has caused much public debate and strife.

To me, being Jewish is very much about a unique, private, and national identity rooted in a common mission and a responsibility for partnering with God in ever perfecting the work of creation. We find a key to the role of the "chosen people" and its mission in Genesis. Here God reveals His master plan and His reason for choosing Abraham and the nation that will emanate from him:

"Now the Lord had said, 'Shall I hide from Abraham what I am about to do, since Abraham is to become a great and populous nation and all the nations of the earth are to bless themselves by him? For I have singled him out, that he may instruct his children and his posterity to keep the way of the Lord by doing what is just and right, in order that the Lord may bring about for Abraham what He has promised him'" (Gen. 18:17–19, see also Pss. 119:137–144).

Being Jewish is not merely a biological fact. Being consciously Jewish is about being part of a family consisting of the descendants of our forefathers and foremothers, as well as those who have chosen to cast their lot in with the Jewish people. We are a people singled out to partner with God and to create a model society and thereby become a blessing for all God's children. For that reason, I attach paramount importance to the debate between two schools of rabbinic thought as to what is the essence of Judaism.

While Rabbi Akiva suggests that the great principle of the Torah is "Love your neighbor as yourself" (Lev. 19:18), Ben Azzai feared that this laudable principle may be reduced to a particularistic, narrow interpretation. The *"reah"* (neighbor) has been interpreted by some as *"reacha b'mitzvot"* (your fellow Jew). Ben Azzai offered a more universal approach as a greater principle of the Torah. He quoted Genesis 5:1:

"This is the book of the generations of Man. On the day that God created mankind, in the likeness of God, He made him: male and female He created them: and blessed them, and called their name Man, in the day when they were created."

Since all are created in the image of the Divine, Ben Azzai emphasizes that the obligation extends to all humanity. Violating each other means desecrating God, in whose likeness man was made (Sifra on Lev. 19:18 and Genesis Rabbah on Gen. 24:7). These two schools are also represented in the different readings of Mishna Sanhedrin. The text originally read:

"It is for this that man was created as a solitary human being, to instruct us that whoever destroys one life it is accounted to him by scripture as if he had destroyed a whole world and whoever preserves one life, it is accounted to him by scripture as if he had preserved a whole world" (Sanhedrin 4:5).

This text was later amended in some of the manuscripts and carried through to today's printed text of the Mishna. The word *me-Israel* was inserted. The text therefore did not read "Whoever preserves [or destroys] one life," but "Whoever preserves [or destroys] the life of one Jew."

Undoubtedly, the change in the text occurred in response to times of persecution and powerlessness. People experiencing trauma naturally look inward, tending to see only their own self-interest and to exclude others. Such a response, however, negates the Jewish mission. We were commanded to transform our age-old sufferings into a blueprint for a just and equitable society. The Torah often repeats this guiding principle, as in Leviticus 19:33–34:

"When a stranger resides with you in your land, you shall not wrong him. The stranger who resides with you shall be to you as one of your citizens; you shall love him as yourself, for you were strangers in the land of Egypt: I the LORD am your God."

Similarly, the Passover celebration focuses on its educational impact. Many of its rituals remind us of this formative phase of our nation. In the Passover Seder, I consider its most important injunction to be:

"In each and every generation, one must see himself as if he has come out of Egypt."

Before he died, Daniel Pearl spoke about his connection with Israel. Was this "admission" coerced or an existential reality for him? Clearly, his captors considered it an admission of guilt by association. Recent occurrences throughout Europe and elsewhere remind us as well of the inseparable link between Jews and Israel. The world around us will always connect and identify Israel with the Jewish People.

How do we as Jews relate to this equation? What does Israel mean to us? Some consider it a destination for a sentimental journey; others think of it as an "insurance policy," a safe haven for persecuted Jewish communities; still others are motivated by a religious commandment, or by a sense of Jewish mutual responsibility. All these considerations are valid and important.

Let me offer an additional outlook. Judaism was never intended merely as a faith and lifestyle for the individual, the family, or the congregation. It aimed to provide a blueprint for society, for a sovereign nation rooted in social and moral principles of Judaism, impacting on the world and providing a shining light to all humanity.

Rarely do we hear this concept in Knesset debates or in the Israeli public and not even in Israel-diaspora dialogue forums. Regrettably, it does not seem to appear on the agenda of Israel's religious parties or that of the Chief Rabbinate. For me, however, this ought to be a key element in defining the relationship between Jews and Israel. It should guide the public discourse over Israel's character as a Jewish state.

I suggest that only in Israel may we as Jews assert full control of our destiny and societal norms; military ethics; national, social, and economic policies; etc. We can and should view Israel as a huge laboratory, enabling us to put to test and implement Judaism's commitment to *tikkun olam* in a contemporary setting.

Can Judaism provide a meaningful model and a relevant blueprint to a modern Jewish sovereignty living in an era of democracy, scientific discovery, egalitarianism, and diversity? Firmly I believe it can, even if Israel has not provided one as yet.

I further believe that the responsibility to undertake such a critical task does not rest solely on Israelis. The challenge should form the core of an Israel-diaspora partnership that both enriches and inspires Jews all over the world. It enables them to redefine their relationship to each other and to Israel, to strengthen their commitment to our national home.

For the individual Jew and for the sovereign Jewish state alike, each step taken to help mend God's world marks a primary building block in defining "I am a Jew."

 THANE ROSENBAUM is a novelist, essayist, and law professor and the author of *The Golems of Gotham, Second Hand Smoke, Elijah Visible,* and the forthcoming *The Myth of Moral Justice: Why Our Legal System Fails to Do What's Right.* His articles, reviews, and essays appear frequently in the *New York Times, Los Angeles Times,* and the *Wall Street Journal,* among other national publications. He teaches human rights, legal humanities, and law and literature at Fordham Law School in New York City.

"The proclaiming of one's Jewishness is now a moral imperative, a post-covenant concession to the realities of our world."

I am Jewish. I say that freely and unreservedly, because I can, and I should. In one sense, the statement is obvious. My writings are clearly informed by a Jewish sensibility and a Jew's attachment to a particular history. And yet, even outside my novels, the affirmation must, on occasion, be acknowledged. It is a moral act of memory.

For me, being Jewish, and affirming it, is wholly unrelated to the biblical covenant between God and Abraham. I don't necessarily consider myself bound by that agreement, not because it is ancient, or one-sided, or legally unenforceable, or the fact that it has been repeatedly breached by inhuman acts committed, usually, in God's name. Jewish continuity has persevered, but I'm afraid not because God has been keeping up with His end of the bargain.

I am a Jew because to do or say anything less is an insult, a severe slight, a slap in the face to millions of ghosts who would very much feel the indignity of such forgetfulness. Those who were forever silenced by persecution and murder can never rest peacefully if they are forsaken by amnesia. And given our indifference, they will never give up in haunting us, which is as it should be.

As a Jew, I am not alone in this world—or any other world— regardless of how small our numbers or the vastness of animus that is sometimes directed against us. Far too many Jews throughout history have died of totally unnatural causes. And many of these deaths would have occurred even without an invocation of Jewish tribalism that is the subject and title of this book.

For this reason, the proclaiming of one's Jewishness is now a moral imperative, a post-covenant concession to the realities of our world. We do so not out of fear of breaching our contract with God or provoking His wrath. What we fear, what would bring us unbearable shame, is the disappointment in ourselves that comes from forgetting. Jewish continuity and remembrance are the only remedy for our loss. It is what a decent and moral people should be expected to do.

I am a Jew. Saying so is a new, mandatory *Sh'ma*. A daily ritual, like a prayer, uttered without restraint, for no reason at all, other than that it must be said. The reaffirming of our faith, in ourselves.

 RICHARD SIEGEL is the executive director of the National Foundation for Jewish Culture. In a previous life, he was one of the editors of *The Jewish Catalog*, the best-selling book of the late 1960s Jewish counterculture.

"I am Jewish because I cannot imagine being otherwise."

I am Jewish. This is a declarative statement. I am Jewish, like I am hungry. But it is more. It is a statement of definition. I am Jewish, like I am a man. But it is more. It is a statement of affirmation. I am Jewish, and I am proud to assert it.

In reality, the affirmation trumps the definition. Because being Jewish is ultimately a choice, even if it sometimes feels essential. What is it that enables us, compels us, to turn this choice, this voluntary identity, into an essential identity?

I hope I never have to face a situation like Daniel Pearl faced. But I hope that if I do, I will have the courage and clarity to make this simple declarative, essentialist, and affirmative statement. I am Jewish.

I have spent my entire adult life as a Jewish communal worker. Why? I have been involved with *minyanim,* explored contemporary Jewish spirituality, written books exploring the contemporary Jewish experience, spent vacations exploring ancient Jewish synagogues. In my own ways, I observe Shabbat, *kashrut,* and loyalty to Israel. Why?

I could be glib and say that being Jewish is one of the few things that I am good at. I could be coy and say that because of my family background, I am comfortable being Jewish. I could be dismissive and say that I enjoy it. But the truth is that I am Jewish because it addresses some of the most profound questions of my being. And, I would argue, these are questions that apply to us all, not as Jews, but as human beings.

Thankfully, it does not answer the questions, because that is the quest of a lifetime. But it addresses them, refines them, deepens them, and provides enormous resources—intellectual, emotional, spiritual—with which to plumb them.

For me, three fundamental questions are:

1. Where do I fit into the chain of human history? I want to know that I am not just an accident of nature, a randomly embodied soul. As my Hebrew name reminds me, I am the son of parents, who were children of others, who were descendants of still others, all the way back at least to the tribes gathered at Sinai, if not to the very creation of the world.

2. Who is my community? In this most existential of times, I want to know that I am not alone. Beyond my family unit, I have the ten who pray their individual prayers together with me. My community is *clal Yisrael,* which intimates, even if it does not fully embody, all of humanity.

3. What is the meaning of my life? I want to know that my existence has value, that there are ultimate implications to my actions. We may live in a broken world, but there is the promise that the broken can be made whole. Through this imperative of *tikkun olam,* repairing the world, my being Jewish extends out to all of God's creation.

I am Jewish because I cannot imagine being otherwise.

 MICHAEL MEDVED is a film critic, author, and nationally syndicated radio talk-show host.

"A choosing people, more than a chosen people."

The statement "I am Jewish" simultaneously affirms connection and declares disassociation.

On the one hand, Jewish identity connects us to parents, grandparents, and ancestors from countless generations, providing a sense of continuity and rootedness that contemporary Americans only rarely enjoy. Jewishness (however we choose to define it) also attaches us to our fellow Jews around the world, guaranteeing membership in a large, contentious, frequently quarreling, always emotional, extended family. At a time when many of our fellow citizens complain of loneliness and isolation, that affiliation offers an instantly available community for those who choose to enter it.

At the same time that a proclamation of Jewish identity gives life to these associations it also emphasizes separateness and nonconformity. To be a Jew is to be different—to stand aside from the surrounding culture with a stubborn, indestructible detachment. Even in Israel, the world's only Jewish-majority society, the sea of hostile Islamism surrounding that embattled state makes it impossible to take Jewish identity for granted as an automatic, effortless, or organic development. Living as a Jew—in the United States, Israel, or anywhere else—requires an act of will, a course of conscious decision. As frequently described, we remain a choosing people, more than a chosen people. As the story of Daniel Pearl (may his memory be a blessing) makes powerfully clear, the choice to be Jewish can enrich life, and ennoble death.

JIM BALL practices public relations and Judaism in Massachusetts.

"Somehow, I'd been Jewish for a long time, but I didn't know it until I met Anita."

Everything in the world—whatever is and whatever happens—is a test, designed to give you freedom of choice. Choose wisely.

—Rebbe Nachman of Breslov

Twenty years ago, I chose to marry the woman I loved. It was inevitable, of course, because she was the most wonderful, vibrant, intelligent, and loving woman I'd ever met. Who wouldn't jump at that chance? We'd begun our journey several years before, and part of that journey was her discovery of her Judaism. I, on the other hand, had been raised a devout, church-going Presbyterian and had even toyed with the idea of entering the ministry. I left the church behind during college in the sixties, as so many of us did. But I like to think I never left behind my sense that something moved in the universe out there beyond me, something ineffable. So when she discovered her Judaism, I discovered mine. And as we prepared to marry, I prepared to become a Jew.

As I studied, things became clear. All those Jewish women I'd dated before. Why I loved Lenny Bruce so much. Why, as a young music student, Leonard Bernstein's Third Symphony, *Kaddish,* had moved me so deeply. Why I enjoyed the arguments with my friends. Why Mel Brooks was funny. Why, when I first heard a sermon by the rabbi who would later convert me, his words made so much sense. It even explained why I liked the layers of paint on old *mezuzah*s in New York apartments. Somehow, I'd been Jewish for a long time, but I didn't know it until I met Anita.

And yet, it wasn't totally clear until our beautiful daughter, Emilia, was born. As she grew, she grew into Judaism naturally, fully, and so comfortably. Now a grown young woman, a freshman in college, she wears her Jewishness so easily, without a doubt; it's like her skin. And

I know one of the main reasons I am a Jew is so Emilia would be one. Because the world needs her Judaism. A test, Nachman? Perhaps. I do know this. I chose wisely.

 RABBI KENNETH J. LEINWAND is a 1977 graduate of the Hebrew Union College–Jewish Institute of Religion. He holds the rank of colonel and is the command chaplain for the United States Army Europe and the Seventh Army in Heidelberg, Germany.

"God has granted me the privilege to serve a congregation of 62,000 soldiers and 130,000 family members."

There is no mistaking my Jewish identity.

At staff meetings and in the field talking to soldiers; during training exercises or at suicide-prevention briefings and commanders' orientations; at Shabbat services or at a memorial service following a training accident; whether deployed to Kosovo or in a garrison in Heidelberg; and throughout combat operations during the Gulf War; every day for the past twenty-six years I proudly wear on my collar and beret the insignia of the Jewish chaplain—the Star of David and the Ten Commandments.

As the command chaplain on a four-star battle staff planning for major military operations, or in my role as the technical supervisor of 200 chaplains of every major denomination, God has granted me the privilege to serve a congregation of 62,000 soldiers and 130,000 family members throughout U.S. Army Europe. What a marvelous opportunity to make a *Kiddush Hashem*—a sanctification of God's name!

I am a Jew who has made a life commitment to protect our constitutional right for the "free exercise" of religion—not only for Jews but for all our citizens. I am thankful to the Almighty for blessing me and my family in allowing us to touch the lives and hearts of so many dedicated, noble, and extraordinary men and women.

NORMAN LAMM is chancellor of Yeshiva University after having served as its president for twenty-seven years. He is also the Jakob and Erna Michael Professor of Jewish Philosophy and the author of ten books.

"As important as 'identity' and 'people-hood' are, they are not the whole story."

When Daniel Pearl uttered those three words, "I am Jewish," just before he was cruelly murdered by professional Islamist killers, he transformed his all too short life from that of an unfortunate victim of political fanaticism to that of a martyr for the Jewish people and faith. This essay is dedicated to his memory. Of him and of so many others like him, throughout our history, does the Talmud record the words of the immortal Rabbi Judah the Prince, who cried at the death of a pagan martyr who had committed an act of supreme heroism, "There are those who attain immortality in one brief moment, while others take a whole lifetime to achieve it."

The Book of Jonah, read in the synagogue on Yom Kippur, is one of the most intriguing books of the Bible. Its historicity and message have been interpreted, reinterpreted, and debated by classical Torah scholars and modern commentators. But perhaps a most fascinating interchange recorded at the very beginning of the book is often overlooked. Here is how the Torah describes the dialogue between the fleeing prophet, asleep in the hold of the ship, and the frightened sailors aboard the storm-tossed vessel who want him to pray to his God as they pray to theirs:

> The shipmaster came to him and said to him, "What do you mean by sleeping? Get up and pray to your God so that He might take note of us so that we will not perish." … Then they said to him, "Tell us, please, why is this catastrophe come upon us? What is your occupation? Where do you come from? What people do you belong to?" And he said to them, "I am a Hebrew, and I worship the Lord God of heaven who created the sea and the dry land."

> —Jonah 1:6, 8–9

At that critical moment, when both he and they were facing possible extinction, the one answer Jonah gave to the whole cascade of questions by the panicking mariners was, "I am a Hebrew," "I am Jewish." That is his occupation, that is his origin, that is his people. And one might add: that was his fate and that was his destiny, without elaboration or analysis. When a Jew's identity is challenged, the answer that issues from the depths of his being is and should be, "I am Jewish."

Yet it would be an error to be satisfied with that existential definition of one's very being. As important as "identity" and "peoplehood" are, they are not the whole story. Indeed, Jonah himself added the words, "and I worship the Lord God of heaven who created the sea and the dry land." A person's identity is tied up with his job, his origins, his people, his gender, his country. For a Jew, that is as important as it is for any other human being. But Jonah went beyond mere identity; he elaborated on what that identity implied, in what transcendental firmament it was anchored, what duties it imposed upon him, and what kind of life he is expected to lead.

To understand what more than mere self-definition is required of the Jew by Judaism, it is best to refer to the three covenants as described in the Torah. Each covenant, or *berit,* is more than just a contract, although it is that too; it connotes major commitments, turning points in human and Jewish history.

The three covenants are: with Noah, with Abraham, and with Moses. The first was the covenant with humanity at large—the universal dimension of Judaism. In it, God pledged that He would never again destroy the entire world by a flood. The second was with Abraham and his posterity. Here the Almighty promised to be the God of the children of Abraham, vouchsafed to them their perpetuity as a people, and gifted to them the Land of Israel. The third was the Torah itself—the full range of religious obligations and spiritual privileges incumbent upon Jews by virtue of their birth into the people of Israel. It is understood that each successive covenant included that which preceded it. Thus, to be a Jew in the fullest sense, one must be committed not only to the laws of the Torah but also to Israel—people and land—and to all humanity, as part of the unique covenantal commitment to the creator.

From this point of view, a Jew who lives ethically and morally but is divorced from the Jewish community and Land of Israel is a good human being but a spiritually underdeveloped Jew. One who adds to this his national-ethnic loyalties as a Jew is better but is still an incomplete Jew. And one who observes the commandments but fails to identify with his people and homeland, or is delinquent as a moral human being, is doing the unthinkable. Such a Jew, who observes the covenant of Moses but betrays his obligations under the national and the universal covenants, is living a contradiction.

The same covenantal analysis holds when transposing from the individual to the polity and society. Thus, a state that does not abide by the Noahide (that is, universal) covenant is not a civilized state, for that covenant implies the security of its citizens and their fundamental human rights. The Abrahamic or national-ethnic covenant includes such things as culture, history, traditions, and the whole idiom of public life and discourse—all of which unify a people and make it distinct from other political-cultural entities. The Mosaic covenant addresses the nation, but, because it commands not only laws but the cultivation of the spirit as well, will as well as conduct, it is addressed to individuals who may or may not accept upon themselves this third covenant. Thus, the Mosaic covenant addresses the heart and mind and will of individuals: "I have set before you life and death, blessing and curse; therefore choose life, so that both you and your seed may live" (Deut. 30:19). To choose means that I choose out of freedom, without any external compulsion.

The brunt of the Book of Jonah is that the prophet cannot escape his divine mission, no matter how much he resents it. Equally important is the book's message that a Jew ought not seek to avoid his commitment to the three-fold covenant that has stood before us and beside us throughout our history as goad and vision. And even if one comes to that second, Abrahamic *berit* at the very end of his life—at the very cusp of extinction, having spent most or all of his years in indifference or even rejection of his Jewish heritage—and yet offers up those sacred words, "I am a Hebrew," or "I am Jewish," he is granted immortality.

In one brief moment.

 LARRY S. MOSES is president of The Wexner Foundation, which focuses upon strengthening Jewish leadership in North America and Israel.

"I am the bearer of meaning, of messages and compassions."

Being a Jew is recognizing one's inheritance—a system of values, commitments, and beliefs of profound importance to the human experiment. As a Jew, I am the bearer of meaning, of messages and compassions; I am a representative of a tradition filled with caring and service; I am one among many who will not rest in a harsh and unredeemed world where even one child knows hunger, even one forgotten person needs justice. I am a Jew in and out of the synagogue, with and without other Jews, with or without my God, alone and in the company of many. Being a Jew is the possibility of situating oneself in this vast universe and in relation to God, others, and self with a spark of divine empowerment, and a sense of responsibility that is both self-affirming and self-transcendent. I am also a Jew who is the son of a survivor of Auschwitz, the son of a family almost wholly murdered in the gas chambers, and an heir to a legacy of degradation that was unmitigated and that would have broken another people. Most profoundly, no degradation can lower the Jew beneath his mission. For being a Jew, first and foremost, is affirming life, embracing hope, and proudly bearing the mantles of justice, compassion, and deeds of lovingkindness.

RABBI TONY BAYFIELD is the professional head of the Reform movement in Britain; the editor of the quarterly *MANNA;* and a writer, particularly in the field of the theology of interfaith relations.

"To be a Jew is to go on a journey of discovery."

I am seven years old and perched on a London bus with my father going to synagogue. I am holding a brown paper bag that conceals his *tallit.* I don't often go to synagogue and don't want to go. It's a scary place, even though my grandfather will be there. Only years later did I discover the significance of the paper bag.

I am fourteen and sitting in a huge, dusty, red upholstered chair in the front room of the house that served as the first home of our Reform synagogue. There are seven of us and we are studying the prophets. I am thrilled to be a Jew like Isaiah.

I am eighteen and canvassing for Arnold Shaw, prospective Labour candidate for Ilford South. I knock on a neat, semi-detached front door and launch into my speech. "Shush," says the householder through the half-opened door. "He's a yiddisher boy, isn't he? I'll vote for him. A poster? Certainly not." The door slams. Thus did the irresistible force of Jewish *petit bourgeois* aspirations meet the immovable object that is Jewish attachment to left-wing idealism.

I am twenty-one and standing in a circle in the garden of the master's house at Magdalene College, Cambridge. "I believe we will be having the pleasure of your company for another three years, Bayfield," declaims Sir Henry. "No," I say and stammer through my embarrassment: "Actually, I'm giving up the law for religion. I am going to Rabbinic Training College." The silence is interminable—as if I have committed the worst social *faux pas* imaginable. "And what are *you* doing next year, Bewers?"

I am twenty-nine and three years into my first pulpit. We have no permanent building but, on Friday nights, use the small synagogue in the nineteenth-century house that serves as Britain's only Jewish Approved School for delinquent children. I have been arguing with myself about the existence of God and wondering what a lawyer with a rational and rather prosaic turn of mind is doing as a rabbi. I let myself into the house and open the heavy, glass-paneled door to the little chapel. I stand there, aware of the tangibility of the souls and prayers and of my love for this little community of Jews from the margins. There is an arm round my shoulder.

I am forty-three. My younger daughter has just come back from her first Jewish residential weekend—with many of the children she goes to school with, on the same campus as her school, and with her beloved elder sister, Lucy, as one of the *madrichim*. "How was she?" we ask Lucy. "She cried on Friday night. She was homesick. She missed the family Friday night." May God make my children like ...; my non-P.C. rendition of the *Eshet Chayil*, a true wife. My wife, my fulcrum, my teacher, my understanding of love.

I am forty-eight and staring in disappointment at the *Jewish Chronicle*. I have just published the "MANNA Platform," a 10,000-word statement of Reform [U.K.] Jewish belief, arranged with stunning originality under the headings of God, Torah, and Israel. I am so proud to have finally, with colleagues and friends, articulated a coherent statement of what it is to be a Reform Jew. The *Jewish Chronicle* carries a short story on an inside page to say that *kashrut* is back in and we seem to be more in favor of Shabbat observance.

I am fifty-six and our son phones from a weekend in Prague to see how his mother is. Linda is desperately ill with cancer and in a reflective mood about the meaning of her life. We ask Daniel what he has been doing. He is with his girlfriend and they have been in the Prague Jewish cemetery, cleaning the grave of her grandfather, a survivor of Auschwitz. Yes, children must make their own decisions in life and be themselves and yes, we want them to be happy. But never was the statement more poignant or personal: One who brings up a righteous child is like one who never dies. Linda has brought up three. With me.

The Book of Genesis, from Abraham onward, consists of a succession of individual journeys. The Books of Exodus, Leviticus, Numbers, and Deuteronomy are dominated by a collective journey, the journey of a people from slavery, from imminent danger, to revelation, to wandering, to the Promised Land. For me, that paradigm, that metaphor, defines my understanding of being Jewish and of

Judaism. To be a Jew is to go on a journey of discovery. One's Jewish identity is never fixed. It develops, evolves, and changes. Looking back, I can see how I have changed and how my understanding of myself as a Jew has been transformed. Halakhic definitions are bound to be approximate and imperfect, and poetic definitions like those of Edmond Fleg ("I am a Jew because ...") or Emmanuel Eydoux ("To open eyes when others close them ...") are moving but personal and frozen at a point on someone else's individual journey.

I am deeply concerned about the relationship between Genesis and the last four books of the Torah, about the relationship between the individual and the collective journey. For the Jewish journey is imperiled when it loses touch with the collective journey, ceases to add to it and be enriched by it. The bonds often seem tenuous and blown by the winds of chance these days.

But what for me is the true quality of the paradigm and the metaphor is that it is future-orientated. Only in Judaism, said the Catholic philosopher Renan, is the golden age yet to come. We may not opt for stasis, still less return to Egypt. We are covenanted to the future. "We cannot choose the dreams of unknowing.... We are hunters after reality, wherever it may lead," said George Steiner.

I am twenty-five and my teacher, Rabbi Michael Goulston, says in his last sermon: "To be a Jew is to live with God, which means to live the future—to serve the ONE whom we cannot really have in us or over us or behind us, but always and only before us." At fifty-seven, that resonates with me more than ever.

HAROLD KUSHNER is rabbi laureate of Temple Israel in Natick, Massachusetts, and author of several best-selling books on spiritual themes.

"To proclaim that I live every moment of my life in God's presence."

At the most basic level, when I say "I am a Jew," I am defining myself by my roots. I am declaring myself the son of my parents, the descendant of my grandparents and great-grandparents. I am placing myself in a chain of a hundred generations going back to that band of freed slaves who stood at Sinai and received the Torah.

But while that is an important part of my identity, it is only a small part. When I say "I am a Jew because my ancestors were Jewish," that focuses only on the past, while my Jewishness is very much about the present and the future. To say "I am a Jew" says something about how I will live this day: how will I treat other people in my life, how honest will I be in my business dealings, how much of my income will I set aside for *tzedakah* (charity), will I find time in my day for prayer and study? And it says something about the future: what sort of world do I envision and work for? What are the most important values I will strive to impart to my children and grandchildren?

For me, to say "I am a Jew" is to say that I find the fingerprints of God all over creation. It is to affirm the lesson of the very first page of the Bible, that there is something special about being human, that God created everything there is by saying "Let there be," but fashioned the first human beings personally, breathing something of the divine spirit into them. I understand God's words "Let us make a human being in our image" to be directed to the animals whom God had created in the previous verse. God is saying to the animals, "Let us together fashion a different kind of creature, one who will be like you in some ways and like Me in others." For me as a Jew, life's challenge is to realize that divine potential in me, and the Torah is the instruction manual to guide me to do that.

History teaches me that to say "I am a Jew" is to side with the oppressed rather than with the oppressor, in the full knowledge that I will be a target for people whose souls are corroded with hatred. They will hate me not because there is anything wrong with me, but because there is something terribly wrong with them. But emboldened by the memory of generations before me and by the examples of Jewish heroes and martyrs of my own time, I accept that role.

To say "I am a Jew" is to proclaim that I live every moment of my life in God's presence, avoiding wrongdoing and seeking holiness, because of the spark of God within me.

PART IV:

HUMANITY AND ETHNICITY

ELIE WIESEL is the Andrew W. Mellon Professor in the Humanities at Boston University, and the author of more than forty books, the latest of which is *Wise Men and Their Tales*. In 1986, he was awarded the Nobel Peace Prize.

"For a Jew, Judaism and humanity must go together."

Daniel Pearl's last words are those of a Jew who was assassinated only for his Jewishness. They will resonate in many hearts. They are meant to be an answer to his murderers' questions: Why are you here? Why do you oppose terrorism? Why do you denounce injustice? "I am Jewish," answered Daniel Pearl.

Did he believe that to be Jewish today means what it meant yesterday and a thousand years ago? I do. It means for the Jew in me to seek fulfillment both as a Jew and as a human being. For a Jew, Judaism and humanity must go together. To be Jewish is to recognize that every person is created in God's image and thus worthy of respect. Being Jewish to me is to reject fanaticism everywhere.

As a Jew I must be sensitive to the pain of all human beings. To remain indifferent to persecution and suffering anywhere, in Afghanistan or in Kiev, is to become an accomplice of the tormentor.

 Samuel G. Freedman, a professor of journalism at Columbia University, is the author most recently of *Jew vs. Jew: The Struggle for the Soul of American Jewry*. He writes frequently for the *New York Times, USA Today,* and *Salon*.

"Universalism without tribalism is a kind of self-loathing."

When I first read a profile of Daniel Pearl, shortly after he had been kidnapped in Pakistan, one detail in particular caught my eye. Pearl, the article mentioned, played the fiddle in bluegrass bands. I had already surmised by his surname that Pearl was Jewish, and when I learned of his taste in music, I could intuit what kind of Jew, and what kind of human being, he was.

Although trained as a classical violinist, he later chose to play bluegrass, the music of rural Appalachians, of evangelical Protestants of Scots-Irish stock. No American music could have stood at a more distant remove from the heritage and experience of the typical American Jew, an urban creature with roots in Eastern Europe.

But during my own years in college in the 1970s, and as someone who often wrote about music in the decades since, I had chanced upon a surprising number of Jews who fell in love with bluegrass. One of them even joked to me they were making their own genre, Jew-grass. The pun got at a larger truth: Through music, these Jews were entering and inhabiting and claiming as their own the wider world, the world beyond ghetto and *shtetl*, tony suburb and Ivy League campus, all those Jewish redoubts, past and present.

Daniel Pearl played bluegrass in the great spirit of Jewish universalism. Every fact that I subsequently absorbed about him—that he was married to a French Buddhist, that he wrote about Persian rugs and child beauty pageants, that he enjoyed having tea with a certain contact in Tehran—made sense in the context of Jew-grass. I could extrapolate from Pearl to a whole proud lineage of radical universalists in modern Jewish history, those who taught in inner-city public schools in the North and volunteered as Freedom Riders in the South, who created the workers-cooperatives of Red Vienna and expanded the frontier of physics in the universities of pre-Hitler Germany, who considered Judaism the religion unspeakably sectarian and retrograde and yet could not have been more Jewish in their very disdain for it.

So, of course, when Daniel Pearl hovered in limbo, missing but presumably alive, his wife and colleagues and friends emphasized what a universalist he was, as if that might spare him death. Similarly, they downplayed his Jewish identity and his Israeli ancestry, as if somehow those facts might have escaped the notice of his captors. And who could blame the people closest to Pearl for both speaking truly of his universalism and effacing the inconvenient truth of his heritage, given all that was at stake.

In death, however, the meaning of Daniel Pearl changed, or, I might say, it grew complete. He lived as a universalist, but he died as a tribalist, inescapably Jewish. Very little of his family history, as it turned out, had escaped his executioners. In his last statement, he told them he was Jewish. He told them his father was Israeli. He told them that in Bnei Brak there was a street named for Chayim Pearl, his great-grandfather, one of the town's founders. He might have told them many additional details about his background, true, but they have selected and pasted together only those "incriminating" facts on a tape designed to glorify their act.

While some of what Pearl said was probably coerced, or else was uttered in the desperate hope of survival, it is impossible to avoid in his words the sense of some agency, some autonomy, some principled self-determination. There is a venerable phrase in black Christianity that Jesus' death took the sting out of death and the victory from the grave. When I heard Daniel Pearl say, "I am Jewish," I heard him seizing back from his tormentors the ability to define him. He would define himself. He would not die denying what he always upheld through life. He would steal their victory from the grave.

In the aftermath of Pearl's murder, his family issued a statement remembering him as "a musician, a writer, a storyteller, and a bridge-builder ... a walking sunshine of truth, humor, friendship, and compassion." Those words attest to Daniel Pearl of Jew-grass, of interfaith marriage, of multicultural interests, of accomplishment as a foreign correspondent. Yet they sound to me incomplete, only part of the person and part of the meaning of his life and death. The universalistic side of Daniel Pearl is inextricably bound to the tribalistic side, each reliant on the other for wholeness.

For me, universalism without tribalism is a kind of self-loathing. Whether fetishizing the blonde-haired "*shiksa* goddess" as a mate or championing all versions of nationalism and identity politics except for Zionism, too many Jews exude a desire to flee their own skin. They do not want to be enriched and altered by a dynamic encounter with Otherness but rather to escape into it, to avoid the social incrimination of being demonstrably Jewish. Tribalism, then, is fidelity to heritage and comfort with oneself. Yet tribalism alone refutes the prophetic injunctions to the social justice and the moral lessons of the Exodus narrative. Tribalism mistrusts the outer world because, deep down, it sees Jewish identity as something so fragile that it cannot survive immersion in a polyglot society.

Jewishness confounds so many gentiles, and a good many Jews as well, because its definition is so inchoate, so ineffable, and at the same time so ineradicable. But if I were asked for a definition of Jewishness, I would say it relies upon, indeed thrives upon, the dialectic of universalism and tribalism, the self-correcting tension between seeming opposites. Each hemisphere of our soul keeps the other honest.

As an explorer of countries and cultures, Daniel Pearl was engaging in one of the consummate forms of Jewish universalism, bearing witness. As an innocent facing adversity, he sought strength in, and was willingly laying claim to, the very part of him that his murderers detested most. In those two ways, raveled together, he stood for our best selves.

JONATHAN SACKS is chief rabbi of Britain and the Commonwealth. A well-known figure in the British media, he is the author of fourteen books. The chief rabbi holds visiting professorships at Kings College London and at the Hebrew University. A former BBC Reith Lecturer, Sacks is well known as a philosopher and has been awarded many honors for his contributions to theology and Jewish life.

"In our uniqueness lies our universality. Through being what we alone are, we give to humanity what only we can give."

Why am I a Jew? Not because I believe that Judaism contains all there is of the human story. Jews didn't write Shakespeare's sonnets or Beethoven's quartets. We did not give the world the serene beauty of a Japanese garden or the architecture of ancient Greece. I love these things. I admire the traditions that brought them forth. *Aval zeh shelanu.* But this is ours. Nor am I a Jew because of anti-Semitism or to avoid giving Hitler a posthumous victory. What happens to me does not define who I am: Ours is a people of faith, not fate. Nor is it because I think that Jews are better than others, more intelligent, virtuous, law abiding, creative, generous, or successful. The difference lies not in Jews but Judaism, not in what we are but in what we are called on to be.

I am a Jew because, being a child of my people, I have heard the call to add my chapter to its unfinished story. I am a stage on its journey, a connecting link between the generations. The dreams and hopes of my ancestors live on in me, and I am the guardian of their trust, now and for the future.

I am a Jew because our ancestors were the first to see that the world is driven by a moral purpose, that reality is not a ceaseless war of the elements, to be worshiped as gods, nor history a battle in which might is right and power is to be appeased. The Judaic tradition shaped the moral civilization of the West, teaching for the first time that human life is sacred, that the individual may never be sacrificed for the mass, and that rich and poor, great and small, are all equal before God.

I am a Jew because I am the moral heir of those who stood at the foot of Mount Sinai and pledged themselves to live by these truths, becoming a kingdom of priests and a holy nation. I am the descendant of countless generations of ancestors who, though sorely tested and bitterly tried, remained faithful to that covenant when they might so easily have defected.

I am a Jew because of Shabbat, the world's greatest religious institution, a time in which there is no manipulation of nature or our fellow human beings, in which we come together in freedom and equality to create, every week, an anticipation of the messianic age.

I am a Jew because our nation, though at times it suffered the deepest poverty, never gave up on its commitment to helping the poor, or rescuing Jews from other lands, or fighting for justice for the oppressed, and did so without self-congratulation, because it was a *mitzvah,* because a Jew could do no less.

I am a Jew because I cherish the Torah, knowing that God is to be found not in natural forces but in moral meanings, in words, texts, teachings, and commands, and because Jews, though they lacked all else, never ceased to value education as a sacred task, endowing the individual with dignity and depth.

I am a Jew because of our people's passionate faith in freedom, holding that each of us is a moral agent, and that in this lies our unique dignity as human beings; and because Judaism never left its ideals at the level of lofty aspirations, but instead translated them into deeds that we call *mitzvot,* and a way, which we call the Halakhah, and thus brought heaven down to earth.

I am proud, simply, to be a Jew.

I am proud to be part of a people who, though scarred and traumatized, never lost their humor or their faith, their ability to laugh at present troubles and still believe in ultimate redemption; who saw human history as a journey, and never stopped traveling and searching.

I am proud to be part of an age in which my people, ravaged by the worst crime ever to be committed against a people, responded by reviving a land, recovering their sovereignty, rescuing threatened Jews throughout the world, rebuilding Jerusalem, and proving themselves to be as courageous in the pursuit of peace as in defending themselves in war.

I am proud that our ancestors refused to be satisfied with premature consolations, and in answer to the question, "Has the Messiah come?" always answered, "Not yet."

I am proud to belong to the people Israel, whose name means "one who wrestles with God and with man and prevails." For though we have loved humanity, we have never stopped wrestling with it, challenging the idols of every age. And though we have loved God with an everlasting love, we have never stopped wrestling with Him nor He with us.

And though I admire other civilizations and faiths, and believe each has brought something special into the world, still this is my people, my heritage, my God. In our uniqueness lies our universality. Through being what we alone are, we give to humanity what only we can give.

This, then, is our story, our gift to the next generation. I received it from my parents and they from theirs across great expanses of space and time. There is nothing quite like it. It changed and still challenges the moral imagination of mankind. I want to say to my children: Take it, cherish it, learn to understand and to love it. Carry it and it will carry you. And may you in turn pass it on to your children. For you are a member of an eternal people, a letter in their scroll. Let their eternity live on in you.

MATT PUTNEY, 15, Atlanta, Georgia

I feel that when I say "I am Jewish" it means more than just I follow Jewish law. It means I'm part of a smaller group and at the same time part of a huge global community.

MICHELLE PEARL has a doctorate in epidemiology and currently researches reproductive health in California. She is vice president of the Daniel Pearl Foundation, which was formed to honor her beloved older brother Danny.

"When the time came to feel a connection beyond ourselves, we drew strength from our Judaism because it enhanced our humanity."

Recently I spent a casual evening watching a TV show with some close friends who happen to be Jewish. We ordered Chinese food, analyzed the political climate, talked about our mothers, laughed loudly and freely during parts of the show not intended to be funny, spoke our minds often out of turn, and at the end of the night took longer to say good-bye than the entire episode's runtime. We didn't have a kosher meal, bless our wine or bread, or mention the looming High Holidays other than "Where will you be?" But when we finally parted, we joked that other cultures leave and never say good-bye, while Jews say good-bye and never leave.

Although our little gathering of short, secular Jews was an unwitting backdrop for so many modern Jewish clichés, none of us considers our Jewishness to be our most salient defining characteristic. Our Jewish upbringing taught us to laugh at ourselves (otherwise someone else will), while at the same time providing so much fodder for jokes and neuroses for therapy. For much of my life, that's what being Jewish meant to me: exorbitant quantities of food, liberal use of humor, and a healthy dose of nervous energy.

As I prepared for my wedding, I realized that being Jewish was something more than a mere condiment to my being. I decided to wholeheartedly embrace the richness of our heritage, the joyful spirit of the Jewish tradition, and celebrate life in a way that would not only honor our families, but would tie us forever to the same historical fabric uniting my ancestors and fellow Jews. At our wedding we drank the fruit of the vine, recited the seven blessings, signed a *ketubah,* sang and danced in concentric circles, and were hoisted on chairs and paraded around like a king and queen. The *simkha* of our little community created a palpable energy that would have made my brother proud. When the time came to feel a connection beyond ourselves, we drew strength from our Judaism because it enhanced our humanity.

I didn't choose to be Jewish, but it is intrinsic to who I am. And if you look closely behind the self-deprecating humor, you'll find a pride in the values that make us Jewish.

 RABBI HAROLD M. SCHULWEIS is the spiritual leader of Valley Beth Shalom in Encino, California, and author of many books, including *For Those Who Can't Believe, In God's Mirror, Evil and the Morality of God,* and *Approaches to the Philosophy of Religion.* He is the founding chairman of the Jewish Foundation for the Righteous, an organization that identifies and offers grants to those non-Jews who risked their lives to save Jews threatened by the agents of Nazi savagery.

"Judaism is the particular language through which Jews address humanity."

Some of my best Jewish friends share my humanistic concerns for the submerged communities, the lot of the poor, the weak, and the pariahs of society. But oddly enough, they see no connection between that universal interest and its Jewish roots. While never denying their Jewish ancestry, they find it difficult to articulate their Jewish identity. For them to declare, "I am Jewish" is a confession that, like Woody Allen's, is appended with the coda, "guilty, with an explanation." What is the explanation for their guilt and this inability to speak their Jewish identity with a full-throated voice? Declaring their Jewish identity appears as a compromise of their moral largesse, a betrayal of their universalistic vision. It is as if they hear the question of their Jewishness framed as a hard disjunctive: "Are you a Jew or a human being?" "Is your loyalty to your people or to humanity?"

My teacher, the philosopher Sydney Hook, confessed, in his book *Out of Step,* that during the Holocaust years he and many Jews like him were so enthralled by the promise of universalism that they came to regard the suffering of the Jewish people as mere parochial sentiment. "We did not for a moment deny our Jewish origin but disapproved of what we thought an excess of chauvinism." It echoed the sentiment of Rosa Luxemberg, the internationalist socialist of Jewish descent. She turned on her fellow Jews in anger, declaring, "Why do you persist in pestering me with your peculiar *Judenschmerz* [Jewish pain]? I feel more deeply the wretchedness on the rubber plantations of Puto Maya ..."

Doubtless, my friends are reacting to the kind of insularly Jewish particularism that confuses loyalty to Judaism and the Jewish people with chauvinistic provincialism. That type of paranoiac particularism suspects any cosmopolitan outlook as a threat to the fidelity of Jewish survival and to Jewish uniqueness. My friends are caught in the vise of either/or thinking that divides the world into "them" and "us" and forces choices of false options. The consequence of this split thinking leads to the twin fallacies of pseudo-particularism and pseudo-universalism, which tear apart the wholeness of Judaism and the unity of Jewish identity.

My universalistic Jewish friends are deaf to the uniqueness of Jewish particularism and Jewish universalism and consequently mute in expressing their Jewish identity. To paraphrase George Santayana, the effort to embrace humanity in general is as foolhardy as the attempt "to speak in general without using any language in particular." Judaism is the particular language through which Jews address humanity. Although the Bible originates out of the needs, intuitions, and revelations of a particular people, its wisdom and ethics burst into the public domain of humanity.

Martin Buber, criticized by those who urged him to liberate Hasidic tradition from its "confessional limitations" and to transcend it, offered an authentic Jewish response. He was not bound to step into the street in order to speak what he had heard to the world. He could remain in the door of his ancestral home and still share it with the world.

An authentic Jewish particularism is not contrary to the idea of universalism. It grasps both polarities in one hand. Jewish particularism does not segregate—its unitive embrace is expressed in this rabbinic statement from *Tanna De-Ve-Eliyahu*: "I call heaven and earth to witness that whether it be man or woman, slave or handmaiden, the Holy Spirit rests on each according to his deeds." So the Russian Jewish refusenik Natan Sharansky understood the moral interdependence between Jewish particularism and universalism. While active on behalf of Jewish immigration, Sharansky struggled as well for the rights of Pentecostals, Catholics, Ukrainians, Crimeans, and Tartars. In the prison of the Soviet Union, he came to realize that "Only he who understands his own identity and already has become a free person can work effectively for the rights of others." In retrospect he observed that helping other persecuted people became part of his own freedom only after he had returned to his Jewish roots. Sharansky cited Cynthia Ozick's telling of the Jewish folk tale in which a naif asks the rabbi why one blows the shofar through the narrow side of the ram's horn rather than through the wide side. The rabbi answered, "If you blow it into the wide end, no sound will be emitted. But if you blow through the narrow side, it will reach into the outer limits." Like charity, compassion begins at home, but it does not end there.

Elie Wiesel, whose concern for Soviet Jewry similarly led him to a concern for peoples' races and religions not his own, counseled, "If you try to start everywhere all at once, you get nowhere, but if you start with a single person, someone near to you, a friend or a neighbor, you can come nearer to the other." In the celebrated biblical verse Leviticus 19:18, love of the other is linked to love of oneself. Egoism and altruism are not contradictions. The tradition cautions against that form of self-abnegation, which some declare to be the entry to selfless altruism. No more than love of one's wife leads to misogyny does love of family lead to misanthropy.

I recall for my friends the masterful Hasidic tale in which a wealthy disciple of the rabbi boasts that he lives an abstemious life, eating dry bread and water. The rabbi chastises his parsimony and urges the wealthy man to drink of the finest of wines and eat of the tenderest of meats. When his other disciples wondered why he was upset with the rich man's modest style of life, the rabbi answered, "I fear that if he is content with consuming bread and water, he will argue that the poor who come to him should be content with rocks and sand."

To be Jewish is to live in a dynamic and dialectical relationship between the private and the public, the individual and the social, the unique and the universal. It is to seek the integration and harmony, articulated in Rabbi Hillel's celebrated aphorism, "If I am not for myself, who will be for me? But if I live only for myself, of what good am I?"

In these parlous days, when great religions denigrate each other, it is important to remember the wisdom of our sages, who selected two separate readings for the first and the second day of Rosh Hashanah, the Jewish New Year. On the first day, we read of how Hagar and Ishmael, the heirs of Islam, were exiled but protected through the divine intervention of the Angel of God, who rescued the Egyptian wife of Abraham and their son Ishmael and promised that Ishmael would be made into a great nation (Gen. 21:14–21). And on the second day of Rosh Hashanah, the congregation reads the story of Abraham and Isaac, the heir of Judaism, whom the Angel of the Lord saves from the sacrificial knife (Gen. 22:1–19). Both Ishmael and Isaac are God's children and their genealogies are recorded in the Scriptures (Gen. 25:12–18). The particular-universal connection is exemplified in these twin readings on the Jewish New Year and, I have argued, also in all the major celebrations of the Jewish calendar. What else is the significance of the Rabbis' selecting for public reading the Prophet Jonah on the Day of Atonement, and emphasizing the sacrifice of seventy animals on behalf of the seventy nations of the world in the liturgy of Sukkot? It is Jonah who initially refuses to prophesy against Nineveh because he is apprehensive lest God repent of His judgment. For this, Jonah is chastised, the pagan citizens do indeed repent, and God Himself repents of His judgment to punish Nineveh. The compassion of God is not restricted to one people. The Jewish tradition, properly understood, will not allow God to be segregated.

To declare one's Jewish identity is to know how to sing the song that rises to holiness. The rabbinic philosopher and poet Abraham Isaac Kook caught the growing melody of the Jewish song: "There is one who sings the songs of his own self, and in himself finds everything. Then there is the one who sings the song of his people and cleaves with a tender love to Israel. And there is one whose spirit is in all worlds, and with all of them does he join in his song. The song of the self, the song of one's people, the song of man, the song of the world—they all merge within him continually. And this song, in its completeness and its fullness, is to become the song of holiness" (Oroth Ha-Kodesh II, p. 458).

 EHUD BARAK, tenth prime minister of the State of Israel, led far-reaching efforts to negotiate peace agreements with both Syria and the Palestinian Authority. He is the most-decorated soldier in the history of Israel.

"Struggles for the very security and peace of bodies and minds that our forefathers proclaimed, three millennia ago, to be the self-evident right and destiny of all mankind."

I am a Jew because I was born one.

Years later, as a grown-up, I became proud of it.

Being a Jew means to belong to the people whose prophets and sages set the moral foundations and values of our modern liberal democratic humanity.

Being a Jew means to belong to a faith that prefers the power of ideas over the reigning of the sword and proved that while facing the toughest imaginable challenges—from Titus to Torquemada to Hitler—it could prevail.

And being a Jew in Israel means never losing hope, while participating in an unprecedented historic experience of rebuilding once again a Jewish vibrant democratic state at our very birthplace. A state that still struggles for the very security and peace of bodies and minds that our forefathers proclaimed, three millennia ago, to be the self-evident right and destiny of all mankind.

BERNARD-HENRI LÉVY is one of France's leading philosophers and the author of numerous best-selling books, including his most recent, *Who Killed Daniel Pearl?*

I am a universalist Jew.

I am Jewish through my mother and my father.

I am Jewish through Lévinas, Buber, Rosenzweig.

I am Jewish because being Jewish means loving the law more than the earth and the letter as much as the spirit.

I am Jewish as a result of the distrust that has always been engendered by, and that I have always felt in reaction to, ecstatic states and extreme religious passion.

I am Jewish as a result of my rejection of all forms of magic or of mystery: "Beware," cried out Lévinas, author of *Difficult Freedom,* "of all the false prophets who tell us that man is 'never closer to the gods than when he ceases to belong to himself'! On your guard, Jews, against forgetting that Judaism is the only religion in the world that preaches refusal of the numinous and obscure forces—a religion of disenchantment, of the saint and not of the sacred!" This is how I am Jewish.

I am Jewish in that I am antinaturalist and antimaterialist—I am Jewish, in other words, because I am at home in the Book and among men, more than in the obscure forest of symbols and even of life.

I am a Jew of the *galout* (exile); I am a Jew who, for years and years, reflects on this question of the *galout;* not exactly a rehabilitation of the *galout;* not, properly speaking, a metaphysic of exile; and, even less, of a distance in relation to Israel, which I love from the bottom of my heart, an unconditional love; but a meditation on an essential exile, without redemption or return, which seems to me to constitute what it is to be Jewish, both in galout and in Israel; the contrary of Ulysses' exile; the correlate and counterpart of the fascination, Jewish as well, with the kingdom of heaven; is Jew not the name, equally, of the son of Abraham (the Hebrew) and of Jacob (the Israelite)? Is Jewish philosophy not, indissolubly, the philosophy of the kings and the prophets, of Israel and of the voice which, through Jeremiah, implores the "rest of Israel" to "fortify its position in exile"?

I am Jewish because I am not a Platonist; Jewish because of what I would call, to be succinct, anti-Platonism coextensive to Jewish thought; an ethic more than a viewpoint; a relation to other men as much as to God or, more exactly, to God, yes, but insofar, and only insofar, as it brings me nearer my neighbor.

I am Jewish like Lévinas when he discusses friendship with Buber. In that discussion, which is worthy of, by its terms, the famous dispute in which Proust, on the same subject, ends up throwing his slippers at the face of Emmanuel Berl, Lévinas expresses his distrust of the Buberian notions of dialogue and reciprocity. I am Jewish, yes, in the way Lévinas declares how strange and pointless is the idea of a purely spiritual, or "de-nerved," friendship, which can only sink into "formalism." Too much idealism, he insists, and you are too much the "artist in your relations with other men." He concludes with these magnificent formulations, which are a part of my Jewishness: Others need "solicitude" more than "friendship," because "to clothe those who are naked and nourish those who are hungry is the real and concrete access to the otherness of the other, more authentic than ethereal friendship."

I am a Jew who is not really a humanist (the word is meaningless for a reader, even among the less learned, of Maharal de Prague or Gaon de Vilna), but I am conscious of a Judaism that makes me responsible for others, their keeper—a Judaism that defines itself, therefore, as an ethic and defines this ethic as that which is established when I resolve to make of myself not the equal but the hostage of my neighbor and that I see, above my "I," a "thou" who dominates me from his saintly height.

I am a Jew who is not obviously political (how could a student of Lévinas forget his "Politique Aprés"?) but open, on the other hand, to the world and making messianism the basic responsibility of man, of each man, in the work of redemption.

I am a universalist Jew.

I am a Jew who does not resign himself to leave to Christianity the monopoly of universalism. The Jewish "chosenness," for me as again for Lévinas or Albert Cohen, is not privilege, but mission. The role of the Jewish people, according to me as well as to Rosenzweig, is to open, for all peoples, the invisible and sacred doors that illuminate the star of redemption. And this is, in my eyes, the meaning of the commandment of Deuteronomy: "Hold not in abhorrence the Edomite, for he is your brother; hold not in abhorrence the Egyptian"; and this too in the story of Jonah whom God enjoined: "Rise up and go speak to Nineveh," even though Nineveh is, as he knows, Israel's enemy, the capital of Assyria, the very kingdom of the wicked.

I am a Jew like Walter Benjamin when Benjamin speaks of his "solicitude for the vanquished and the hungry"—I am Jewish in the sense of *Poésie et Revolution* and the "Theses on the Concept of History" showing that "each second is the narrow door through which may pass the messiah."

I am a Jew who believes, like Benjamin again and, in a certain way, like Scholem, that Jewish messianism is the "incarnation of an invisible and secret history" that "opposes the history of the strong and mighty," which is to say "visible history"—all my life I've believed in this Judaism, and this is what I practiced.

I was Jewish, in other words, in my *Réflexions sur la Guerre, le Mal et la Fin de l'Histoire*. I was Jewish in Burundi, in Angola, and in Muslim Bosnia and a martyr like the Black Tigers of Sri Lanka.

I was Jewish among the Nubians on their way to being exterminated in southern Sudan.

I am Jewish each time that, in the most desolate zones of the world, in the heart of its most forgotten wars, I prove the Jewish intuition according to which the most serious evidence of the existence of God is the existence of faces—and the sign of God's eclipse, their programmed effacement.

I am Jewish because I believe in a God that by another definition is "Do Not Kill."

I am Jewish when I try, in the course of one year, to put my steps into those of Daniel Pearl, and I am Jewish when, in my own way, modest and secular, yes, but that is my way, I try to contribute to the sanctification of his name.

DAVID GROSSMAN is a writer; among his books are *See Under: Love; The Yellow Wind; The Book of Infinite Grammar;* and *Be My Knife*. He lives in Israel.

"This attitude has caused the Jew and his history to become, in the eyes of humanity, a story that is larger than life."

For me, to be a Jew is to be an outsider.

An outsider in relation to human situations in which a collective of any sort comes into being, composed of many who speak (or roar) in a single voice; an outsider with that slight suspicion of whatever makes that collective possible; with that sense of loneliness that takes hold of the individual in the presence of such a collective, even if he does not want—or is unable—to be part of it; with the feelings of uniqueness and election that accompany that loneliness; with that trace of (not entirely comprehensible) pride that accompany those feelings, pained incessantly by the fact that that uniqueness and election place an invisible but real barrier between him and the others; with the constant skepticism that lies—or ought to lie—within regard to those feelings (which have turned, for the Jewish people, into the concept of "the chosen people"), because all too often it seems as if those feelings are nothing but a scab that has formed over the wound of loneliness, of the Jews' tragic distinctiveness; with the knowledge that this distinctiveness—and who knows whether it was imposed from the start on the Jews by others or whether the Jews chose and refined it—has made "the Jew" into an almost universal symbol of the absolute alien; with pain at the fact that this attitude has caused the Jew and his history to become, in the eyes of humanity, a story that is larger than life, and therefore something that is not really part of life itself, something detached from the course of nature and history experienced by other nations.

To this I must add the sense of profound, instinctive, familial identification that I feel toward Jews throughout the generations. I share their fate, their way of thinking, their culture, their language, and their humor. But perhaps what I really identify with, more than anything else, is precisely that sense of loneliness, injury, and persecution, the feeling of being foreign in this world, ever anxious about the tenuousness of existence.

But whenever I feel that by identifying this way as a Jew, I become part of this particular collective, the Jewish collective, I take a step back, and have some serious (and very Jewish) doubts about belonging to it.

TOVAH FELDSHUH is an award-winning film, television, and stage actress, most recently starring as Prime Minister Golda Meir in William Gibson's *Golda's Balcony* on Broadway.

"I love the universal, because for us it means we belong, we are part of, we are included—not separate."

What does it mean to Tovah Feldshuh to be Jewish?

It means loving to live in the question. It means searching for the specific truth with such commitment that when one finds it, it resonates with the universal. I love the universal, because for us it means we belong, we are part of, we are included—not separate.

Being Jewish also means an overview, a *weltanschauung*, a slight distance from the many societies in which we live because we have been distanced either by the ruling class or by our own volition. And from this distance is born a sense of humor and irony that is on the highest plane of laughter and insight.

Being Jewish is at least a five-sense experience: the hearing of the *Kol Nidre*, the sight of the Torah, the smell of the chicken soup, the taste of the gefilte fish, the touch of a *mezuzah*. Then there is the most precious sixth sense to being Jewish: the instinct to survive. How we want to live a full life! How we know what it is for life to be taken from us. The Jews have more collective eulogies than the mind can fathom, on which we say *Kaddish*.

I was just in Israel, and during my stay there were two bombings in one day.

The bus stop the homicide bombers attacked was repaired by the next day and functioning. The cafe, because of its large windows, took a little longer to get back on its feet: seventy-two hours. It brings to mind a quote by Teddy Roosevelt that to me personifies the Sabra, who exemplifies the core of the Jewish experience:

The credit belongs to the man who is actually in the arena—
Whose face is marred by dust and sweat and blood
Who knows the great enthusiasms, the great devotions—
And spends himself in a worthy cause—
Who at best if he wins knows the thrills of high achievement—
And if he fails at least fails while daring greatly—
So that his place shall never be with those cold and timid souls
who know neither victory nor defeat.

—Theodore Roosevelt, April 23, 1910

NADINE GORDIMER, the author of thirteen novels, nine volumes of stories, and three nonfiction collections, was awarded the Nobel Prize in Literature in 1991. She lives in Johannesburg, South Africa.

"My answer is: recognize yourself in others."

I am a Jew. To be a Jew, to be black—it is simply something you *are*. There is no pride in belonging to one particular race, color, or designation, and no denigration whatever in your identity. Recently I was asked in a questionnaire what wish I would want to leave behind me in the world. My answer is: recognize yourself in others.

That would be the end of racism, which we know in all its pain and despicable horror. I believe that Daniel Pearl's last words "I am a Jew" were an assertion of his inalienable right to recognition of the human oneness in his specific identity. His was the ultimate judgment on the senseless brutality that took his young life.

THEODORE BIKEL is a folksinger; a theater, film, and television actor; a radio host; the president of Actors' Equity; a political activist; a Jewish spokesman; and an author.

"I make no claim that Jewish culture is superior to other cultures or that the Jewish song is better than the song of my neighbor. But it is mine."

In my world, history comes down to language and art. No one cares much about what battles were fought, who won them, and who lost them—unless there is a painting, a play, a song, or a poem that speaks of the event. Only then does the distinction between past and present cease to have any meaning. No heirloom of humankind captures the past—the good and the bad—as do art and language. Some of it survives as painful memory in the crazy language of generals and politicians and some as joy or anguish or pain in the legacy of poetry and song.

Throughout my life I have cared as deeply about the songs of all peoples as I have about the rights of all peoples. I have always striven to raise the voice of hope for a world where hate gives way to respect and oppression to liberation. I know only too well that we live in a world of guns, bombs, and terror. To conquer hate seems a nigh-impossible task. But I prefer to make common cause with those whose weapons are guitars, banjos, fiddles, and words.

Despite a large body of work I have in the general artistic arena, I am viewed by many not just as an artist who happens to be a Jew but as a "Jewish artist." I do not resent the label, except for the fact that I disapprove of labels in general. They are confining. But when I toil in the field of Jewish culture, which I frequently do, I am indeed a "Jewish" artist.

Lest my predilection toward my own Jewishness be misunderstood or misinterpreted, let me emphasize that I am a universalist, quite passionately devoted to the cause of equality within the human family. But I came by this attitude precisely because of the Jew in me.

I remain convinced that I can be a true universalist only when I am a better Jew. I perceive the world, especially American society, as a kaleidoscope. The brighter each particle shines, the better for society as a whole and certainly for each ethnic component of it. My particle is the Jewish one.

I am also determined to give the Yiddish language a fighting chance to survive. Yiddish should not be reduced in our minds to mis-remembered mumblings of *Zayde's* (grandfather's) admonitions or *Bubbe's* (grandmother's) terms of endearment. I cherish the Hebrew language and master it well, but where is it written that I have to abandon Yiddish in order to love Hebrew?

The following is a Yiddish poem by I. Papiernikov that I have rendered into English as a small example of a culture we so carelessly let slip through our fingers.

Zol zayn az ikh boyu der luft mayne shleser
Zol zayn az mayn Got iz ingantsn nito
In troym iz mir heler, in troym iz mir beser
In troym iz der himl gor bloyer vi blo.
Zol zayn az kh'vel keynmol tsum tsil nit derlangen
Zol zayn az mayn shif vet nit kumen tsum breg
Es geyt nit in dem tsu hobn dergangen
Es geyt nor in gang oyf a zunikn veg.

Could be that my whole world is only confusion
Could be what I thought was God's word isn't true.
Yet my dream is as bright as the brightest illusion
And the sky in my dream is much bluer than blue.
Could be that I'll not see the fruit of my yearning
Could be that I'll never be rid of my load.
What matters is not the end of the journey
It's the journey itself on a bright sunlit road.

What moves me is neither ethnocentric pride nor sectarian arrogance. I make no claim that Jewish culture is superior to other cultures or that the Jewish song is better than the song of my neighbor. But it is mine. And since it is the song of my people, it is up to me to cultivate it, lest the garden become desolate and the blooms wither and die.

JUDEA PEARL was born in Tel Aviv, Israel. He is a professor of computer science at the University of California, Los Angeles, and president of the Daniel Pearl Foundation. He is the author of three books on artificial intelligence: *Heuristics, Probabilistic Reasoning,* and *Causality.*

"I see Jews as the scouts of civilization."

To be Jewish is to identify myself with the past, present, and future of a collective of individuals who call themselves "Jews." As an act of choice, I select a certain thread of history and label it "mine," that is, relevant to me. Similarly, I select the destiny of other members of the collective and label it "ours," that is, relevant to our children.

The logic of being Jewish thus rests on a fortunate symbiosis between two forces: choice and history. The first lays claim to universalism, the second to tribalism.

We strive for a culture of universal, all-inclusive humanity, yet we recognize that the innate architecture of the human mind requires a tribal framework to codify, implement, and sustain the principles of that culture. We thus nurture a tribal subculture, equipped with vivid ethos and personalized teachings, and use it to inspire humanistic standards of behavior, warmth of an extended family, and a sense of mission and continuity. Our record and endurance attest to the power of this symbiosis.

And religion? What about God, and covenant, and holiness, and the 613 *Mitzvot?*

I am a secular Jew. I find it hard to believe that an entity up there takes record of my thoughts and deeds. Still, I chant the Friday night *Kiddush* with all the seriousness that my grandfather did. Why? Because my tradition, with all its theology, myths, and rituals, offers me an effective language of symbols and metaphors with which to understand the teachings of my past, and in which to formulate my commitments for the future.

This is perhaps what Danny meant when he said: "Afterlife? I don't have answers, mainly questions. But I sure hope Gabriel likes my music." In other words, "I doubt the existence of the afterlife, but

I conduct my life as though a Gabriel will be asking one day: 'Anyone here care to bring some joy to the world?' I want to be chosen."

But why Jewish? Why don't I offer my children the choice of some other subculture to anchor our identity and to exercise our humanity? The answer is twofold: it wouldn't be easy, and it wouldn't be wise.

I would probably make a clumsy, unconvincing father reciting the songs of the Hiawatha to my children. In contrast, I do a fairly decent job with the *Kiddush,* or *Pirkei Avot* (Ethics of the Fathers) or the story of Hanukah. These reside deep in my brain, marked with a big "mine," evoking hundreds of stories, smells, and melodies that one expects from a father, grandfather, or a teacher. I cherish the thought that these sweet melodies were also evoked in Danny's mind when he wrote to us in an e-mail in September of 1998: "I intend to give my children all the Jewish tradition I know, maybe more with your help."

But who are we? I look down the history of ideas and I find our little subculture scoring an impressive list of accomplishments. I see Jews as the scouts of civilization—the ones who question conventional wisdom and constantly seek the exploration of new pathways. Abraham questioned the wisdom of idolatry, Moses questioned the wisdom of servitude and lawlessness, the prophets questioned institutional injustice, and so the chain goes on from the Maccabees, Jesus, and Spinoza, to Marx, Herzl, and Freud, down to Einstein, Gershwin, and the civil rights activists of the 1960s.

As individuals, we do not consciously choose this lonely role as scouts, border-challengers, idol-smashers, and boat-rockers. It has permeated our veins partly from the Bible and the Talmud in their persistent encouragement of curiosity, learning, and debate, and partly transmitted through the free-spirited character and attitude of our parents, uncles, and historical role models. But mostly, this role has been imposed on us by the travesties of history—conventional wisdoms were mighty unkind to us, and their guardians quite oppressive. Our sanity demanded that we challenge those conventions and, in due course, we have learned to challenge all conventions.

Ironically, this habit of questioning authorities has evoked much anti-Jewish antagonism. Few can appreciate those who are on the lookout for improvement, especially when experiments occasionally fail (e.g., Marxism). Still, many are grateful when experiments turn successful (e.g., relativity) and most understand that, failures notwithstanding, experiments propel the progress of civilization.

Thus, is my Jewishness a blessing or a burden? Do I prefer the trails of the scouts to the safety of the bandwagon? You bet I do. It is only from those trails that I can see where the voyage is heading, and it is only from there that I can discover greener pastures.

I am Jewish, and I doubt I would be in my element elsewhere.

ERAN ROTSHENKER, 22, Jerusalem, Israel

For me, being Jewish and being an Israeli always get mixed up together. It's being proud of who you are and loving Israel so much that you start hating all that's going on there, and understand how much you love it again. But above all, being Jewish means first and foremost being a good, valuable human being.

RABBI CHAIM SEIDLER-FELLER directs the Yitzak Rabin Hillel Center for Jewish Life and teaches Jewish studies at UCLA.

"Can I be intensely Jewish without losing the sense that I am created in the 'image of God' like everybody else?"

I love being Jewish, and I also love being human. In fact, as a Jew, I have always struggled with and celebrated the tension between my embrace of the universally human and my commitment to the particularly Jewish. It is an energizing tension that compels creativity and prevents complacency. And it is enriching because neither facet exhausts the totality of my being.

How do I create a balance between these different dimensions of my identity? How can I integrate my humanity with my Jewishness so that they both have value? Can I manifest both aspects simultaneously? Can I be intensely Jewish without losing the sense that I am created in the "image of God" like everybody else? Does my Jewishness open me up to my humanity? These are some of the dilemmas that I consistently confront.

That confrontation and struggle is mandated by the dynamic flow of the Torah, which begins with creation, focuses on the human condition—mortality, conflict, exile, alienation—and then moves on to introduce the Abrahamic family and the particular story of the emergence of the Israelite/Jewish people. The spotlight is on one group not because it embodies the one truth but because the biblical point of view is that the particular is the guarantor of the universal. When God destroys the Tower of Babel, God proclaims that the purpose of creation was that humans diversify and proliferate cultures and languages. This is the glory of civilization, what Jonathan Sacks calls "the dignity of difference." The problem with the Tower was that the dominant, if magnificent, universal culture that it generated has, throughout human history, promoted uniformity of thought, conformity of behavior, centralization of power, and, eventually, persecution and oppression of the other, who is identified as the deviant. In response, the Torah argues that the best way to inspire cultural creativity and inculcate tolerance of difference is by affirming a world of "particulars," each of which illuminates another aspect of the universal truth. Once an individual comprehends that he/she is only a particular, he/she immediately understands that other particulars are "just like me" and that together they comprise the whole. Each one needs the other to broaden his/her perspective, to keep him/her honest, to motivate him/her to look beyond him/herself, and to gain an awareness that only together can they envision the One.

Contrary to the popularly held belief that particularism leads to exclusivism and conflict and that universalism is a healing ideology, Judaism, consequent to its experience as a minority religion, asserts that a pluralistic, inclusive world is anchored in the particular. Indeed, the deeper, humbling truth is that there are no stand-alone universals, for we are all only particulars.

ANNE ROIPHE is the author of twelve books of fiction and nonfiction and a contributor to the *Jerusalem Report*.

"The color of my humanity is Jewish."

I am Jewish, which is a biological fact. It is not just a biological fact. It means that I am attached to the history of my people as it unfolds from Abraham to Theodore Herzl, from Nehemiah through Albert Einstein. It means I see Spinoza in Martin Buber and Joshua in Ben Gurion and Rashi in the LSATs. It means that I am convinced that there is a purpose and a meaning, although we cannot see it clearly in the Jewish role in human existence. It means that the ordeals of the Jewish people in exile have alerted me to the vulnerability of the powerless and connected my imaginative life with those who may be hunted by Hitlers or Hamans, however they may be disguised across the globe. It means that to the best of my limited knowledge, the Jewish ethics as debated in the Talmud and studied in the Torah will shape my vision of right and wrong and are alive within my small and large decisions. It means that my seasons are marked by the holidays when Jews take the Torah out of the ark and walk around the congregation and replace it and when Jews remember to save the gleanings of the fields for the hungry or stand silent for the murdered children of pogroms. It means that I understand exile in its literal and metaphorical meaning. It means that the color of my humanity is Jewish and that I fully expect that humanity to be of worth to all, connected to all, and open to anyone who would share it.

It means that in one corner of my mind I remember my brother's worst Jewish jokes and in another corner I remember my Queen Esther costume as well as the way my uncle misbehaved at Passover gatherings. I remember the destruction of the First and Second Temple and the barbarism of Kristallnacht and all that followed. I remember it all as if it were yesterday.

 Dr. URI D. HERSCHER is founding president and CEO of the Skirball Cultural Center in Los Angeles, California.

"The Jewish people have deeply understood the value of recognizing a common thread in all of humanity."

To be Jewish is, above all, to be part of a community of memory. It is a four-thousand-year-old community of memory that recognizes what we owe to those who have come before us. Jews focus on what we have learned as a community not only to memorialize it, but in addition to apply it to what we face now. To be Jewish is to accept the responsibility for continuing to make the world a more civil and humane place—not in spite of the anguish endured during a four-thousand-year history, which our memory makes available to us—but because of it.

When you are about to be murdered, it is hard to imagine three more telling words to say than: "I am Jewish." It affirms that you are a part of a community larger than yourself—one that remembers what is to be learned from ghastly experiences of which your own death is but the most recent. It is a community that will continue despite your murder, and it is a community that will remember you because you have remembered it.

It is a courageous and responsible reporter's last filed sentence—one that records the most important thing he can see in what he is experiencing—that he is a member of a heritage that continues to work for civility and humanity of which he has been privileged to be a part. Daniel knew that he was part of an ancient tradition that would carry forward the ethical anchors he had helped carry during his life's journey.

So, what does it mean to say "I am Jewish"? Our biblical patriarch, Abraham, gave us our first two clues. To discover there is one God rather than multiple gods, suggesting that we probably are one humanity rather than "us" versus "them." We are not friends and foes, family and strangers, but rather simply human beings. Biblical commentators note that Abraham, having just been circumcised at a rather advanced age, was instructed by God to heal while resting on his cot and not to rise during his time of recovery—not even for prayer.

But Abraham's response to God's urging was to give us a second clue as to what it means to be a Jew. While resting in his tent, Abraham sees strangers from afar. He rises from his bed to welcome them and to invite them into his tent for refreshments and a meal. His first act as a Jew is to be hospitable to the stranger, to dissolve barriers, and to embrace others. Our biblical commentators conclude from this midrash that it is actually more important in Jewish tradition to welcome the stranger into your home than to rise for prayer.

In our own American Revolution, it was said that we had better hang together, lest we certainly will hang separately. It may be the most important discovery of the human race so far. Community creates safety, while barriers produce estrangement, fear, enmity, and hatred, and the zealotry that gives it form. To have survived four thousand years, always as a small and marginal community within often hostile larger societies, the Jewish people have deeply understood the value of recognizing a common thread in all of humanity. And further, that this common thread must be nurtured if all of us are to survive. Forged within the four-thousand-year-old Jewish heritage, this discovery may now (in an increasingly interconnected world) be the only one in which humanity can vest hope for our future.

When the biblical Jonah learned that God wanted him to help those in Nineveh, Jonah responded by saying that he would be glad to help the Jews of Nineveh, but none of the other communities in the city. God's retort: "No, I didn't say that you ought to help just the Jewish community in Nineveh. I said help the *entire* community in Nineveh." It is clear there is no safety in isolation. Only as the total community learns our way into a more civil future can any of us be safe. Daniel Pearl had, in the courageous and responsible journalism he conveyed to the world, grasped what Jonah did not. Until we understand each other and find ways to connect with each other, to act inclusively, we all remain at risk.

I was born with the memory of the Holocaust and a deep understanding of how cruel the world can be. I've personally lost eighty percent of my paternal family in the Holocaust, and a good portion of my maternal family in Israel's War of Independence. I hear their voices from the grave: "We died, but you are to live to make this world less cruel and more humane." I have now added Daniel Pearl's voice to that group of lost family who speak to me thus.

Daniel Pearl's memorial service took place at the Skirball Cultural Center, where we welcomed hundreds of Daniel's friends and colleagues, as well as his dear family. We rose in honor of all Jews everywhere and through all time as we remembered him. We rose as human beings whose humanity has been enlarged by Daniel Pearl's time among us.

ALEXANDER MILITAREV is president of the Jewish University in Moscow and a professor of Semitic and Afroasiatic languages at the Russian State University for the Humanities.

"I frequently doubt whether preservation of national consciousness assists or hampers the establishment of universal humanistic values in our world."

Being Jewish is not the chief among my identities; belonging to the human race and more personal identification have always meant more to me. Like my parents and grandparents and all my friends, I am more Cosmopolitan than Jewish. Like many people of similar liberal values, I frequently doubt whether preservation of national consciousness assists or hampers the establishment of universal humanistic values in our world.

For more than two thousand years, the Jews have played an exceptional part in the formation of Western civilization, producing a strategy for the survival of Homo sapiens. Will this strategy lead mankind to general prosperity, long life, a symbiosis with living nature, a comprehension of its place in the world and, perhaps, expansion throughout the universe? Or bring about its self-annihilation in a global war, from terrorism, overpopulation, hunger, or the greenhouse effect? What if a different, more isolationist, less wasteful, and less conflicting strategy holds more promise for the survival of our species? Which scale is one to use to measure the benefits and achievements attained thanks to this strategy against all kinds of calamities accompanying mankind's progress: wars; genocide; ecological damage (done and expected); the loss by many of the comfortable hope for eternal life of the soul, "salvation," and life after death?

I do not know the answers to these questions; and I distrust those claiming to have them. I believe that, to a certain degree, the Jews are responsible for the victories, the defeats, and the future of this civilization, having stood at its source together with the ancient Greeks. They are not the only ones responsible, but it does not detract from their responsibility. As for individual responsibility, each one should, in my view, be completely free to choose whether or not to bear this responsibility.

PART V:

TIKKUN OLAM (REPAIRING THE WORLD) AND JUSTICE

 RUTH BADER GINSBURG, associate justice of the United States Supreme Court, was nominated by President Clinton in 1993 and took the oath of office on August 10, 1993. Prior to her appointment to the Supreme Court, she served for thirteen years on the bench of the United States Court of Appeals for the District of Columbia Circuit, and earlier, taught on the law faculties of Rutgers (1963–1972) and Columbia (1972–1980).

"The demand for justice runs through the entirety of the Jewish history and Jewish tradition."

Former Supreme Court Justice Arthur Goldberg once said: "My concern for justice, for peace, for enlightenment stems from my heritage." Justice Stephen Breyer and I are fortunate to be linked to that heritage and to live in the United States at a time when Jewish people residing here face few closed doors and do not fear letting the world know who we are.

For example, I say who I am in certain visible signs. The command from Deuteronomy appears in artworks, in Hebrew letters, on three walls and a table in my chambers. *"Zedek, zedek, tirdof,"* "Justice, Justice shalt thou pursue," these artworks proclaim; they are ever-present reminders to me of what judges must do "that they may thrive." There is also a large silver *mezuzah* mounted on my doorpost. It is a gift from the super-bright teenage students at the Shulamith School for Girls in Brooklyn, New York, the school one of my dearest law clerks attended in her growing-up years.

A question stated in various ways is indicative of what I would like to convey. What is the difference between a New York City garment district bookkeeper and a Supreme Court justice? One generation my life bears witness, the difference between the opportunities open to my mother, a bookkeeper, and those open to me.

I am a judge, born, raised, and proud of being a Jew. The demand for justice runs through the entirety of Jewish history and Jewish tradition. I hope, in all the years I have the good fortune to serve on the bench of the Supreme Court of the United States, I will have the strength and courage to remain steadfast in the service of that demand.

JONATHAN FREEDLAND is a columnist for *The Guardian* of London. He is currently at work on a book about family, identity, and Jewishness.

"Wherever there is a revolutionary political movement, you will usually find Jews involved in it: We are raised to believe the world can be made better."

I am Jewish because my parents were Jewish and their parents and their parents and their parents. Yet that hardly contains the truth of it. It is rather more of a choice than that.

Every day we make a choice about how Jewish we want to be. In most places and at most times, that choice is relaxed and entirely voluntary: Should we eat kosher, should we see that new movie about Israel? Sometimes, it is more pointed: Should we stand up to the person who just made an anti-Semitic remark? Occasionally it is a profound choice: Should we change our name to one less overtly Jewish? And, sometimes, very rarely, it is a matter of life and death. As it was for Daniel Pearl.

How do we make these choices? For many Jews, it is a mixture of guilt, sentiment, and obligation to parents and ancestors. Rather than let down the past, we continue to identify, however weakly, as Jews. We stay Jewish because we feel we ought to; to walk away would be an act of betrayal.

But I am keen to find a more positive reason to say "I am Jewish." Recently I have begun to look closely at three members of my own family—one from each of the last three generations—and I have seen the different ways Jewishness shaped their lives. Two were immigrants; one was born in Palestine; one died in Israel.

Each one of their stories reveals a different aspect of what it is to be Jewish. For one, Jewishness meant a life of dual identities and allegiances: He was forever with a foot in two different worlds. To say "I am Jewish," at least in the diaspora, is often to say, "I can belong to two different societies at once. I can be both Jewish and something else." In the United States, that has become a commonplace, with hyphenated identities—Irish-American, Hispanic-American—quite the norm. On the globalized planet of the twenty-first century, it is how millions now live. But Jews introduced this hybridity into the world a long time ago; it has become absorbed into who we are.

For another relative of mine, a great-uncle, to be a Jew meant to be a force for good in the world. He was not religious, rather an atheist communist, but still he believed he was following an ancient Jewish imperative: *tikkun olam,* repair the world. There is a reason why, wherever there is a revolutionary political movement, you will usually find Jews involved in it: We are raised to believe the world can be made better. That the work of creation is a joint venture, with God and humanity partners—maybe even equal partners.

And finally there is my mother. She is, to be literal, what defines me as a Jew. Her life has crisscrossed continents and known tragedy, but I'm not one of those who sees perennial wandering or a familiarity with suffering as part of the Jewish essence. Rather, her life tells me that ties of family and memory can withstand even the pressure of destruction, and that a version of these ties has bound the Jews to each other for millennia. It may defy rational, intellectual explanation, but kinship is a powerful force, one that can be turned to good or ill—and Jews know a thing or two about it. When I say "I am Jewish," I say I am connected to my fellow Jews: human beings I will never have met. And if I can be connected to them, then I can be connected to everyone.

 **Stephen H. Hoffman** is president and CEO of United Jewish Communities. He is a graduate of Dickinson College, received his MSW from the University of Maryland, and a master's in Jewish studies from the Baltimore Hebrew University.

"Identify with the yearning to see all people free—free from want, free from terror, free from dictatorships, free from modern-day slavery and injustice."

I am connected to a people that stretches back four thousand years, that identifies with the experience of our forefather Abraham. I identify with him not because I want to be associated with a historical figure and thereby claim a share of fame in a relative, but because I want to live by his values, by his example of caring for the lives of the people of Sodom and Gomorrah, and by his example of being a just man, though a man who made mistakes.

I am connected to a people that tell their story of the Exodus from Egypt each year, beginning with the phrase "We were slaves," and so identify with the yearning to see all people free—free from want, free from terror, free from dictatorships, free from modern-day slavery and injustice.

I am connected to a people that draws its inspiration from the words of the prophets—words that urge us to be just, to not serve the false gods of greed and jealousy, that remind us that we can always make the choice to repent when we stray and to share in our creator's love.

I am Jewish because I want to be a part of a people that has much to share with the world.

GARY SHTEYNGART is the author of the novel *The Russian Debutante's Handbook,* which won the Stephen Crane Award for First Fiction and the National Jewish Book Award.

"'Repair the world,' a mandate that does not stop at the borders of our communities, a mandate that has no borders at all."

I was born in the Soviet Union, where, in official circles and in the press, the term "Cosmopolitans" served as the code word for Jews, a term that in the twilight years of the Stalin administration nearly resulted in a second Holocaust under the so-called "doctor's plot." The term refers to the supposed rootless nature of the Jewish people, our lack of allegiance to authoritarian power, our propensity to settle in urban areas and act as a conduit between different cultures.

Despite the negative connotations the Soviet government attached to such Cosmopolitanism, these are the traits I have always treasured in the Jewish diaspora, and these are the traits that come to mind when I think of Daniel Pearl and his senseless murder. History may have conspired to scatter the Jews about the earth, but from this misfortune we have emerged a curious, worldly, and yes, cosmopolitan people. We are blessed with an endless hunger to travel the globe, to document, to experience, and, often, to make right. In a new century defined by fanaticism, corruption, and official hypocrisy, the truth-seeking mission of a superb journalist like Mr. Pearl dovetails neatly with the Jewish mandate to "repair the world," a mandate that does not stop at the borders of our communities, a mandate that has no borders at all.

 LYNN SCHUSTERMAN is the president of the Charles and Lynn Schusterman Family Foundation, which is dedicated to helping Jewish people flourish by supporting programs throughout the world that spread the joy of Jewish living, giving, and learning. She is also president of Synagogues: Transformation and Renewal (STAR), chairman of the international board of directors of B'nai B'rith Youth Organization, and co-chair of the Hillel International board of governors.

"Serving others is one of the pillars upon which Judaism rests and the future of all humanity depends."

I first learned about philanthropy when I was very young. Some of my earliest and fondest memories of my father involve the time I spent with him, visiting and helping to care for people I remember calling the "little old ladies," women who, I shudder to think, were probably no older than I am today! My father never talked in terms of charity. He spoke only of improving lives and, in turn, making the world a better place for all of us. Time and again, he would say, "Each of us is worth only what we are willing to give to others."

My father was not a religious man, so he never placed his giving in any greater context. He helped others not because of any specific ideology but because it was the way he thought he should act. He was unfamiliar with the litany of prescriptions in Jewish texts concerning the proper way for Jews to help people in need, whether within or outside of their families.

Given this background, my initial approach to philanthropy was as uninformed by Jewish tradition as was the process I learned from my father. His values and traditions naturally became my own, and my early sense of giving mirrored his. I supported and worked for the same groups to which he exposed me, groups I knew were providing important services to those in need.

That all changed when my family traveled to Israel in 1977. What I saw and what I felt completely transformed me into the person I am today. From that moment forward, being Jewish became much more than just a means of self-identification. It engulfed every aspect of my life and inspired me to increase my involvement with Jewish groups and causes. My philanthropy quickly became an expression of my innermost convictions, a reflection of those values and traditions of greatest importance to me. Indeed, my Judaism is better defined through my philanthropy than through my congregational affiliation or community participation. My experiences in Israel also placed my father's philanthropic model within the distinctly Jewish context of *tikkun olam,* our biblical imperative to repair the broken aspects of the world, and provided me with a new perspective from which to practice my philanthropy.

As a member of an extended family, I embrace the common heritage and future I share with my fellow Jews around the world. I also recognize the special obligation I have toward them, a responsibility that in large part led to the establishment of our family foundation more than a decade ago.

My husband, Charles, and I knew it was incumbent upon us to share our good fortune with those "family members" in need of help. We began to seek out ways to help as many Jewish people as possible, especially Jewish children, in times of need. Jewish people and institutions became a primary focus of our philanthropic work, both in our commitment of financial resources and in the expenditure of our time.

Like Charles, I believe passionately that the renaissance of Jewish life around the world is within our grasp. Now that Charles is gone, I have redoubled my efforts to help revitalize Jewish communities in the United States, Israel, and the former Soviet Union in an effort to preserve his legacy and realize our shared vision. Our foundation has sharpened its mission to focus on helping the Jewish people flourish by supporting programs that spread the joy of Jewish living, giving, and learning. To ensure that Jewish life thrives, not merely survives, we are investing in young people and seeking to make the full spectrum of Jewish experience available to them in comfortable and familiar ways. We believe this approach is vital to assuring that our teens and young adults choose to embrace Judaism and to love Israel from among the increasingly wide range of lifestyle options available to them.

While some people say service to others is the rent we pay for space on this planet, I see service to others as the down payment we make to ensure a safe, secure home on earth for our children and our grandchildren. Either way, serving others is one of the pillars upon which Judaism rests and the future of all humanity depends.

> One day, a man walking on the road
> saw Honi the Circle Maker planting a carob tree.
> Puzzled, the man asked, "How long will it be before this
> tree will bear fruit?"
> Replied Honi, "Seventy years."
> The man then asked, "And do you believe you
> will be alive in another seventy years?"
> Honi answered, "When I came into this world,
> there were carob trees with fruit ripe for picking.
> Just as my parents planted for me,
> so I will plant for my children."
> —Babylonian Talmud, Ta'anit 23a

With this talmudic parable and my Jewish *neshama* (soul) guiding me, I continue to push forward on the philanthropic path I began walking with my father to make the world a little bit better for generations to follow. Our youth deserve, and our faith requires, nothing less from every member of *clal Yisrael* (the Jewish people).

RABBI JACQUELINE TABICK was ordained in 1975, the first female graduate of the Leo Baeck College in London. At present she is rabbi of North West Surrey Synagogue, vice president of the Reform Synagogues of Great Britain, chair of the World Congress of Faiths, patron of the Jewish Council for Racial Equality, and on the executive board of the InterFaith Council of the United Kingdom.

"It is only if we act, if we try to carry out what God wants of us, that the existence of God has meaning and reality."

The ultimate goal of Judaism is not to ensure we have Jewish grandchildren, though that would be nice! It is not even to give meaning to our lives, though that can be a more than acceptable byproduct. Judaism has a wider goal, to make the world into the sort of place we feel God had in mind when the divine creative act took place. Just thinking about God has little or no effect on our world. It is only if we act, if we try to carry out what God wants of us, that the existence of God has meaning and reality.

We are taught that the Torah is a tree of life, and it is, but only to those who take hold of it. The teachings contained in our tradition challenge us to carry out our responsibility to God by accepting our messianic obligations. Then we can be true partners with God in the work of creation and help bring about a world of justice, truth, and peace, and along the way find purpose, meaning, and joy in remaining Jewish.

DAVID COLBURN is an entrepreneur and independent investor. He and his wife are also philanthropists committed to helping disadvantaged children and advancing religious causes.

"I am here by the grace of Hashem, that I must honor Hashem, my fellow man, and myself through the way I live my life."

Being Jewish means that we get up every day pushing, seeking, toiling to be the best person we can possibly be. Actually, it is more than that, it is pushing, seeking, toiling to become a better person than we have any right to imagine we could become. Stretching the boundaries of our imagination, creativity, and willingness to sacrifice in order to find within us greater kindness, dedication, love, discipline, understanding, caring, strength, and intellect.

It is not by mistake that I as a Jew begin every day by reciting in my prayers, *"Modeh ani l'fanecha melakh chai v'kayahm ...,"* which literally means "Thankful am I, living and eternal Hashem...." Alternatively, we do not recite, *"Ani modeh ... "*—"I thank You ...," although that would be more correct, grammatically speaking. Through these first meditations from my lips each morning I acknowledge that I am not the center of the universe, that I do not come first—as I am just one very small piece of the puzzle—rather, what does come first is my thanks and recognition that life's course is not under my control, that I am here by the grace of Hashem, that I must honor Hashem, my fellow man, and myself through the way I live my life.

In this regard, we see life as an incredible, rugged, obstacle-ridden journey—of which the Torah and its teachings provide us the map to successfully navigate, to determine the right priorities, to understand our responsibilities to man and the world. We do not take the "road less traveled"; instead, we follow a road paved with four thousand years rich in history, tradition, and law. A road that imbues us with the notion that no person should be taken for granted, that each day is a gift and a responsibility, that each person is equal in the eyes of Hashem, that there are no guarantees.

We therefore have the responsibility to get up each day and ask the questions, "Why are things the way they are/why are we the way we are?" and then, "What are we going to do about it to make it better/how are we going to improve?"—as human beings, as individuals, as parents, as friends, as children, as members of a community, as citizens of the world, as Jews. Knowing that if we do not move forward we move backward, that if we are silent we are complicit, that if we turn our head away we are still responsible.

We do not accept things the way they are without imagining they could be better, should be better, must be better. We do not look at our good fortune without understanding the responsibility it puts on us to give to others, to give back, to provide leadership, to improve, to make sure others do not go without. Nor do we look at our good fortune and decide somehow that is the measure of a person, that it allows one to look down on others less fortunate, that it anoints our everyday lives, that it frees us from the struggle for goodness and righteousness. In the same way, we do not allow misfortune to break our belief, to be used as a crutch or excuse not to better ourselves or the world around us, to free us from the struggle.

The Midrash tells us of a famous Rabbi Zusya who, musing one day about his concerns in meeting his maker at the time of his death, said to one of his students, "I am not worried that Hashem will ask me whether I was as great a leader as Moshe—how could I be?—and I am not worried that Hashem will query as to whether I was as righteous as Abraham—who was?—but how do I respond when Hashem asks whether I was the best person *I* could have been?"

We are humbled by humanity, we are angered by hypocrisy, we are called to action by suffering, we are not accepting of injustice, we start our days at nightfall looking to the light and hope of a new day, we will never forget, we will always believe, we will never walk by, and we will always ask why, and then what we can do to be/make it better, and then we will do it!!!

 JUDY FELD CARR, C.M., MUS.M, MUS.BAC., L.L.D., L.H.D., of Toronto, Canada, is a former university lecturer who spent almost three decades secretly arranging the rescue of the bulk of the Syrian Jewish community, for which she was awarded the Order of Canada, honorary university doctorates in Canada and the United States, and the Humanitarian Award of Merit from the University of Haifa.

> "Indeed, the recognition that one is Jewish automatically implies—unspoken and unheralded—the sense that one has *obligations,* as opposed to the demands of others that they have *rights.*"

For those among us who may be deeply religious, it is likely to be a studied aim in life to find ways and means of expressing their Jewishness by consciously following well-known specific precepts, such as the requirement for every Jew to be the guarantor of, or be responsible for, every other Jew.

While I much prefer Abraham J. Heschel's statement: "We are God's stake in human history," I must admit that, in my case, the proclamation "I am Jewish" derived solely from an unconscious injunction.

In leading the clandestine rescue of more than three thousand Jewish souls from the veritable prison that was their homeland—Syria—it did not occur to me that I was following any edict.

Despite my late father's plaintive response, "What could we do?" to my immature ten-year-old's query about why he and his generation did nothing of consequence to save Europe's Jewry, my twenty-eight-year involvement of spiriting my coreligionists out of an oppressive dictatorship was not prompted by any expressed *mitzvah* (religious requirement) that echoed from my Jewishness.

I have learned that the motivation to help another Jew, no matter what the nature of his or her distress, has been absorbed unconsciously over the centuries by witnessing or learning about myriad acts of heroic proportions toward fellow Jews, rather than by learning quotations or voicing precepts.

"I am Jewish" lingers, unspoken, in the very depths of our beings and is not required to be uttered, except in response to a specific question, or, G-d forbid, when placed in extremis, as were the Rabbis of old and as was Daniel Pearl.

Indeed, the recognition that one is Jewish automatically implies—unspoken and unheralded—the sense that one has *obligations*, as opposed to the demands of others that they have *rights*.

I am secure in the knowledge that there will be succeeding generations able to say to themselves, or proudly to others, "I am Jewish," because I was privileged to lead their forbears to the free world from the bondage of Syria.

 **ROBIN KRAMER** has been a senior fellow at the California Community Foundation since 1998, anchoring the foundation's long-range planning and initiatives to nurture and connect civic leadership in the region. She is a co-chairperson of the Daniel Pearl Foundation.

"Jews are obligated to become inventors, makers of memory and meaning and future, not disconnected consumers of ancient history or trapped in unspeakable tragedy."

I am Jewish. This is at my very core, how I wrestle with questions divine and perhaps not; how I wonder at the mystery and connection of all things in the world, and how I journey in it. I am rooted in the Jewish people; in Jewish teachings about living, ethics, study, empathy, and kindness; about Israel as home. About the pursuit of justice. About humor.

I am part of the Jewish and the American story; I have a long memory. I was born and raised in Denver, Colorado, the daughter of a tent maker and a maker-of-families, and the descendent of observant, studious, quietly pugnacious gentle men and women most recently from Russia, Poland, and Hungary. From my first remembered Passover seder, I have been certain I was once a slave to Pharaoh and also delivered to freedom. I experienced the desert trek to Sinai as if inside one of those beautiful tents my dad made—an elegant cloth palace, a stop on the way to somewhere, a home for the moment, beckoning and secure. I also know my annoying relative was the one asking every hour of the forty-year wander, "So, are we there yet?"

I am Jewish. From my mother, an adoptions social worker, I inherited a zeal for being an activist part of the repair of the world, to help ensure freedom, access, and opportunity; to protect the frail, the small voice, and the different; to welcome the stranger. In my community-building endeavors in wonderfully diverse, eclectic, sublime/absurd Los Angeles, I am at once insider and outsider.

I am Jewish, a citizen of this planet. In every generation, Jews are obligated to become inventors, makers of memory and meaning and future, not disconnected consumers of ancient history or trapped in unspeakable tragedy. Sitting at the Pearl family's kitchen table during the searing months just following the kidnapping and murder of their Daniel, and now as the days go forward, I have been lifted up by their courage, their quips and small joys, and their steadfast, creative efforts to stamp out hate and build mutual understanding across race, religion, ethnicity, and nation. I am both humbled by the depths of their hurt and loss and by their work as menders of the breach.

I am Jewish. One of my three sons is also named Daniel. I am hopeful.

RICHARD N. GOLDMAN and his late wife, Rhoda, established the Richard and Rhoda Goldman Fund in 1951. The fund has granted more than $62 million to Israeli and domestic Jewish charitable organizations since 1990. Mr. Goldman is a board member of the Jerusalem Foundation, a trustee for the Washington Institute for Near East Policy, and a director and former president of the Jewish Community Federation of San Francisco.

"It doesn't matter who a person is or what one's position in this world is. What matters is what you do with it."

Although I did not have the good fortune to know Danny, I felt that he was one of my own family from the beginning of his horrible experience to the end. I was particularly proud when he stated, "I am Jewish," as it gave me the opportunity to reflect upon my own life.

I was born in San Francisco and expect to reside here for the rest of my days. I am now eighty-three years of age, enjoying good health, and spending the majority of my time in philanthropic endeavors. As a youth, I respected my Jewishness but was sensitive to anti-Semitism, which led me to speak with caution. At that time, I was not always comfortable being Jewish. Following the end of World War II and after marrying my wife, Rhoda, I became more confident, prideful, and outspoken about my religious conviction.

I often ask myself, "How is it that a sentence spoken by a young man whom I never met, in a faraway place called Pakistan, can become a source of inspiration to me, my children, and my eleven grandchildren? And why is it that this young man's example encourages Jews everywhere to be proud of their heritage and to feel safer in the world?" I believe the answer is that it doesn't matter who a person is or what one's position in this world is. What matters is what you do with it—that is, how you live your life.

A half century ago, my late wife and I founded the Richard and Rhoda Goldman Fund. While our philanthropic giving over the years has expanded to meet the needs of an increasingly complex world, our commitment to *tikkun olam*—repairing the world—has remained steadfast. Philanthropy is the art of giving. Giving to others to make the world a better place is what being Jewish means to me.

TULLIA ZEVI, a former journalist, served as vice president of the European Jewish Congress and the first woman president of the Italian Jewish Community.

"'The supreme virtue of tolerance.'"

I am a Jew belonging to the same generation that produced the murderers and the victims of the *Sho'ah*. I was spared the tragic destiny of the immense majority of European Jews by a provident father who, in 1939, brought the entire family to the safety of the United States.

By war's end, I deeply felt the urge, the need, and the duty to return to Europe, seeking to know and understand, but also to do my share in restoring the life of the shocked and shattered European Jewish communities.

I returned as a journalist and covered events ranging from the trials of the Nazi chieftains in Nuremberg to the Eichmann trial in Jerusalem.

I settled in my native Italy, where my family had sought refuge after the expulsion of the Jews from Spain in 1492. At the first postwar Congress of the Union of Italian Jewish Communities I was elected a member of its governing board, and years later I served as its president for four successive four-year terms.

Jewish communal life has been restored, well integrated into Italian society, though memory and vigilance remain imperative against old threats and new dangers.

Europe is undergoing deep changes: No longer a relatively "white and Christian" continent, it is now being turned into a multiracial, multicultural society by the arrival from the four corners of the earth of millions of human beings seeking better lives. It is substantially a positive phenomenon that, however, is bound to create problems and arouse anxieties and defensive mechanisms.

Although anti-Judaism and anti-Semitism cannot be considered uprooted, Jews are no longer perceived, as they were for centuries, as the scapegoats on which European societies discharged their problems, fears, and aggressiveness.

As Jews with a long history and tragic memories, we have the duty and the responsibility to remind our fellow Europeans of what concentration camp survivor and author Primo Levi called "the supreme virtue of tolerance."

 **PETER YARROW** is a member of the renowned folk singing trio Peter, Paul and Mary and a lifetime activist, mainly in the areas of human and civil rights, the peace movement, and now educational initiatives.

"Primarily, being Jewish means acting ethically Jewish (much more than being observant) and ... I am willy-nilly an OK Jew."

Not unlike many Americans my age, I was brought up by parents, in my case by my mother, Vera, who embraced her Jewish identity in cultural ways but was not at all observant. Vera came from a family of first-generation immigrants from Russia, for whom pride of having recently come to America was gratefully acknowledged by virtually eliminating all religious and previous national identity from their lifestyle. "We are Americans, now!" was their exuberant exclamation of loyalty to this glorious country of opportunity. Furthermore, my mother, being an idealist and born shortly after the turn of the century, embraced a not uncommon notion that religion was frequently the cause of war and, therefore, she eschewed religious observance.

It is no wonder she sent me to "Sunday school" at Ethical Culture, which gave me an ecumenical perspective but did not require me to abandon a sense of my cultural Jewishness; it encouraged a life that corresponded to universally held tenets of ethical behavior.

When I was fourteen my mother remarried, and because my step-father was all but horrified that I had not been Bar Mitzvahed, I was sent to Central Synagogue to be confirmed. In that context, I had my first meaningful exchanges with religious Judaism through Rabbi David Seligson, who was compassionate and enlightened, and who very much understood who I was. He took my questioning of religious practice very seriously. Actually, I remember, after having delivered my confirmation speech to him and the other members of the confirmation class, asking Rabbi if I would be considered a good Jew if I never entered a synagogue again, or celebrated any holidays, but lived an ethical life. He told me he had to think about that, and that he would give me an answer at next week's confirmation class. The next week he explained, with solemnity, that I would indeed be considered a good Jew if my actions in life were consummate with an ethical Jewish perspective.

And so it was that my life went on that path, until Peter, Paul and Mary, some twenty years ago, were slated to perform at Carnegie Hall in what was an emulation of The Weavers' Christmas concert, our "Holiday Celebration."

It so happened that that concert fell on the third night of Hanukah, and therefore Paul and Mary asked me to write a Hanukah song to add to our repertoire for that night. I didn't realize it then, but the dialogue about whether I should write that song, within myself and with my rabbinical friends and mentors, would help me articulate my own Jewishness.

Frankly, I had grave doubts about my authority to write a Hanukah song. I began to ask myself the following questions: Would it be presumptuous of me to write such a song? Would it be shirking a responsibility to identify myself as a Jew by not writing the song? Were my grave concerns about the terrible Shatilla-Sabra massacres that had just occurred such that they would color my writing of a song about a Jewish holiday that I understood was in a way about the prevention of an attempted quasi-genocide of Jews? Would I be viewed as simplistic in my understanding of Jewishness if I simply spoke from the heart? Did I need to study before I attempted to write such a song, or were my heart and personal inclination enough of a validation? Finally, I asked myself, was my mother's perspective a valid one, or was I going to define myself differently as a Jew?

I turned to my rabbi friends for advice.

The interesting turn of events made it clear from all the rabbis' perspectives, which included those of Rabbi Danny Syme, Rabbi Elliott Kleinman, and Rabbi Alex Schindler, that my particular internal self-questioning and dialogue was so convoluted and so typically Jewish and intense that, besides the fact that I should have no worries about writing such a song (nonaffiliated Jews are still Jews), this internal dialogue was about as Jewish as dialogues get. "Go for it!" they all advised.

The song itself turned out to be a kind of manifesto of my own Jewishness. It pays tribute to my mother and to the perspective of my own evolution as a Jew. I still believe that, primarily, being Jewish means acting ethically Jewish (much more than being observant) and that I am willy-nilly an OK Jew. But if the truth be known, with my mother's passing, being a part of a Seder or a High Holy Day service has become profoundly meaningful for me. Such observance has become a window to stop the wheels of life from turning at a frenzied speed and a time to contemplate the larger picture of my own life as a human being, as a citizen of the world, and as a Jew.

I cherish these moments now and would still be hard-pressed to define where I classify myself along the spectrum of Jewishness. But I guess my being invited to be a part of the writings for this book gives me one more reason to thank my gracious teachers, who have allowed me to understand the richness of my tradition and its history a little bit better and so bring a greater fullness to my life, as whatever kind of Jew I am, or might be in the future.

Light One Candle
Light one candle for the Maccabee children
With thanks that their light didn't die
Light one candle for the pain they endured
When their right to exist was denied
Light one candle for the terrible sacrifice
Justice and freedom demand
But light one candle for the wisdom to know
When the peacemaker's time is at hand

(chorus)
Don't let the light go out!
It's lasted for so many years!
Don't let the light go out!
Let it shine through our love and our tears.
Light one candle for the strength that we need
To never become our own foe
And light one candle for those who are suffering
Pain we learned so long ago
Light one candle for all we believe in
That anger not tear us apart
And light one candle to find us together
With peace as the song in our hearts
(chorus)
What is the memory that's valued so highly
That we keep it alive in that flame?
What's the commitment to those who have died
When we cry out, "They've not died in vain!"?
We have come this far always believing
That justice would somehow prevail
This is the burden, this is the promise
This is why we will not fail!
(chorus)
Don't let the light go out!
Don't let the light go out!
Don't let the light go out!
—© 1983 Peter Yarrow

 **FRANCINE KLAGSBRUN** is the author of more than a dozen books, most recently, *The Fourth Commandment: Remember the Sabbath Day.* She is a columnist for *The Jewish Week* and *Moment* magazine and lectures widely on social and religious issues.

"At the core of Jewish consciousness there exists a vision of becoming a holy nation and a light unto others."

To be Jewish is to be part of a people that gave the world monotheism and the Torah, and with those contributions changed the course of civilization.

Ah, you say, but that was long ago. What has ancient history to do with being Jewish today?

My answer is that from those ancient teachings stem spiritual and ethical ideals that still challenge us to live up to our fullest human potential. From the Hebrew Bible comes the concept that every human being is created in the image of God. On one level that means that each person, no matter how lowly, is worthy of respect and consideration. On another level, regarding humans as created in God's image means recognizing a spark of divinity within ourselves, and that means reaching for the best we can be, in relation to ourselves and others. Accordingly, Jewish texts, the heart blood of this tradition, provide moral lessons to govern every aspect of existence—from dealing honestly in business to avoiding gossip, from protecting the poor to protecting the environment.

Closely related, Judaism places great value on life itself. Although it holds out the dream of a messianic age in a world to come, it emphasizes the importance of the life we have in this world. Human life is so important, the Talmud teaches, that to destroy a single life is equivalent to destroying an entire universe. Life is so important that it is to be constantly sanctified and celebrated, in marriage and family living, in blessings over the food we eat, in year-round festivals and the weekly Sabbath (another Jewish contribution to the world). "Choose life," the Bible commands (Deut: 30:19), and Jews through the ages have responded by clinging to life individually and as a people even in the face of dire dangers and persecutions.

To be Jewish is to belong to this people that has held onto its life-affirming principles against all odds. But belonging to the Jewish people does not mean shutting out the rest of the world. Wherever Jews have lived, they have interacted with their societies, influencing them and being influenced by them. In the process they have created a culture whose language and literature, science and scholarship, humor and song is rich in beauty and diversity. Today that culture flourishes especially in Israel, the Jewish homeland, and radiates outward to places everywhere.

To be committed to being Jewish does not preclude railing against God for life's injustices (Jewish sages and scholars have done that for centuries) or reinterpreting sacred texts to ferret out meaning for each new generation (they have done that, too). It does not preclude acknowledging that as a people we have not always lived up to our highest ideals. Still, at the core of Jewish consciousness there exists a vision of becoming a holy nation and a light unto others. That vision is the essence of being Jewish.

I am Jewish, and I say those words with passion, pride, and awe at their profundity.

HANOCH GREENBERG, 23, Netanya, Israel

Know who you are, where you are going, and what is your heritage.

Be ready to pay the price sometimes.

Go against the stream.

Know that you are special but not more than everyone else but like them.

Know that due to the Jewish history you have more responsibility for other people than other nations have, knowing that first and foremost you need to be a good person and only then "good" Jewish.

SJALOM AWRAHAM SOETENDORP, born in 1943 in Amsterdam, the Netherlands, survived the Holocaust as a "hidden child." He is rabbi of the Liberal Jewish Community, The Hague, the Netherlands; president, European Region, World Union for Progressive Judaism; and co-chair, Global Forum of Spiritual and Parliamentary Leaders, with Sheikh Ahmed Kuftaro, grand mufti of Syria.

"A witness to the courage of compassion inherent in the human spirit."

The beginning of May 1943 the *grüne Polizei,* the special police force whose task it was to round up Jews, reached our home in the *Juden viertel,* the heart of the Jewish quarter in occupied Amsterdam. My parents had postponed the moment of departure for a hiding place. It had proved to be impossible to find a foster home where my parents could stay together with me, Sjalom Awraham, their firstborn, three months old, and my mother could not part with me. Now it was too late, the suitcases stood readily packed at the entrance. The head of the Gestapo located me, asleep in the cradle, and said: *"Schade daß er ein Jude ist"*: "A pity that this is a Jewish child." The response of my father was immediate. *"Glücklich daß er ein Jude ist"*: "Luckily he is a Jewish child, because whatever will happen to him, he will never grow up to become a son of murderers." The leader hit my father and shouted at the top of his voice: "Jewish swines, you are too dirty to touch, we will return tomorrow morning to take you away," and they left.

My father always said there were tears in the eyes of the Gestapo leader, and those tears of compassion saved our lives. That night we escaped. A few days later, a man of the Resistance knocked on a door in Velp, near Arnhem, carrying a suitcase with holes in it. A woman, Ria van der Kemp, German-born and forty-seven years old, opened the door. He asked her whether she would be prepared to take care of the Jewish baby in the suitcase. If she had replied that it was too dangerous, her teenage son was living with them and German soldiers had their quarters nearby, and closed the door, nobody could have blamed her. But because she kept the door wide open and cared and sustained me for more than two years despite everything, I am alive to be a *zekher*, a witness to the courage of compassion inherent in the human spirit. Yes, evil is contagious, but thank God and humans that goodness is also contagious.

My parents and I survived in different hiding places. My father, a progressive rabbi, became the builder of Jewish life in the remnant community in the Netherlands after the *Sho'ah*. He always taught us, two brothers and a sister who were born after the war, "One can take away everything you have, even your life, but one cannot take what you are. And thus strengthen, cherish, sanctify your identity!" I have been privileged to work as a rabbi for thirty-five years, rebuilding communities in the Hague, Rotterdam, and Utrecht; helping to restore Jewish life in Moscow, Kiev, and all over the continent; and engaging in interreligious activities. Only a few weeks ago I held such a meeting of hope with Palestinians near the Dead Sea in Jordan. Together with my wife, Sira, herself a child survivor, we have been able to build a family, our children and grandchildren, each one a miracle. I am increasingly involved in efforts everywhere to reach the United Nations Millennium Goals by the year 2015: that all children will have primary education; that the one billion people who have no access to fresh water, to proper sanitation facilities, will have access; that the AIDS epidemic will be reversed. My realistic dream is that the one billion people between the United States and Japan who live in relative wealth will decide to contribute 0.1 percent, one-thousandth of their income, in the coming years as extra voluntary taxation toward these goals. For this purpose, I established the foundation Jewish Institute for Human Values. My driving force is the permanent awareness of the open door. Millions upon millions of children look to us in hopeful desperation. Do we keep the door open?

Ani Ma'amin. I believe with a perfect faith that we will, that our children and our children's children will, and the *mashi'ach* will walk through the open door. And yes, there will be *t'chiyat hametim*, the living of the dead, when all those whose tree of life has been cruelly cut before its time will be comforted and gladdened with the living by the messianic time of peace and justice. *Ani Ma'amin.*

ALAN COLMES is co-host of America's number-one debate show, *Hannity and Colmes*, seen nightly on the Fox News Channel, and host of the nightly nationally-syndicated radio show *Fox News Live with Alan Colmes*. He is the author of *Red, White and Liberal: How Left is Right and Right is Wrong*.

"It encompasses the basic dignity and humanity with which we regard all God's creatures."

What beautiful and poetic last words they were that Daniel Pearl offered the world. For me, being Jewish isn't just about a religion, a set of rituals that we observe to honor our traditions. Being Jewish is just that: a way of being; it encompasses the basic dignity and humanity with which we regard all God's creatures. "Jewish" can mean so much while, at the same time, be so specific, for it bespeaks kindness, decency, and justice on scales ranging from the global to the personal and the intimate. It's no accident that the word "shalom" means "hello," "good-bye," and "peace." Thank you, Daniel, for saying so much in your final words. *Shalom*.

RUTH W. MESSINGER is president of the American Jewish World Service, an organization that works to alleviate poverty, hunger, and disease in the developing world by providing financial support, technical assistance, emergency relief, and skilled volunteers to grassroots nongovernmental organizations. Prior to assuming this position in 1998, she was in public service for twenty years in New York City, including having served as Manhattan borough president.

"Service is my way of encountering God in the world, since God can only be found in our response to the needs of others."

Daniel, I believe that the pursuit of justice is a goal that we both shared passionately. And I know this pursuit is based on our strong

Jewish foundation. As taught to our people for centuries: "Justice, justice you shall pursue" (Deut. 16:20).

Your pursuit led you to truth-seeking, to journalism, and ultimately to the perils of Pakistan. My pursuit has taken me from local politics to communities around the world: from El Salvador to Afghanistan, Uganda to Ukraine. Where you sought justice with the pen, I seek justice through service.

As a Jew, I feel a deep responsibility to assist those in the world who are the most beleaguered—the millions living in abject poverty who are determined to carve out respectful lives for themselves and their families.

Holding a deep attachment to the land and people of Israel, I feel compelled to go beyond the focus on Israel and Jews in need to help *all* people in need fulfill their visions, particularly those who are among the poorest of the poor in the developing nations of the world.

As a Jew, I am working with grassroots groups in Africa, Asia, Latin America, the Middle East, Russia, and Ukraine, feeding the hungry, caring for the stranger, and defeating the oppressions that plague so many. And I envision a day when service by Jews, in a Jewish context, will become a rite of passage in and for the Jewish community. It will be done by people of all ages, from teens to seniors, and involve work with Jews and non-Jews.

The Torah reminds us at least thirty-six times to "remember the stranger," as we were strangers in a strange land. Jewish service in these non-Jewish, strange lands will take us outside ourselves to work for social justice in a place or with people who are in some ways different from us. We will do this in a Jewish context, fulfilling the highest form of *tzedakah* by helping people help themselves; in the process, the work will transform our community and our world.

Through service, Jews will become effective agents in the world, working against growing alienation and creating global community. We will make a contribution in a world in which there is an increasing need for experiences that promote cross-cultural understanding. We will foster critical thinking, concern for others, and political and social diplomacy. We will make a dramatic difference in attracting Jews to more active Judaism, changing the ways in which Jews are seen around the world and changing the ways in which Jews understand their global obligations.

Service is my way of encountering God in the world, since God can only be found in our response to the needs of others. Through this response we can hope to fulfill the *mitzvah* of *tikkun olam* (repairing the world). As our tradition teaches in *Pirkei Avot,* "It is not for us to complete the work, but neither are we free to desist from it."

ROSALIE SILBERMAN ABELLA is a justice on the Ontario Court of Appeal in Canada.

"An intense loyalty to humanity and a passionate commitment to its civilized expansion."

For me, being Jewish means keeping the vision of justice alive in tribute to the memory of those who were denied it.

About a year ago, I found something written by a young Jewish lawyer, a graduate of the Jagellonian University in Krakow, who, along with his wife, survived several years in concentration camps. Their two-and-a-half-year-old son was killed in Treblinka. The man was head of the displaced persons camp in Stuttgart after the war, and this is the introduction he wrote for Eleanor Roosevelt when she visited the camp in 1948:

> We welcome you, Mrs. Roosevelt, as the representative of a Great Nation, whose victorious army liberated the remnants of European Jewry from death. We shall never forget that aid rendered by both the American people and army. We are not in a position of showing you many assets. The best we are able to produce are these few children. They alone are our fortune and our sole hope for the future.

That man was my father, and I was one of those few children. I know, now that I am a parent, what an act of faith in humanity and justice it was for people like my parents to decide to have children after the dehumanizing injustice they had endured.

We are the generation that saw and survived the Holocaust. We must therefore be the generation that rails most vigilantly against the intolerance that produced it. There may be risks in insisting on this expanded vision, but they are nothing compared to the risks in ignoring inhumanity. The banality of evil must never blur our capacity to see it. And having seen it, to identify it, fight it, and extinguish it. What can we leave our children if not an intense loyalty to humanity and a passionate commitment to its civilized expansion?

Indifference is injustice's incubator. It is not just what you stand for, it is what you stand up for.

SENATOR DIANNE FEINSTEIN has served the people of California in the United States Senate since 1992. She was the first woman on the San Francisco Board of Supervisors, the first woman mayor of San Francisco, the first woman elected senator of California, and the first woman member of the Senate Judiciary Committee.

"It takes all of us who cherish beauty and humankind to be mindful and respectful of one another."

I was born during the Holocaust. If I had lived in Russia or Poland—the birthplaces of my grandparents—I probably would not be alive today, and I certainly wouldn't have had the opportunities afforded to me here. When I think of the six million people who were murdered, and the horrors that can take hold of a society, it reinforces my commitment to social justice and progress, principles that have always been central to Jewish history and tradition.

For those of us who hold elected office, governing in this complex country can often be very difficult. My experience is that bigotry and prejudice in diverse societies ultimately lead to some form of violence, and we must be constantly vigilant against this. Our Jewish culture is one that values tolerance with an enduring spirit of democracy. If I've learned anything from the past and from my heritage, it's that it takes all of us who cherish beauty and humankind to be mindful and respectful of one another. Every day we're called upon to put aside our animosities, to search together for common ground, and to settle differences before they fester and become problems.

Despite terrible events, so deeply etched in their souls, Jews continue to be taught to do their part in repairing the world. That is why I have dedicated my life to the pursuit of justice; sought equality for the underdog; and fought for the rights of every person regardless of their race, creed, color, sex, or sexual orientation, to live a safe, good life. For me, that's what it means to be a Jew, and every day I rededicate myself to that ideal.

BERNARD KOUCHNER is a medical doctor, former minister of health (1987–2002) in France, and founder of Médecins sans Frontières (Doctors without Borders), which received a Nobel Peace Prize.

"What do the Jews do? They keep watch. They are the sentinels against intolerance."

"I am a Jew." Such few syllables: It is hard to think of any other sentence that could sum up an entire life in a simpler and more intense manner.

One does not decide by himself to be a Jew or not to be one by using various stratagems, starting of course with integration. The others decide for you by designating you as such. You cannot escape. One day, it falls upon you. "A Jew is a man whom the others believe to be a Jew," Sartre wrote.

I am Jewish because my father was. My mother, being a Protestant, meant I could have escaped. What happened was the opposite. I am half a Jew: a way to feel twice a Jew when anger and history compel you to. I am a Jew when I choose.

What do the Jews do? They keep watch. They are the sentinels against intolerance.

We were a small group of men who did not want to remain idle facing other people's tragedies. We combined our efforts in many places of the world, caring for people of all origins who suffered from the same evils and cried with the same voice. We were medical doctors: a profession useful beyond borders, doted with a universal ethical code. Whenever the sick, the wounded, the starving would call for help, we would get there, especially when it was forbidden or dangerous. Make no mistake: such charitable activities were intensely political. To try and prevent massacres and genocides, to protect the weak, is it not the very goal, and the grandeur, of politics? As the protection of human rights is no longer the monopoly of governments, it is up to public opinion, to intellectuals, to society as a whole to force them to act.

For the past forty years, I have practiced and looked for this kind of humanitarian brotherhood, I have tried to define, theorize, and promote the right of humanitarian intervention. It has been a way to fight the obvious: every man is a battle, an unfinished killer, eager to do evil without always being able to. Any ordinary man can become a unique machinery of extermination. One kills to live, to have a taste of immortality. One kills out of boredom, and testosterone feeds religious fanaticism. When one is only a smallish man, he wants to try and slap Kafka's face.

The right to intervene in Kosovo and East Timor, positive though unfinished experiences, failed ones like Afghanistan and Iraq: such endeavors prove that the international community considers each man as its particular responsibility. The children of Chechnya or Liberia are also our children.

Who are the Jews? They are sentinels. They watch, and they care about their business, which is the world. They look for the signs of forthcoming massacres. What do the Jews do? They walk the killing fields. They measure the barometer of human cruelties. The moment Jews are attacked, women, democrats, people of moderate views and faith are bound to follow.

The blow the United Nations suffered in Baghdad in August 2003 is similar to 9/11, the end to a sort of fake innocence and neutrality. Jews are murdered first, then Americans, then all those who, with or without their knowing, have become the enemies of intolerance and religious fanaticism.

"I am a Jew," Daniel Pearl said. Alongside him, holding his hand, we all are Jews.

ZEV YAROSLAVSKY is a member of the Los Angeles County Board of Supervisors and a former member of the Los Angeles City Council. Prior to his entry into politics in 1975, he was a well-known advocate for human rights and freedom of emigration for Jews in the former U.S.S.R.

"We are a people of laws, not whim. We are a people of ethical principle, not convenience."

I am a Jew! At its core, being a Jew means seeing myself as though I were a slave in Egypt; as though I were a student of Maimonides; as though I lived in Chmelnitzky's seventeenth-century Ukraine; as though I resided in my ancestors' Lithuanian *shtetl* (a small eastern European Jewish village), with all of the hardship and scholarship that permeated the place; as though I were confronted with the moral meltdown of World War II; and as though I were a participant in the rebirth of the Jewish state. These and other seminal events in Jewish history inform who I am and the kind of decisions I make in my personal and professional public service life.

We are a people of laws, not whim. We are a people of ethical principle, not convenience. As a Jew, I am committed to justice—to doing the right thing, even, or especially, when doing so puts me at risk. Being a Jew means identifying and soldiering with those who are marginalized and persecuted. It means, in the words of Moses in Deuteronomy, being "strong and of good courage."

SIMONE VEIL was born in Nice in 1927 and deported to Auschwitz-Birkenau in 1944. After the war she studied law, served as France's Minister of Health, and in 1979 became the first woman elected president of the European Parliament.

"The preservation of the respect and the tolerance owed to other communities, because that also is the fundamental message of Judaism that my parents transmitted to me."

Born and raised in a family that has been French for many generations, I was French, without having to ask myself questions. But to be Jewish, what did that mean for me, and for my parents, at that time agnostic, as were my grandparents, religion being completely absent from our family home?

From my father, I have especially retained that his belonging to Judaism was tied to the wisdom and the culture that the Jews have acquired over the centuries, in times when too few had access to such things. They had remained the People of the Book, despite the persecutions, the misery, and the wanderings.

For my mother, it was more about the attachment to the values for which, throughout their long and tragic history, the Jews had never stopped struggling: tolerance, respect for the rights of each person and of all identities, solidarity.

Both of them died during deportation, leaving to me as their sole inheritance the humanistic values that for them Judaism represented. From this inheritance, it is not possible for me to separate the memory that is always present, even obsessive, of the six million Jews exterminated merely for being Jewish, six million including my parents, my brother, and many close friends. I cannot separate myself from them, and that will be sufficient so that until my death, my Judaism cannot be taken away. *Kaddish* will be said on my grave.

As a deportee to Auschwitz myself, I never heard any of my comrades question either their attachment to Judaism or, when all else failed, their faith. To the contrary, in our complete destitution, in spite of our suffering and humiliation, certain ones among us still had the strength to fast for Yom Kippur and to express the hope to go live in Palestine, if, by miracle, they left the camp alive.

The State of Israel did not yet exist, but it didn't matter. There was nowhere else on this earth that they could imagine establishing a home and finding happiness.

Since the birth of the State of Israel, this light remains, despite the anguish felt for its survival and its security, for the preservation of the respect and the tolerance owed to other communities, because that also is the fundamental message of Judaism that my parents transmitted to me.

DANIEL KAHNEMAN is the Eugene Higgins Professor of Psychology at Princeton University and professor of psychology and public affairs at Princeton's Woodrow Wilson School of Public and International Affairs. In 2002 he was awarded the Nobel Prize in Economic Sciences.

"The complexity of evil and the fallibility of the good have been with me all my life and are perhaps the first things I think about when I think of being a Jew."

I trace my vocation as a psychologist to my experience as a Jewish child in France, before and during World War II. Like many other Jews, I suppose, I grew up in a world that consisted exclusively of people and words, and most of the words were about people. Nature barely existed, and I never learned to identify flowers or to appreciate animals. But gossip was fascinating—the people my mother liked to talk about with her friends and with my father were fascinating in their complexity. Some people were better than others, but the best were far from perfect, and no one was simply bad. Most of her stories were touched by irony, and they all had two sides or more.

There was a rich range of shades to one experience I remember vividly. It must have been late 1941 or early 1942. Jews were required to wear the Star of David and to obey a 6 p.m. curfew. I had gone to play with a Christian friend and had stayed too late. I turned my brown sweater inside out to walk the few blocks home. As I was walking down an empty street, I saw a German soldier approaching. He was wearing the black uniform that I had been told to fear more than others, the one worn by specially recruited SS soldiers. As I came closer to him, trying to walk fast, I noticed that he was looking at me intently. Then he beckoned me over, picked me up, and hugged me. I was terrified that he would notice the star inside my sweater. He was speaking to me with great emotion, in German. When he put me down, he opened his wallet, showed me a picture of a boy, and gave me some money. I went home more certain than ever that my mother was right: People were endlessly complicated and interesting. It seemed that even the SS soldier had more than one side to him.

I also remember struggling as a child with the troubling thought that the monstrous Hitler enjoyed flowers and was tender to babies. If there was some good even in Hitler, then evil could not be described simply as the thing that evil people do; evil people were a puzzle to be understood. Understanding did not imply forgiving: It was all right to hate, and a duty to resist. But the complexity of evil and the fallibility of the good have been with me all my life and are perhaps the first things I think about when I think of being a Jew.

 RABBI NAAMAH KELMAN is a descendent of ten generations of rabbis. Born and raised in New York City, she has lived in Jerusalem since 1976. She was ordained by the Hebrew Union College in Jerusalem, becoming, in 1992, the first woman rabbi to be ordained in Israel, where she is the director of Educational Initiatives and acting dean of Hebrew Union College—Jewish Institute of Religion.

"Not to take oneself too seriously, but to take one's responsibilities very seriously."

Being Jewish has taught me how to laugh! First and foremost to laugh at myself and at my situation. More important, to laugh in order to act in the world. This is not to say we are to make fun of someone or make light of our fate. Rather, one is not to take oneself too seriously, but to take one's responsibilities very seriously. The first Jewish child born was called "Yitzchak" (he will laugh). Biblical names are heavy with meaning. Yitzchak was born to elderly parents, after years of barrenness. Sarah, our first foremother, had clearly lost all hope. Yet when she is told of her impending birth, she laughs out loud, out of total disbelief and relief. This first child might have been called many names. Names burdened with the weight of history, national and human. Instead, we are reminded to laugh. Laughter gives us perspective on life, but mostly it opens the door to hope and healing. It opens up new possibilities. Listen to what's funny to children and it will reveal a new world and a new generation. As Jews, we find comfort in our children as much as we receive guidance from our past. Why do we sit down every year at the Passover Seder? To teach our children. To teach in a way they can learn, and to teach in ways that we adults can keep learning. Laughter—we pack it in our luggage, we season our Friday night soup with it. Often it is mixed with tears. This is one of our most powerful weapons of survival.

We have fought despair relentlessly. Laughter is one of our secret weapons. According to the tradition of the Rabbis of the talmudic era, when the messiah comes, all Jewish holidays will be canceled except two: Yom Kippur and Purim. Yom Kippur is the Day of Atonement, the day of fasting, prayer, and reflection. Purim, of course, is the day we celebrate our deliverance from evil and destruction: a day when we wear costumes, allow ourselves to become totally intoxicated, and make fun of ourselves. There is a deep lesson here; it's almost funny. Even in a messianic era, let us have a yearly reminder of humility and forgiveness and the recognition that our fate can be precarious. Even in messianic times, keep a sense of humor.

I am a Jew because I have learned to ask tough questions. We are a tradition that does not take "No" for an answer. We ask tough questions in the face of hard realities. These questions spur us to take action. Two Israelite midwives came before Pharaoh to protest the fate of the Israelite slaves. The symbolism should not be lost on us. The servants of new life have the passion and power to speak to power. We are a tradition that revisits reality again and again, each time with a compass that points us in the direction of justice and righteousness. The first passages of Genesis paint a remarkable world created for us. God creates a world of equality and harmony; a world without race, nation, or hierarchy. Toward this ideal world we must move, and it is our responsibility as Jews that we gather the forces to build that world.

As a young woman some twenty-five years ago, I was fortunate to ask questions and fight for the answers. I was part of a generation that began to question the status of women in our tradition. We asked, and then demanded, that we be granted equality as full partners in living and creating Jewish life. My two grandmothers, one a fifth-generation American and a graduate of law school in 1907, the other an immigrant to Canada from eastern Europe, both led remarkable lives as rabbi's wives and Jewish mothers. Different as they were, they shared the fate of women. They could function and impact the community, provided they remained wives and mothers.

By 1972, when the first woman, Sally Preisand, was ordained by the Hebrew Union College–Jewish Institute of Religion, Jewish life would never be the same. In 1992, I became the first woman to be ordained a rabbi in Israel. Since 1973, hundreds of women have joined the ranks of rabbis and cantors. We have revived, renewed, and recaptured our roles as leaders among the Jewish people. We have altered the way Jews pray, we have reformulated rituals, we have embraced new traditions. Women are now an unstoppable force in Jewish life, bringing new energies and creativity after being sidelined for hundreds of years.

I am a Jew, because as Jews we are commanded to choose life. "Behold, God has given you good and evil," it is written in Deuteronomy 30, "choose life! I have set before you the blessing and the curse; choose life!!" The Jewish tradition wants us to take part in every aspect of human living: food, drink, sex, self-realization. But be moderate, and sanctify human action in the world. Enjoy food, but limit what you eat in order to recognize that we share this planet with other species. Use drink to celebrate the passages of our days as we mark the transition from the daily to holiness. As we turn to Shabbat, holidays, as we sanctify the marriage of human beings, wine is a symbol of joy, not an escape from reality. Sexual activity is natural, too, just keep it in the context of a loving monogamous relationship, between consenting partners.

And self-realization ... the power to create, achieve, shake up the world. Go for it, says our tradition ... but keep your impulses in check. Never be smug and never exploit others. One of the most remarkable rabbinic discussions I have come across regards a question concerning prayer. These discussions can be technical and even tedious, but more often than not our Rabbis throw out some amazing questions, for themselves and for us. They ask in the Tractate Berakhot 7a, "How do we know that God prays?" Now, this very question suggests audacity. Aren't we supposed to pray to God and not the other way around? What does the all-knowing, all-powerful God pray for and to whom? The Rabbis are saying as much about themselves as they are telling us about their concept of God. They are unequivocally stating that God prays, so naturally, they then ask, what is the content of God's prayer? According to the Rabbis, God prays that God will be merciful and compassionate to humankind. What a remarkable idea. Even God needs to "look inside" and find the power to be kind and loving. And if we are made in God's image, it behooves us to act with loving-kindness in God's world.

Being a Jew means belonging to a people so rich and varied. We share a history that spans time and space. We are European, Middle Eastern, Asian, African. Our story spans from the prophets of ancient Israel through poets, philosophers, dreamers, entrepreneurs, scientists of today. We have invented ourselves in culture after culture, while clinging to a center called Jerusalem. Despite vast differences, we share a passion for knowledge, learning, and pursuit of holiness. We can be stubborn; we can be difficult. We have demanded a deep commitment to "mending the world" *(tikkun olam)*. Now we have come back to our Jewish homeland. In Israel, we have revived the Hebrew language, we have created new Jewish cities (Tel Aviv) and returned to old ones (Jerusalem). We can walk in the footsteps of Jeremiah. Not only has the desert bloomed, but out of teeming refugees and wanderers we have created a vibrant Jewish-Hebrew culture. We live the Jewish holidays rooted in the land and landscape. Our wandering can end. Yet we have discovered that it is not so simple. Jerusalem is holy to the three monotheistic faiths. Two peoples claim the Land of

Israel. We face perhaps the greatest challenge to the core issues of our faith as we strive to resolve the conflict in this region. We have done much to retain our humanity; we have also abused our power. Yet with our ability to ask tough questions, to choose life, and to right wrongs, I firmly believe that we will find a way to resolve our differences and end the bloodshed. I am a Jew because with our return to our homeland we have faced renewal and incredible hardships. *Hatikvah* (hope) is our national anthem, and when all inhabitants of this area can live in hope, side by side ... then we can truly laugh.

I am a Jew because we pray everyday that creation is renewed. We can always start again, there is always a second chance. It is in our hands. Daniel Pearl did not have a second chance. But in our great tradition, he left us with a second chance and a last will. I believe that he wanted the world to know he was a Jew because his instincts to probe, to challenge, to reach out, to love, and to laugh came from the depths of his Jewish soul. He was brutally murdered simply because he was a Jew. But until that horrendous moment, he lived and acted in the world to bring a brighter future for all humankind. Daniel Pearl summoned us to do no less. This is a profound Jewish teaching.

ROGER CUKIERMAN is the present chairman of the CRIF (The Council of French Jewish Institutions), the roof organization of all French Jewish organizations. He spent his professional life with the Edmond de Rothschild banking group of which he was chairman of the board.

"A powerful code of moral values."

The Jews have brought to the world a powerful code of moral values. One of the most important of these values is self-respect, and another, implied by the first, is respect for every human being. These moral values, which are the building blocks of all civilized societies, are currently under attack by barbarism and fanaticism.

For me, being Jewish is a commitment to defend these values.

Daniel Pearl is for all Jews the symbol of courage. Why? Because he carried our values in the face of adversity with dignity and pride. He embodied respect for all people; he was proud of being principled, proud of being Jewish, proud of his parents, proud of his ancestors, and proud of Israel. By being proud of us he gave our children a weapon with which to defend civilization.

EDGAR M. BRONFMAN is president of the World Jewish Congress and The Samuel Bronfman Foundation and is chairman of Hillel: The Foundation for Jewish Campus Life. He is the former chairman and CEO of The Seagram Company, Ltd.

"By asserting my Jewishness I am keeping faith with my ancestors, and thus I am being true to myself."

"I am Jewish." Those were the last words said by Daniel Pearl before he was murdered. That was a brave and very meaningful statement, full of pride, and somewhat similar to the words of the martyrs who died in the Holocaust saying the *Sh'ma*. What those words mean is different, I suppose, to every man and woman who says them. I have been asked to write about what those words mean to me.

My being Jewish, like all other Jews, is an accident of birth. My parents, grandparents, and all my progenitors were Jewish. What makes me a bit different from many, though by no means the majority, is that I am glad I am a Jew. Why? First of all, because by asserting my Jewishness I am keeping faith with my ancestors, and thus I am being true to myself. The religion called Judaism I find quite fascinating. Although I have some quarrels with the strict interpretations of the Orthodox and even more so with the Ultra-Orthodox, I am very happy with the essentials of my religion. I like the fact that we each are directly responsible and responsive to the Almighty. The rabbi is there to teach, not to forgive our sins. Only G-d can do that, hence we ourselves are responsible for our actions. I love the ethics with which a Jew is supposed to live. When Harry Truman was advised that the government needed a set of ethics, he replied that we have the Ten Commandments, and we don't need anything else. I am proud of the fact that Jews gave the Ten Commandments to the world, and that our forefathers thought of how men and women should treat each other fairly long before others did. I'm proud of the Talmud, that body of biblical interpretation which contains our ethics, and so much more. I do the "mirror test" every day. Let me explain. I look in the mirror to see whether I like the person I'm looking at, and if not, why not? And if I've hurt someone or done something I now wish I had not done, can I make it right? On the bottom of my mirror is a reminder to say the *Sh'ma*.

I love the commandment dealing with the repair of the world, *tikkun olam,* based on the concept that man is G-d's partner in creation and we must not only take care of the world but also improve it. That encouraged me to look more carefully around me, to appreciate nature, the varied seasons, the beauties of spring and fall in the northeastern United States, the pristine glamor of white snow covering the mountains and flatlands of the American West, the beauty of sand and sea at the shore in summer and the awesome power of water made so evident by the gorge of the Grand Canyon. I have thrilled to the animal life in the wilds of Kenya, Botswana, and Zimbabwe and studied the bird life and the animals in South Africa.

I also get very annoyed at those who don't respect our environment, the gas-guzzling SUVs, the litter we encounter on roadways and country lanes, the senselessness of it all. I look at slums here and shanties in Venezuela and Brazil and think of our obligation to make the earth more beautiful and to give mankind its due dignity. That makes me think of our duty to be charitable and the beauty of Maimonides' admonition that the greater charity is to make a man self-sufficient, and the greatest charity is that the recipient not know who was his benefactor. I try to live by the commandment to love the stranger as thyself, and I find it challenging, but what a way to fight bias!

I like reading about the time when we were all just Jews, not labeled Orthodox, or Conservative, or Reform. I hope there will come a time when we can go back to that, and then Jews will worship where they wish, where they get the spirituality they desire—or not worship at all, but still revel in the traditions of our people and do the *mitzvot* Judaism requires of them.

I write these words in memory of Daniel Pearl. I don't know what being Jewish meant to him—I was never fortunate enough to meet him. I do know by his last words that he was a proud Jew. What a role model for our young people!

 **DEBBIE FRIEDMAN,** singer, songwriter, and guitarist, has recorded nineteen albums and performed in hundreds of cities in the United States, Canada, Europe, and Israel, including New York City's Carnegie Hall. Her music is so fully integrated into synagogue liturgy that it's already considered "traditional" in many congregations.

"In every interaction—be it a concert, or when I function as a *sh'licha tzibur,* or at a healing service—in any of my relationships, no matter what I do, I am a Jew."

Dear Daniel,

This is the first time I have had to think about the "why" of the words "I am a Jew." I have never defined myself or my work before.

I was born into a Jewish family, exposed to Jewish experiences and Jewish people.

The concept "I am a Jew" never crossed my mind until I was asked to reflect on your words.

I actually chose to be who I am. I felt that my life was incomplete. I was looking for connection. I was always drawn to the Jewish people and our history and particularly to the values that were so easily translated and incorporated into life. It chose me back when at a point I began to interpret those values. Through songs and prayers I was able to reconstruct the same ideas and share them with others.

In your last moments, when you uttered the words "I am a Jew," you gave some people their first experience of acknowledging their

Jewish selves. Those who never identified before were awakened by your strength and conviction.

In every interaction—be it a concert, or when I function as a *sh'licha tzibur,* or at a healing service—in any of my relationships, no matter what I do, I am a Jew. I feel the presence of the Divine and a link to the past. I know there are many who have come before me who have made their mark. They, like you, have left pieces of themselves so that we, the living, might incorporate them into our lives in order to reconstruct the places in our world that have been shattered.

I am a Jew because I know that it is not meant for me to do this work alone. I am engaged both with the Holy One and with all of those with whom I am involved.

I am a Jew because I know the world that you and I and many others like us envision is a world yet to be created by us.

I am a Jew because in spite of all the hatred and violence in this world, I believe we must hope and live together as if the world were sheltered beneath the wings of the *Shekhinah.* We must live as if we were enveloped in a world of love and compassion. I am a Jew because together we must pray for the day when all people will sit beneath the vine and fig tree—when none shall be afraid and when all the words that come forth shall be words that speak of the family of humanity.

The world you had envisioned is a world that we will continue to build through song and prayer, through action and acts of loving-kindness.

Often we dreamers are laughed at for our lofty thoughts. In truth it is love and peace that are two values that cannot be touched or defiled by anyone. They are held in one's heart and soul in the most sacred parts of us, and they soar to the highest heights in the heavens.

I had to write you because, though we never met, we were engaged in a shared dream of a world in which all human beings would be seen as precious—to be celebrated and loved.

This piece was not to have been a tribute to you, but it would have been hard to write about "I am a Jew" without making reference to you, since you were and will always be the one who made me think about why I am a Jew.

Your memory is a blessing.

ACKNOWLEDGMENTS

A project of this kind and magnitude can only be done with the help of many people who understand and are committed to the inspiring potential of the idea, and who help make it a reality.

First we wish to thank Alana Frey, the teenager whose Bat Mitzvah project was the inspiration for this book, and Daniel Eisenkraft, who further developed this idea in his Bar Mitzvah project.

Many people around the world generously shared their ideas about who we might invite to participate in this book, and many others gave their time—and address books—to help us reach contributors. In particular, we would like to thank Dan Adler, Andrew Gilbert, Arthur Goldwag, David and Daniel Papermaster, Ina and Zeev Fabian, Barry Greenberg and Lori Rhees, Peter Almiga, Leon Adler, Shira Harzog, Kenneth Cukier, Jon Rosenbloom, Jon Blair, Jeffrey Dvorkin, Jessica and Latif Jiji, Amir Pnueli, Rachel Levine, Yuval Rotem, Allegra Goodman, Ali Berson, Uriella Obst, Debra Gonsher Vinik, Eric Linder and the staff at UAHC Camp Coleman, the staff at UAHC Camp Swig, Susanna Zevi, Matthew Miller, Chris Custance and her team at deep books, the distributor of Jewish Lights books in England, and Rabbis Lee Bycel, Sheldon Zimmerman, Kerry Olitzky, Glynis Conyer, Paul Steinberg, Elyse Goldstein, Michael Cohen, David Woznica, and David Gelfand.

To Bernard-Henri Lévy, Cynthia Ozick, Martin Peretz, Dr. Richard A. Lerner, David Horovitz, Deborah E. Lipstadt, Rabbi Tony Bayfield, Daniel Jonah Goldhagen, Dennis Prager, Rabbi Uri Regev, and Richard Siegel for not only participating with their essays, but also getting us in touch with other contributors.

To Malcolm Hoenlein, Paul Auster, Jonathan Safran Foer, Dr. Heskel M. Haddad, Heather Munroe-Blum, Ed Koch, and Judy Blume for the time and thought they gave to our undertaking.

To our daughters Tamara and Michelle for their guidance, encouragement, advice, and ideas.

Thanks to the hundreds of secretaries, assistants, agents, managers, and other "gatekeepers" without whose help we couldn't have gotten this done.

Last and not least, we would like to express our special gratitude to Stuart M. Matlins, the publisher of Jewish Lights, for taking a personal interest in this project and steering it from its very inception through high seas and fairly rough waters to its final port of artistry, and to assistant editor Lauren Seidman for her devotion to this project and for putting it all together.

GLOSSARY

Am Yisrael—People of Israel.

Ani Ma'amin—I believe.

clal Yisrael—The Jewish People.

Eretz Yisrael—The Land of Israel.

Gemara—Second part of the Talmud; commentary on the Jewish oral law.

goy (goyim)—Non-Jew(s).

Halakhah—Jewish law.

hamantashen—Traditional Purim pastry.

Hatikvah—"Hope"; the Israeli national anthem.

Havdalah—The concluding ceremony of Shabbat.

hesed—Loving-kindness.

Kaddish—Public declaration of praise for God said in memory of people who have died.

kashrut—Jewish dietary laws.

ketubah—Traditional marriage contract.

kibbutznik—Member of a kibbutz.

Kiddush—Special blessing recited on Shabbat and major festivals, usually before a meal.

Kol Nidre—Evening prayer on beginning of Yom Kippur.

madrichim—Counselors.

mezuzah—Encased strip of parchment inscribed with two passages from the Torah and hung on the right doorpost of a house or room.

midrash—The commentary developed in classical Judaism to interpret the Bible differently from it's literal meaning, or the method of interpreting the Bible this way.

minyan (minyanim)—Group(s) of ten Jews over the age of thirteen required for prayer services.

Mitzrayim—Egypt.

mitzvah (mitzvot)—Commandment; obligation or good deed(s).

moshav—Family community, like a kibbutz, where members live on and own their farms.

Palmach/Haganah—Elite force of the underground Israeli army prior to the founding of the State of Israel.

pilpul—Method of talmudic study.

rachamim—Compassion for one in need.

Sabra—Jew born in Israel.

Shekhinah—The presence of God in this world.

sh'licha tzibur—Leader of a community prayer service (f); *sh'liach tzibur* (m).

Sh'ma (Sh'ma Yisrael)—Central prayer of Jewish worship.

simkha—Celebration.

Sho'ah—The Holocaust.

shul—Synagogue.

tallit—Prayer shawl.

t'fillin—Small square leather boxes that contain parchments inscribed with certain biblical verses, worn on the forehead and upper arm during morning prayer services (except on Shabbat and major festivals).

tzedakah—Righteous generosity; giving to those in need.

yahrzeit—Anniversary of a death.

INDEX OF CONTRIBUTORS

CREDITS

"Judaism is like a chain of peace and existence that spans space and time, where each individual Jew is a different link" © 2004 Avraham Burg. Translated by Clive Lessem.

"We may choose to live as Jews, visibly and vitally, or else slip anonymously into the gentile mainstream" © 2004 Ruth R. Wisse. Photo credit: Jim Gipe.

"Judaism is the foundation of my identity" © 2004 Joshua Malina

"I am a Jew. My mother is a Jew. My father is a Jew. We all met at Sinai" © 2004 Irwin Cotler

"It would have been inconceivable a generation or two ago that Harvard could have a Jewish president" © 2004 Lawrence H. Summers

"If I, as an individual, do not have a good reason to continue to live as a Jew, then collectively the Jewish people has a problem—assimilation" © 2004 Zalman M. Schachter-Shalomi

"To say with pride and confidence, regardless of the consequences, 'I am Jewish'" © 2004 The Right Honourable The Lord Woolf

"At that moment I realized I could no sooner stop being a Jew than I could stop being Korean, or female, or *me*" © 2004 Angela Warnick Buchdahl

"To be a Jew means to belong to a national group that can be left or joined, just as any other national group is left or joined" © 1981 A. B. Yehoshua, from *Between Right and Right,* translated by Arnold Schwartz (New York: Doubleday, 1981). Used by permission of Doubleday, a division of Random House, Inc.

"Judaism is a tool of resistance wherever you come across words, behavior, events that you feel are evil" © 2004 Michael Chlenov

"We Jews are searchers for truth" © 2004 Daniel Schorr. Excerpt, reprinted with the permission of Pocket Books, an imprint of Simon and Schuster Adult Publishing Group, from *Staying Tuned: A Life in Journalism* by Daniel Schorr © 2001 by Daniel Schorr. Photo credit: Marvin Jones.

"Being Jewish is very important ..." © 2004 Stefanie Stoler

"To know, to talk to myself, to contradict, to question" © 2004 Maureen Lipman

"But I'm an American reporter, a Jew who believes in going after facts on the ground" © 2004 Mike Wallace

"Only a person who is connected to his past, to his people, and to his roots can be free, and only a free person has the strength to act for the benefit of the rest of humanity" © 2004 Natan Sharansky. Translated by Haim Watzman.

"A 'cultural Jew' ... total Jew" © 2004 Norman Lear

"I am Jewish, and it colors everything I've done, do, and will do" © 2004 David Horovitz

"More than matzo balls, chopped liver, and chicken soup" © 2004 Kitty Dukakis. Photo © 2002 John Kreis.

"Growing up in an interfaith household ..." © 2004 Jamie Sistino

"A very important part of my identity, but not the only part of my identity" © 2004 Thomas L. Friedman

"We hear a joyous cry of survival" © 2004 Bernice Rubens

"Being Jewish represents an inspiration to assert genuine individuality, to resist reductive group labels, and to transform one's life from the ordinary to the extraordinary.... In Judaism, learning is prayer" © 2004 Leon Botstein

"I am a son of this people, a nation that is adamant about remembering the past, inspired by its heritage, receptive to change, undaunted by the great prophecy that forges the destiny of the Jewish people, as in the words of the verse: 'old from new produce'" © 2004 Shimon Peres

"To be a Jew is to be old in history, but not only that" © 2004 Cynthia Ozick. Photo credit: Julius Ozick.

"Empowerment to question, zeal for honesty, reverence for learning, and deep commitment to create a better world for the next generation" © 2004 Ruth Pearl

"We are small in number; our impact has been incredible" © 2004 Larry King

"When I say that I am Jewish ..." © 2004 Sarah Rosenbaum

"While still young, I wondered whether my Jewish heritage was only a burden to be borne, rather than a privilege and blessing to be acknowledged with pride. Today I know better" © 2004 W. Michael Blumenthal. Photo credit: Paul Papier, Papier Photographic Studios, Princeton, New Jersey.

"A school of alchemy that knows how to transmute pain into life-affirming substance" © 2004 Tamara Pearl

"When I say I am Jewish ..." © 2004 Spencer Newman

"The unequivocal sense I have of being Jewish is fundamentally a kinship bond" © 2004 Sylvia Boorstein

"To accept a Jewish identification is to embrace much more than belief alone" © 2004 David J. Azrieli

"This is the lesson of Israel, the lesson that Zionism spoke to the exiles. Jewish meaning is made out of life, not martyrdom" © 2004 Martin Peretz. Yakov Glatstein excerpts from *The Selected Poems of Jacob Glatstein,* translated and with an introduction by Ruth Whitman (New York: October House, 1972). Aaron Zeitlin excerpt from *A Treasury of Yiddish Poetry,* edited by Irving Howe and Eliezer Greenberg, translated by Robert Friend (New York: Holt, Rinehart and Winston, 1969). Marie Syrkin excerpt from *Gleanings: A Diary in Verse.* Box 2, folder 16, Marie Syrkin Papers, The Jacob Rader Marcus Center of the American Jewish Archives, Cincinnati, Ohio.

"United through space and time by shared ancestry, shared culture, and shared historical memories" © 2004 Sherwin T. Wine. Photo credit: Gorback Studio of Photography, Franklin, Michigan.

"To me, 'I'm Jewish' means ..." © 2004 Jade Ransohoff

"Distinctly Jewish voices: funny, ironic, yearning, sometimes self-deprecating, sometimes grandiose, but always with a great heart" © 2004 Wendy Wasserstein

"Remember the guy who smashed all the idols in the idol store?" © 2004 Sarah Silverman

"To be a Jew means to belong to a nation whose people are linked to each other spiritually and emotionally, to belong to a group that shares a common magnificent past, one tradition, and a common destiny and fate" © 2004 Moshe Katsav

"When I say I am Jewish ..." © 2004 Amanda

"I hope that I, as a leading, proud, and active Jew, am not getting paranoid.... We should recognize the new and sad realities—and fight back, with heads held high" © 2004 Lord Greville Janner

"I learned how similar and different we all feel as Jews" © 2004 Alana Frey

"I am Jewish means for me ..." © 2004 Itay

"The really interesting stuff was in the history, the debates, the great arguments between Jews and about Jews" © 2004 Richard Dreyfuss

"A looking to the future. Out of the past" © 2004 Roald Hoffmann. Excerpt from Martin Buber, *Tales of the Hasidim: The Early Masters* (New York: Schocken, 1947). Photo credit: Clemens Loew.

"Humble yet proud of a heritage that has dignified me" © 2004 Vidal Sassoon

"I was born here [Israel] thousands of years ago. This is where I belong" © 2004 Ida Haendel

"Not the forgetting of the origin, but its maintenance as a living flame" © 2004 Daniel Libeskind. Photo © Studio Daniel Libeskind.

"Everyone knows by now that no one can kill our spirit" © 2004 Jackie Mason

"A sense of belonging, a deeply ingrained attachment to traditions, and, above all, a set of values that guide my actions" © 2004 Maurice Lévy

"The journey itself is not only the means, but also the end. I am blessed to be a voyager on an ancient pathway" © 2004 Rachel B. Cowan

"A deep and brilliant stream of culture and intellectual activity" © 2004 Milton Friedman

"Sometimes I unroll my Jewish self in places where people expect a secular artist, which of course I am, but they also discover a Jew" © 2004 Liz Lerman. Photo credit: R. Newton Brown.

"Being a 'survivor' is not what I think when I say 'I am a Jew.' I think about how we're different" © 2004 Daniel Gill

"We've been praying, learning, suffering, debating, and asking for two thousand years for what you have right now: the chance to take that final step back to our homeland" © 2004 David Suissa

"Being a musician and being Jewish have something in common: constant wandering, and never-ending struggle" © 2004 Yefim Bronfman

"I believe that Judaism is not only heritage, tradition, ethics, and faith but also a whole encompassing spirit" © 2004 Shelley R. Deutch Tayar

"Judaism is not a boundary; it is the force that breaks boundaries" © 2004 Douglas Rushkoff

"An intellectual and spiritual home" © 2004 Gloria Goldreich

"The disquieting questions lurk in the background of one's mind and at times intrude into the foreground" © 2004 Daniel Jonah Goldhagen

"As a Jew, the message of Daniel is very clear to me: Our only safe shelter is Israel" © 2004 Ephraim Kishon

"We believe, pray, and are because our parents and grandparents, and their parents and grandparents, believed, prayed, and were" © 2004 Menachem Z. Rosensaft

"Being Jewish runs deeper than superficial identification and is, in fact, an essential element driving other values" © 2004 Robert Rabinovitch

"A birthright, a glorious gift from one's forefathers of faith, culture, and heritage" © 2004 Naim Dangoor

"'You're Jewish?'" © 2004 Kerri Strug

"The themes from Jewish history combine the wide-ranging facts of creativity and courage, resistance and renewal, with a deep spiritual continuity" © 2004 Martin Gilbert. Photo © 2003 Sigrid Estrada.

"'Who knows if not for this very purpose' I had long been preparing" © 2004 Deborah E. Lipstadt

"A heritage, preserved through millennia by courage, achievement, and loyalty, and for all these reasons, a source of legitimate pride, to be cherished and passed on to those who come after us" © 2004 Bernard Lewis

"Joyful gratitude that there is a God who created the universe" © 2004 Joe Lieberman

"When I say I'm Jewish I think of three things …" © 2004 Robyn J. Friedman

"God has burdened human beings with the task of being the carriers of God's vision for human history. The law and the commandments express not only God's legislative authority but also, and above all, God's need for human beings" © 2004 David Hartman

"The concept of the Jews being one people is a *religious* idea and not an ethnic, political, or cultural one" © 2004 Eric H. Yoffie

"I think that being Jewish is not just the religion I practice ..." © 2004 Sarah Levin

"Being part of this people, I am part of the unfolding mystery" © 2004 Alan Dershowitz. Photo credit: Stu Rosner.

"Life in all its forms is sacred; in the face of each creature I see my creator" © 2004 Lawrence Kushner

"Being Jewish is not keeping kosher ..." © 2004 Felicia Lilien

"The all-encompassing perfection of the world's physical laws reflects the power of the creative force that brought them into being" © 2004 Arno Penzias

"To discover a frame through which to understand experience" © 2004 Patricia Karlin-Neumann

"Judaism to me is the name of the telephone in my heart that allows me to speak to God" © 2004 Shia LaBeouf

"At the heart of what it means to be a Jew is to ask questions" © 2004 Sandy Eisenberg Sasso

"A Jew, in my unhalakhic opinion, is someone who *chooses* to share the fate of other Jews, or who is *condemned* to do so" © 2004 Amos Oz. Excerpt from Amos Oz, *Under This Blazing Light* (Cambridge: Cambridge University Press, 1995).

"When I say I'm Jewish I think ..." © 2004 Samantha Schram

"'I am Jewish, and I fear Hashem, the G-d of the Heavens, who made the sea and the dry land'" © 2004 Israel Meir Lau. Translated by Ben Rose.

"When I say that I am a Jew, I mean to say that a Jew is what I desire to become" © 2004 Leon Wieseltier

"Keep loving, despite all the hatred" © 2004 Naomi Ragen

"I do not look Jewish in the eyes of the international Jewish community and I am frequently asked, 'How did you become Jewish?' and 'Who converted you?'" © 2004 Gershom Sizomu

"Today, we are all Jews by choice" © 2004 Michael H. Steinhardt

"A conscious decision to be a Jew and an ongoing commitment to leading a Jewish life" © 2004 Dennis Prager

"'Kirk, I think you like being Jewish 'cause it's so dramatic'" © 2004 Kirk Douglas

"The past dictates the future" © 2004 Richard Lerner

"To suffuse history with holiness" © 2004 Julius Lester

"Chosenness means taking responsibility for making our world a better place" © 2004 Chaim Kramer

"The core of the relationship is freedom and equality, the two essential conditions of the moral life that, in turn, revolves around responsibility—to oneself and others" © 2004 Josef Joffe

"A unique, private, and national identity rooted in a common mission and a responsibility for partnering with God in ever perfecting the work of creation" © 2004 Uri Regev

"The proclaiming of one's Jewishness is now a moral imperative, a post-covenant concession to the realities of our world" © 2004 Thane Rosenbaum

"I am Jewish because I cannot imagine being otherwise" © 2004 Richard Siegel

"A choosing people, more than a chosen people" © 2004 Michael Medved

"Somehow, I'd been Jewish for a long time, but I didn't know it until I met Anita" © 2004 Jim Ball

"God has granted me the privilege to serve a congregation of 62,000 soldiers and 130,000 family members" © 2004 Kenneth J. Leinwand

"Important as 'identity' and 'peoplehood' are, they are not the whole story" © 2004 Norman Lamm

"I am the bearer of meaning, of messages and compassions" © 2004 Larry S. Moses. Photo © Thomas J. Fitzsimmons.

"To be a Jew is to go on a journey of discovery" © 2004 Tony Bayfield

"To proclaim that I live every moment of my life in God's presence" © 2004 Harold Kushner

"For a Jew, Judaism and humanity must go together" © 2004 Elie Wiesel

"Universalism without tribalism is a kind of self-loathing" © 2004 Samuel G. Freedman. Photo credit: Carol J. Freedman.

"In our uniqueness lies our universality. Through being what we alone are, we give to humanity what only we can give" © 2000 Jonathan Sacks. Excerpt from Jonathan Sacks, *A Letter in the Scroll: Understanding Our Jewish Identity and Exploring the Legacy of the World's Oldest Religion* (New York: The Free Press, 2000). Reprinted with the permission of Chief Rabbi Jonathan Sacks and the Free Press, a Division of Simon & Schuster Adult Publishing Group. All rights reserved.

"I feel that when I say 'I am Jewish' ..." © 2004 Matt Putney

"When the time came to feel a connection beyond ourselves, we drew strength from our Judaism because it enhanced our humanity" © 2004 Michelle Pearl

"Judaism is the particular language through which Jews address humanity" © 2004 Harold M. Schulweis

"Struggles for the very security and peace of bodies and minds that our forefathers proclaimed, three millennia ago, to be the self-evident right and destiny of all mankind" © 2004 Ehud Barak

"I am a universalist Jew" © 2004 Bernard-Henri Lévy. Translated by James Mitchell.

"This attitude has caused the Jew and his history to become, in the eyes of humanity, a story that is larger than life" © 2004 David Grossman. Translated by Haim Watzman.

"I love the universal, because for us it means we belong, we are part of, we are included—not separate" © 2004 The Tovah Corp.

"My answer is: recognize yourself in others" © 2004 Nadine Gordimer. Photo credit: Jerry Bauer.

"I make no claim that Jewish culture is superior to other cultures or that the Jewish song is better than the song of my neighbor. But it is mine" © 2004 Theodore Bikel

"I see Jews as the scouts of civilization" © 2004 Judea Pearl

"For me, being Jewish and being an Israeli ..." © 2004 Eran Rotshenker

"Can I be intensely Jewish without losing the sense that I am created in the 'image of God' like everybody else?" © 2004 Chaim Seidler-Feller

"The color of my humanity is Jewish" © 2004 Anne Roiphe

"The Jewish people have deeply understood the value of recognizing a common thread in all of humanity" © 2004 Uri D. Herscher. Photo © 1996 Grant Mudford.

"I frequently doubt whether preservation of national consciousness assists or hampers the establishment of universal humanistic values in our world" © 2004 Alexander Militarev

"The demand for justice runs through the entirety of the Jewish history and Jewish tradition" © 2004 Ruth Bader Ginsburg. Photo credit: Steve Petteway.

"Wherever there is a revolutionary political movement, you will usually find Jews involved in it: We are raised to believe the world can be made better" © 2004 Jonathan Freedland

"Identify with the yearning to see all people free—free from want, free from terror, free from dictatorships, free from modern-day slavery and injustice" © 2004 Stephen H. Hoffman

"'Repair the world,' a mandate that does not stop at the borders of our communities, a mandate that has no borders at all" © 2004 Gary Shteyngart

"Serving others is one of the pillars upon which Judaism rests and the future of all humanity depends" © 2004 Lynn Schusterman. Adapted in part from Lynn Schusterman, "A Jewish Family's Experience" in *Faith and Family Philanthropy: Grace, Gratitude, and Generosit,* (Washington, D.C.: National Center for Family Philanthropy, 2001). For additional information about the National Center, please visit its website at www.ncfp.org.

"It is only if we act, if we try to carry out what God wants of us, that the existence of God has meaning and reality" © 2004 Jacqueline Tabick

"I am here by the grace of Hashem, that I must honor Hashem, my fellow man, and myself through the way I live my life" © 2004 David Colburn

"Indeed, the recognition that one is Jewish automatically implies—unspoken and unheralded—the sense that one has *obligations,* as opposed to the demands of others that they have *rights*" © 2004 Judy Feld Carr

"Jews are obligated to become inventors, makers of memory and meaning and future, not disconnected consumers of ancient history or trapped in unspeakable tragedy" © 2004 Robin Kramer

"It doesn't matter who a person is or what one's position in this world is. What matters is what you do with it" © 2004 Richard N. Goldman

"The supreme virtue of tolerance" © 2004 Tullia Zevi

"Primarily, being Jewish means acting ethically Jewish (much more than being observant) and ... I am willy-nilly an OK Jew" © 2004 Peter Yarrow. *Light One Candle* lyrics © 1983 Peter Yarrow.

"At the core of Jewish consciousness there exists a vision of becoming a holy nation and a light unto others" © 2004 Francine Klagsbrun

"Know who you are, where you are going, and what is your heritage ..." © 2004 Hanoch Greenberg

"A witness to the courage of compassion inherent in the human spirit" © 2004 Sjalom Awraham Soetendorp. Photo credit: Foto-Persbureau Dirk Hol Naamsvermelding Verplicht. © Vrij Bij Openbaarmaking in Kader Van St. Fonds Van Hoop Voor Kinderen.

"It encompasses the basic dignity and humanity with which we regard all God's creatures" © 2004 Alan Colmes

"Service is my way of encountering God in the world, since God can only be found in our response to the needs of others" © 2004 Ruth W. Messinger

"An intense loyalty to humanity and a passionate commitment to its civilized expansion" © 2004 Rosalie Silberman Abella. Photo © Ashley and Crippen.

"It takes all of us who cherish beauty and humankind to be mindful and respectful of one another" © 2004 Dianne Feinstein

"What do the Jews do? They keep watch. They are the sentinels against intolerance" © 2004 Bernard Kouchner

"We are a people of laws, not whim. We are a people of ethical principle, not convenience" © 2004 Zev Yaroslavsky

"The preservation of the respect and the tolerance owed to other communities, because that also is the fundamental message of Judaism that my parents transmitted to me" © 2004 Simone Veil. Translated from the French.

"The complexity of evil and the fallibility of the good have been with me all my life and are perhaps the first things I think about when I think of being a Jew" © 2004 Daniel Kahneman. Photo credit: Denise Applewhite/Princeton University.

"Not to take oneself too seriously, but to take one's responsibilities very seriously" © 2004 Naamah Kelman

"A powerful code of moral values" © 2004 Roger Cukierman

"By asserting my Jewishness I am keeping faith with my ancestors, and thus I am being true to myself" © 2004 Edgar M. Bronfman

"In every interaction—be it a concert, or when I function as a *sh'licha tzibur* (leader of the prayer service), or at a healing service—in any of my relationships, no matter what I do, I am a Jew" © 2004 Debbie Friedman

AVAILABLE FROM BETTER BOOKSTORES.
TRY YOUR BOOKSTORE FIRST.

Bar/Bat Mitzvah

The Bar/Bat Mitzvah Memory Book
An Album for Treasuring the Spiritual Celebration
By Rabbi Jeffrey K. Salkin and Nina Salkin
A unique album for preserving the spiritual memories of the day, and for recording plans for the Jewish future ahead. Contents include space for creating or recording family history; teachings received from rabbi, cantor, and others; mitzvot and *tzedakot* chosen and carried out, etc.
8 x 10, 48 pp, Deluxe Hardcover, 2-color text, ribbon marker, ISBN 1-58023-111-X **$19.95**

Bar/Bat Mitzvah Basics: A Practical Family Guide to Coming of Age Together
Edited by Helen Leneman. Foreword by Rabbi Jeffrey K. Salkin.
6 x 9, 240 pp, Quality PB, ISBN 1-58023-151-9 **$18.95**

For Kids—Putting God on Your Guest List: How to Claim the Spiritual Meaning of Your Bar or Bat Mitzvah *By Rabbi Jeffrey K. Salkin*
6 x 9, 144 pp, Quality PB, ISBN 1-58023-015-6 **$14.95** *For ages 11–12*

Putting God on the Guest List: How to Reclaim the Spiritual Meaning of Your Child's Bar or Bat Mitzvah *By Rabbi Jeffrey K. Salkin*
6 x 9, 224 pp, Quality PB, ISBN 1-879045-59-1 **$16.95**

Tough Questions Jews Ask: A Young Adult's Guide to Building a Jewish Life
By Rabbi Edward Feinstein 6 x 9, 160 pp, Quality PB, ISBN 1-58023-139-X **$14.95** *For ages 13 & up*
Also Available: **Tough Questions Jews Ask Teacher's Guide**
8½ x 11, 72 pp, PB, ISBN 1-58023-187-X **$8.95**

Bible Study/Midrash

Hineini in Our Lives: Learning How to Respond to Others through 14 Biblical Texts, and Personal Stories *By Norman J. Cohen*
6 x 9, 240 pp, Hardcover, ISBN 1-58023-131-4 **$23.95**

Hineini
in Our Lives

Ancient Secrets: Using the Stories of the Bible to Improve Our Everyday Lives
By Rabbi Levi Meier, Ph.D. 5½ x 8½, 288 pp, Quality PB, ISBN 1-58023-064-4 **$16.95**

Moses—The Prince, the Prophet: His Life, Legend & Message for Our Lives
By Rabbi Levi Meier, Ph.D.
6 x 9, 224 pp, Quality PB, ISBN 1-58023-069-5 **$16.95**; Hardcover, ISBN 1-58023-013-X **$23.95**

Self, Struggle & Change: Family Conflict Stories in Genesis and Their Healing Insights for Our Lives *By Norman J. Cohen* 6 x 9, 224 pp, Quality PB, ISBN 1-879045-66-4 **$16.95**

Becoming
a
Congregation
of
Learners

Voices from Genesis: Guiding Us through the Stages of Life *By Norman J. Cohen*
6 x 9, 192 pp, Quality PB, ISBN 1-58023-118-7 **$16.95**

Congregation Resources

Becoming a Congregation of Learners: Learning as a Key to Revitalizing Congregational Life *By Isa Aron, Ph.D. Foreword by Rabbi Lawrence A. Hoffman.*
6 x 9, 304 pp, Quality PB, ISBN 1-58023-089-X **$19.95**

Finding a Spiritual Home: How a New Generation of Jews Can Transform the American Synagogue *By Rabbi Sidney Schwarz*
6 x 9, 352 pp, Quality PB, ISBN 1-58023-185-3 **$19.95**

Jewish Pastoral Care: A Practical Handbook from Traditional & Contemporary Sources
Edited by Rabbi Dayle A. Friedman 6 x 9, 464 pp, Hardcover, ISBN 1-58023-078-4 **$35.00**

The Self-Renewing Congregation: Organizational Strategies for Revitalizing Congregational Life *By Isa Aron, Ph.D. Foreword by Dr. Ron Wolfson.*
6 x 9, 304 pp, Quality PB, ISBN 1-58023-166-7 **$19.95**

Or phone, fax, mail or e-mail to: **JEWISH LIGHTS** Publishing
Sunset Farm Offices, Route 4 • P.O. Box 237 • Woodstock, Vermont 05091
Tel: (802) 457-4000 • Fax: (802) 457-4004 • www.jewishlights.com
Credit card orders: (800) 962-4544 (8:30AM–5:30PM ET Monday–Friday)
Generous discounts on quantity orders. SATISFACTION GUARANTEED. Prices subject to change.

Children's Books

Because Nothing Looks Like God
By Lawrence and Karen Kushner

What is God like? The first collaborative work by husband-and-wife team Lawrence and Karen Kushner introduces children to the possibilities of spiritual life. Real-life examples of happiness and sadness invite us to explore, together with our children, the questions we all have about God, no matter what our age.

11 x 8½, 32 pp, Full-color illus., Hardcover, ISBN 1-58023-092-X **$16.95** *For ages 4 & up*

Also Available: **Because Nothing Looks Like God Teacher's Guide**

8½ x 11, 22 pp, PB, ISBN 1-58023-140-3 **$6.95** *For ages 5–8*

Board Book Companions to *Because Nothing Looks Like God*

5 x 5, 24 pp, Full-color illus., SkyLight Paths Board Books, **$7.95** each *For ages 0–4*

What Does God Look Like? ISBN 1-893361-23-3

How Does God Make Things Happen? ISBN 1-893361-24-1

Where Is God? ISBN 1-893361-17-9

The 11th Commandment: Wisdom from Our Children
by The Children of America

"If there were an Eleventh Commandment, what would it be?" Children of many religious denominations across America answer this question—in their own drawings and words.

8 x 10, 48 pp, Full-color illus., Hardcover, ISBN 1-879045-46-X **$16.95** *For all ages*

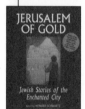

Jerusalem of Gold: Jewish Stories of the Enchanted City
Retold by Howard Schwartz. Full-color illus. by Neil Waldman.

A beautiful and engaging collection of historical and legendary stories for children. Each celebrates the magical city that has served as a beacon for the Jewish imagination for three thousand years. Draws on Talmud, midrash, Jewish folklore, and mystical and Hasidic sources.

8 x 10, 64 pp, Full-color illus., Hardcover, ISBN 1-58023-149-7 **$18.95** *For ages 7 & up*

The Book of Miracles: A Young Person's Guide to Jewish Spiritual Awareness
By Lawrence Kushner. All-new illustrations by the author.

6 x 9, 96 pp, 2-color illus., Hardcover, ISBN 1-879045-78-8 **$16.95** *For ages 9–13*

In Our Image: God's First Creatures
By Nancy Sohn Swartz

9 x 12, 32 pp, Full-color illus., Hardcover, ISBN 1-879045-99-0 **$16.95** *For ages 4 & up*

From SKYLIGHT PATHS PUBLISHING

Becoming Me: A Story of Creation
By Martin Boroson. Full-color illus. by Christopher Gilvan-Cartwright.

Told in the personal "voice" of the Creator, a story about creation and relationship that is about each one of us. In simple words and with radiant illustrations, the Creator tells an intimate story about love, about friendship and playing, about our world—and about ourselves.

8 x 10, 32 pp, Full-color illus., Hardcover, ISBN 1-893361-11-X **$16.95** *For ages 4 & up*

Ten Amazing People: And How They Changed the World
By Maura D. Shaw. Foreword by Dr. Robert Coles. Full-color illus. by Stephen Marchesi.

Black Elk • Dorothy Day • Malcolm X • Mahatma Gandhi • Martin Luther King, Jr. • Mother Teresa • Janusz Korczak • Desmond Tutu • Thich Nhat Hanh • Albert Schweitzer • This vivid, inspirational, and authoritative book will open new possibilities for children by telling the stories of how ten of the past century's greatest leaders changed the world in important ways.

8½ x 11, 48 pp, Full-color illus., Hardcover, ISBN 1-893361-47-0 **$17.95** *For ages 7 & up*

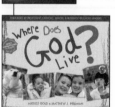

Where Does God Live? *By August Gold and Matthew J. Perlman*

Using simple, everyday examples that children can relate to, this colorful book helps young readers develop a personal understanding of God.

10 x 8½ , 32 pp, Full-color photo illus., Quality PB, ISBN 1-893361-39-X **$8.95** *For ages 3–6*

Children's Books
by Sandy Eisenberg Sasso

Adam & Eve's First Sunset: God's New Day

Engaging new story explores fear and hope, faith and gratitude in ways that will delight kids and adults—inspiring us to bless each of God's days and nights.

9 x 12, 32 pp, Full-color illus., Hardcover, ISBN 1-58023-177-2 **$17.95** *For ages 4 & up*

But God Remembered

Stories of Women from Creation to the Promised Land

Four different stories of women—Lillith, Serach, Bityah, and the Daughters of Z—teach us important values through their faith and actions.

9 x 12, 32 pp, Full-color illus., Hardcover, ISBN 1-879045-43-5 **$16.95** *For ages 8 & up*

Cain & Abel: Finding the Fruits of Peace

Full-color illus. by Joani Keller Rothenberg

Shows children that we have the power to deal with anger in positive ways. Provides questions for kids and adults to explore together.

9 x 12, 32 pp, Full-color illus., Hardcover, ISBN 1-58023-123-3 **$16.95** *For ages 5 & up*

God in Between

Full-color illus. by Sally Sweetland

If you wanted to find God, where would you look? This magical, mythical tale teaches that God can be found where we are: within all of us and the relationships between us.

9 x 12, 32 pp, Full-color illus., Hardcover, ISBN 1-879045-86-9 **$16.95** *For ages 4 & up*

God's Paintbrush

Wonderfully interactive, invites children of all faiths and backgrounds to encounter God through moments in their own lives. Provides questions adult and child can explore together.

11 x 8¼, 32 pp, Full-color illus., Hardcover, ISBN 1-879045-22-2 **$16.95** *For ages 4 & up*

Also Available: **God's Paintbrush Teacher's Guide**
8½ x 11, 32 pp, PB, ISBN 1-879045-57-5 **$8.95**

God's Paintbrush Celebration Kit

A Spiritual Activity Kit for Teachers and Students of All Faiths, All Backgrounds
Additional activity sheets available:
8-Student Activity Sheet Pack (40 sheets/5 sessions), ISBN 1-58023-058-X **$19.95**
Single-Student Activity Sheet Pack (5 sessions), ISBN 1-58023-059-8 **$3.95**

In God's Name

Full-color illus. by Phoebe Stone

Like an ancient myth in its poetic text and vibrant illustrations, this award-winning modern fable about the search for God's name celebrates the diversity and, at the same time, the unity of all people.

9 x 12, 32 pp, Full-color illus., Hardcover, ISBN 1-879045-26-5 **$16.95** *For ages 4 & up*

Also Available as a Board Book: **What Is God's Name?**
5 x 5, 24 pp, Board, Full-color illus., ISBN 1-893361-10-1 **$7.95** *For ages 0–4 (A SkyLight Paths book)*

Also Available: **In God's Name video and study guide**
Computer animation, original music, and children's voices. 18 min. **$29.99**

Also Available in Spanish: **El nombre de Dios**
9 x 12, 32 pp, Full-color illus., Hardcover, ISBN 1-893361-63-2 **$16.95** *(A SkyLight Paths book)*

Noah's Wife: The Story of Naamah

When God tells Noah to bring the animals of the world onto the ark, God also calls on Naamah, Noah's wife, to save each plant on Earth. Based on an ancient text.

9 x 12, 32 pp, Full-color illus., Hardcover, ISBN 1-58023-134-9 **$16.95** *For ages 4 & up*

Also Available as a Board Book: **Naamah, Noah's Wife**
5 x 5, 24 pp, Full-color illus., Board, ISBN 1-893361-56-X **$7.95** *For ages 0–4 (A SkyLight Paths book)*

For Heaven's Sake: Finding God in Unexpected Places
9 x 12, 32 pp, Full-color illus., Hardcover, ISBN 1-58023-054-7 **$16.95** *For ages 4 & up*

God Said Amen: Finding the Answers to Our Prayers
9 x 12, 32 pp, Full-color illus., Hardcover, ISBN 1-58023-080-6 **$16.95** *For ages 4 & up*

Current Events/History

The Story of the Jews: A 4,000-Year Adventure—A Graphic History Book
Written & illustrated by Stan Mack
Through witty, illustrated narrative, we visit all the major happenings from biblical times to the twenty-first century. Celebrates the major characters and events that have shaped the Jewish people and culture.
6 x 9, 288 pp., illus., Quality PB, ISBN 1-58023-155-1 **$16.95**

The Jewish Prophet: Visionary Words from Moses and Miriam to Henrietta Szold and A. J. Heschel *By Rabbi Michael J. Shire* 6½ x 8½, 128 pp, 123 full-color illus., Hardcover, ISBN 1-58023-168-3 **$25.00**

Shared Dreams: Martin Luther King, Jr. & the Jewish Community
By Rabbi Marc Schneier. Preface by Martin Luther King III.
6 x 9, 240 pp, Hardcover, ISBN 1-58023-062-8 **$24.95**

"Who Is a Jew?": Conversations, Not Conclusions *By Meryl Hyman*
6 x 9, 272 pp, Quality PB, ISBN 1-58023-052-0 **$16.95**

Ecology

Ecology & the Jewish Spirit: Where Nature & the Sacred Meet
Edited by Ellen Bernstein 6 x 9, 288 pp, Quality PB, ISBN 1-58023-082-2 **$16.95**

Torah of the Earth: Exploring 4,000 Years of Ecology in Jewish Thought
Vol. 1: Biblical Israel: One Land, One People; Rabbinic Judaism: One People, Many Lands
Vol. 2: Zionism: One Land, Two Peoples; Eco-Judaism: One Earth, Many Peoples
Edited by Rabbi Arthur Waskow
Vol. 1: 6 x 9, 272 pp, Quality PB, ISBN 1-58023-086-5 **$19.95**
Vol. 2: 6 x 9, 336 pp, Quality PB, ISBN 1-58023-087-3 **$19.95**

Grief/Healing

Against the Dying of the Light: A Parent's Story of Love, Loss and Hope
By Leonard Fein
In this unusual exploration of heartbreak and healing, Leonard Fein chronicles the sudden death of his 30-year-old daughter and shares the hard-earned wisdom that emerges in the face of loss and grief.
5½ x 8½, 176 pp, Hardcover, ISBN 1-58023-110-1 **$19.95**

Grief in Our Seasons: A Mourner's Kaddish Companion *By Rabbi Kerry M. Olitzky*
4½ x 6½, 448 pp, Quality PB, ISBN 1-879045-55-9 **$15.95**

Healing of Soul, Healing of Body: Spiritual Leaders Unfold the Strength & Solace in Psalms *Edited by Rabbi Simkha Y. Weintraub, C.S.W.*
6 x 9, 128 pp, 2-color illus. text, Quality PB, ISBN 1-879045-31-1 **$14.95**

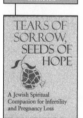

Jewish Paths toward Healing and Wholeness: A Personal Guide to Dealing with Suffering *By Rabbi Kerry M. Olitzky. Foreword by Debbie Friedman.*
6 x 9, 192 pp, Quality PB, ISBN 1-58023-068-7 **$15.95**

Mourning & Mitzvah, 2nd Edition: A Guided Journal for Walking the Mourner's Path through Grief to Healing *By Anne Brener, L.C.S.W.*
7½ x 9, 304 pp, Quality PB, ISBN 1-58023-113-6 **$19.95**

The Perfect Stranger's Guide to Funerals and Grieving Practices
A Guide to Etiquette in Other People's Religious Ceremonies *Edited by Stuart M. Matlins*
6 x 9, 240 pp, Quality PB, ISBN 1-893361-20-9 **$16.95** *(A SkyLight Paths book)*

Tears of Sorrow, Seeds of Hope: A Jewish Spiritual Companion for Infertility and Pregnancy Loss *By Rabbi Nina Beth Cardin*
6 x 9, 192 pp, Hardcover, ISBN 1-58023-017-2 **$19.95**

A Time to Mourn, A Time to Comfort: A Guide to Jewish Bereavement and Comfort *By Dr. Ron Wolfson* 7 x 9, 336 pp, Quality PB, ISBN 1-879045-96-6 **$18.95**

When a Grandparent Dies: A Kid's Own Remembering Workbook for Dealing with Shiva and the Year Beyond *By Nechama Liss-Levinson, Ph.D.*
8 x 10, 48 pp, 2-color text, Hardcover, ISBN 1-879045-44-3 **$15.95** *For ages 7–13*

Abraham Joshua Heschel

The Earth Is the Lord's: The Inner World of the Jew in Eastern Europe
5½ x 8, 128 pp, Quality PB, ISBN 1-879045-42-7 **$14.95**

Israel: An Echo of Eternity *New Introduction by Susannah Heschel*
5½ x 8, 272 pp, Quality PB, ISBN 1-879045-70-2 **$19.95**

A Passion for Truth: Despair and Hope in Hasidism
5½ x 8, 352 pp, Quality PB, ISBN 1-879045-41-9 **$18.95**

Holidays/Holy Days

7th Heaven: Celebrating Shabbat with Rebbe Nachman of Breslov
By Moshe Mykoff with the Breslov Research Institute
Based on the teachings of Rebbe Nachman of Breslov. Explores the art of consciously observing Shabbat and understanding in-depth many of the day's traditional spiritual practices.
5⅛ x 8¼, 224 pp, Deluxe PB w/flaps, ISBN 1-58023-175-6 **$18.95**

The Women's Passover Companion
Women's Reflections on the Festival of Freedom
Edited by Rabbi Sharon Cohen Anisfeld, Tara Mohr, and Catherine Spector
A groundbreaking collection that captures the voices of Jewish women who engage in a provocative conversation about women's relationships to Passover as well as the roots and meanings of women's seders.
6 x 9, 352 pp, Hardcover, ISBN 1-58023-128-4 **$24.95**

The Women's Seder Sourcebook
Rituals & Readings for Use at the Passover Seder
Edited by Rabbi Sharon Cohen Anisfeld, Tara Mohr, and Catherine Spector
This practical guide gathers the voices of more than one hundred women in readings, personal and creative reflections, commentaries, blessings, and ritual suggestions that can be incorporated into your Passover celebration as supplements to or substitutes for traditional passages of the haggadah.
6 x 9, 384 pp, Hardcover, ISBN 1-58023-136-5 **$24.95**

Creating Lively Passover Seders: A Sourcebook of Engaging Tales, Texts & Activities
By David Arnow, Ph.D.
7 x 9, 416 pp, Quality PB, ISBN 1-58023-184-5 **$24.95**

Hanukkah, 2nd Edition: The Family Guide to Spiritual Celebration
By Dr. Ron Wolfson. Edited by Joel Lurie Grishaver.
7 x 9, 240 pp, illus., Quality PB, ISBN 1-58023-122-5 **$18.95**

The Jewish Family Fun Book: Holiday Projects, Everyday Activities, and Travel Ideas
with Jewish Themes *By Danielle Dardashti and Roni Sarig. Illus. by Avi Katz.*
6 x 9, 288 pp, 70+ b/w illus. & diagrams, Quality PB, ISBN 1-58023-171-3 **$18.95**

The Jewish Gardening Cookbook: Growing Plants & Cooking for
Holidays & Festivals *By Michael Brown*
6 x 9, 224 pp, 30+ illus., Quality PB, ISBN 1-58023-116-0 **$16.95**;
Hardcover, ISBN 1-58023-004-0 **$21.95**

Passover, 2nd Edition: The Family Guide to Spiritual Celebration
By Dr. Ron Wolfson with Joel Lurie Grishaver
7 x 9, 352 pp, Quality PB, ISBN 1-58023-174-8 **$19.95**

Shabbat, 2nd Edition: The Family Guide to Preparing for and Celebrating the Sabbath
By Dr. Ron Wolfson 7 x 9, 320 pp, illus., Quality PB, ISBN 1-58023-164-0 **$19.95**

Sharing Blessings: Children's Stories for Exploring the Spirit of the Jewish Holidays
By Rahel Musleah and Michael Klayman
8½ x 11, 64 pp, Full-color illus., Hardcover, ISBN 1-879045-71-0 **$18.95** *For ages 6 & up*

Inspiration

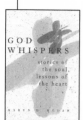

God in All Moments
Mystical & Practical Spiritual Wisdom from Hasidic Masters
Edited and translated by Or N. Rose with Ebn D. Leader
Hasidic teachings on how to be mindful in religious practice and how to cultivate everyday ethical behavior—*hanhagot*.
5½ x 8½, 192 pp, Quality PB, ISBN 1-58023-186-1 **$16.95**

The Dance of the Dolphin: Finding Prayer, Perspective and Meaning in the Stories
of Our Lives By Karyn D. Kedar   6 x 9, 176 pp, Hardcover, ISBN 1-58023-154-3 **$19.95**

The Empty Chair: Finding Hope and Joy—Timeless Wisdom from a Hasidic Master,
Rebbe Nachman of Breslov *Adapted by Moshe Mykoff and the Breslov Research Institute*
4 x 6, 128 pp, 2-color text, Deluxe PB w/flaps, ISBN 1-879045-67-2 **$9.95**

The Gentle Weapon: Prayers for Everyday and Not-So-Everyday Moments—
Timeless Wisdom from the Teachings of the Hasidic Master, Rebbe Nachman of Breslov
Adapted by Moshe Mykoff and S. C. Mizrahi, together with the Breslov Research Institute
4 x 6, 144 pp, 2-color text, Deluxe PB w/flaps, ISBN 1-58023-022-9 **$9.95**

God Whispers: Stories of the Soul, Lessons of the Heart By Karyn D. Kedar
6 x 9, 176 pp, Quality PB, ISBN 1-58023-088-1 **$15.95**

An Orphan in History: One Man's Triumphant Search for His Jewish Roots
By Paul Cowan. Afterword by Rachel Cowan. 6 x 9, 288 pp, Quality PB, ISBN 1-58023-135-7 **$16.95**

Restful Reflections: Nighttime Inspiration to Calm the Soul, Based on Jewish Wisdom
By Rabbi Kerry M. Olitzky & Rabbi Lori Forman
4½ x 6½, 448 pp, Quality PB, ISBN 1-58023-091-1 **$15.95**

Sacred Intentions: Daily Inspiration to Strengthen the Spirit, Based on Jewish Wisdom
By Rabbi Kerry M. Olitzky and Rabbi Lori Forman
4½ x 6½, 448 pp, Quality PB, ISBN 1-58023-061-X **$15.95**

Kabbalah/Mysticism/Enneagram

Seek My Face: A Jewish Mystical Theology
By Dr. Arthur Green
This classic work of contemporary Jewish theology, revised and updated, is a profound, deeply personal statement of the lasting truths of Jewish mysticism and the basic faith claims of Judaism. A tool for anyone seeking the elusive presence of God in the world. 6 x 9, 304 pp, Quality PB, ISBN 1-58023-130-6 **$19.95**

Zohar: Annotated & Explained
Translation and annotation by Dr. Daniel C. Matt. Foreword by Andrew Harvey, SkyLight Illuminations series editor.
Offers insightful yet unobtrusive commentary to the masterpiece of Jewish mysticism that explains references and mystical symbols, shares wisdom of spiritual masters, and clarifies the *Zohar*'s bold claim: We have always been taught that we need God, but in order to manifest in the world, God needs us.
5½ x 8½, 160 pp, Quality PB, ISBN 1-893361-51-9 **$15.95** *(A SkyLight Paths book)*

Cast in God's Image: Discover Your Personality Type Using the Enneagram and Kabbalah
By Rabbi Howard A. Addison
7 x 9, 176 pp, Quality PB, Layflat binding, 20+ journaling exercises, ISBN 1-58023-124-1 **$16.95**

Ehyeh: A Kabbalah for Tomorrow By Dr. Arthur Green
6 x 9, 224 pp, Hardcover, ISBN 1-58023-125-X **$21.95**

The Enneagram and Kabbalah: Reading Your Soul By Rabbi Howard A. Addison
6 x 9, 176 pp, Quality PB, ISBN 1-58023-001-6 **$15.95**

Finding Joy: A Practical Spiritual Guide to Happiness By Dannel I. Schwartz with Mark Hass
6 x 9, 192 pp, Quality PB, ISBN 1-58023-009-1 **$14.95**; Hardcover, ISBN 1-879045-53-2 **$19.95**

The Gift of Kabbalah: Discovering the Secrets of Heaven, Renewing Your Life on Earth
By Tamar Frankiel, Ph.D.
6 x 9, 256 pp, Quality PB, ISBN 1-58023-141-1 **$16.95**; Hardcover, ISBN 1-58023-108-X **$21.95**

The Way Into Jewish Mystical Tradition By Lawrence Kushner
6 x 9, 224 pp, Hardcover, ISBN 1-58023-029-6 **$21.95**

Life Cycle
Parenting

The New Jewish Baby Album: Creating and Celebrating the Beginning of a Spiritual Life—A Jewish Lights Companion

By the Editors at Jewish Lights. Foreword by Anita Diamant. Preface by Sandy Eisenberg Sasso.
A spiritual keepsake that will be treasured for generations. More than just a memory book, *shows you how—and why it's important*—to create a Jewish home and a Jewish life. Includes sections to describe naming ceremony, space to write encouragements, and pages for writing original blessings, prayers, and meaningful quotes throughout.
8 x 10, 64 pp, Deluxe Padded Hardcover, Full-color illus., ISBN 1-58023-138-1 **$19.95**

The Jewish Pregnancy Book: A Resource for the Soul, Body & Mind during Pregnancy, Birth & the First Three Months

By Sandy Falk, M.D., and Rabbi Daniel Judson, with Steven A. Rapp
Includes medical information on fetal development, pre-natal testing and more, from a liberal Jewish perspective; prenatal *Aleph-Bet* yoga; and ancient and modern prayers and rituals for each stage of pregnancy.
7 x 10, 208 pp, Quality PB, b/w illus., ISBN 1-58023-178-0 **$16.95**

Celebrating Your New Jewish Daughter: Creating Jewish Ways to Welcome Baby Girls into the Covenant—New and Traditional Ceremonies
By Debra Nussbaum Cohen 6 x 9, 272 pp, Quality PB, ISBN 1-58023-090-3 **$18.95**

The New Jewish Baby Book: Names, Ceremonies & Customs—A Guide for Today's Families *By Anita Diamant* 6 x 9, 336 pp, Quality PB, ISBN 1-879045-28-1 **$18.95**

Parenting As a Spiritual Journey: Deepening Ordinary and Extraordinary Events into Sacred Occasions *By Rabbi Nancy Fuchs-Kreimer*
6 x 9, 224 pp, Quality PB, ISBN 1-58023-016-4 **$16.95**

Embracing the Covenant: Converts to Judaism Talk About Why & How
Edited and with introductions by Rabbi Allan Berkowitz and Patti Moskovitz
6 x 9, 192 pp, Quality PB, ISBN 1-879045-50-8 **$16.95**

The Guide to Jewish Interfaith Family Life: An InterfaithFamily.com Handbook
Edited by Ronnie Friedland and Edmund Case 6 x 9, 384 pp, Quality PB, ISBN 1-58023-153-5 **$18.95**

Making a Successful Jewish Interfaith Marriage: The Jewish Outreach Institute Guide to Opportunities, Challenges and Resources
By Rabbi Kerry Olitzky with Joan Peterson Littman 6 x 9, 176 pp, Quality PB, ISBN 1-58023-170-5 **$16.95**

The Perfect Stranger's Guide to Wedding Ceremonies
A Guide to Etiquette in Other People's Religious Ceremonies *Edited by Stuart M. Matlins*
6 x 9, 208 pp, Quality PB, ISBN 1-893361-19-5 **$16.95** *(A SkyLight Paths book)*

How to Be a Perfect Stranger, 3rd Edition
The Essential Religious Etiquette Handbook
Edited by Stuart M. Matlins and Arthur J. Magida

The indispensable guidebook to help the well-meaning guest when visiting other people's religious ceremonies.
A straightforward guide to the rituals and celebrations of the major religions and denominations in the United States and Canada from the perspective of an interested guest of any other faith, based on information obtained from authorities of each religion. Belongs in every living room, library, and office.
6 x 9, 432 pp, Quality PB, ISBN 1-893361-67-5 **$19.95** *(A SkyLight Paths book)*

Divorce Is a Mitzvah: A Practical Guide to Finding Wholeness and Holiness When Your Marriage Dies *By Rabbi Perry Netter. Afterword by Rabbi Laura Geller.*
6 x 9, 224 pp, Quality PB, ISBN 1-58023-172-1 **$16.95**

A Heart of Wisdom: Making the Jewish Journey from Midlife through the Elder Years
Edited by Susan Berrin. Foreword by Harold Kushner. 6 x 9, 384 pp, Quality PB, ISBN 1-58023-051-2 **$18.95**

So That Your Values Live On: Ethical Wills and How to Prepare Them
Edited by Jack Riemer and Nathaniel Stampfer 6 x 9, 272 pp, Quality PB, ISBN 1-879045-34-6 **$18.95**

Meditation

The Handbook of Jewish Meditation Practices
A Guide for Enriching the Sabbath and Other Days of Your Life
By Rabbi David A. Cooper
Easy-to-learn meditation techniques for use on the Sabbath and every day, to help us return to the roots of traditional Jewish spirituality where Shabbat is a state of mind and soul. 6 x 9, 208 pp, Quality PB, ISBN 1-58023-102-0 **$16.95**

Discovering Jewish Meditation: Instruction & Guidance for Learning an Ancient
Spiritual Practice *By Nan Fink Gefen, Ph.D.* 6 x 9, 208 pp, Quality PB, ISBN 1-58023-067-9 **$16.95**

A Heart of Stillness: A Complete Guide to Learning the Art of Meditation
By Rabbi David A. Cooper
5½ x 8½, 272 pp, Quality PB, ISBN 1-893361-03-9 **$16.95** *(A SkyLight Paths book)*

Meditation from the Heart of Judaism: Today's Teachers Share Their
Practices, Techniques, and Faith *Edited by Avram Davis*
6 x 9, 256 pp, Quality PB, ISBN 1-58023-049-0 **$16.95**

Silence, Simplicity & Solitude: A Complete Guide to Spiritual Retreat at Home
By Rabbi David A. Cooper
5½ x 8½, 336 pp, Quality PB, ISBN 1-893361-04-7 **$16.95** *(A SkyLight Paths book)*

Three Gates to Meditation Practice: A Personal Journey into Sufism,
Buddhism, and Judaism *By Rabbi David A. Cooper*
5½ x 8½, 240 pp, Quality PB, ISBN 1-893361-22-5 **$16.95** *(A SkyLight Paths book)*

The Way of Flame: A Guide to the Forgotten Mystical Tradition of Jewish Meditation
By Avram Davis 4½ x 8, 176 pp, Quality PB, ISBN 1-58023-060-1 **$15.95**

Ritual/Sacred Practice

The Jewish Dream Book
The Key to Opening the Inner Meaning of Your Dreams
By Vanessa L. Ochs with Elizabeth Ochs; Full-color Illus. by Kristina Swarner
Vibrant illustrations, instructions for how modern people can perform ancient Jewish dream practices, and dream interpretations drawn from the Jewish wisdom tradition help make this guide the ideal bedside companion for anyone who wants to further their understanding of their dreams—and themselves.
8 x 8, 120 pp, Full-color illus., Deluxe PB w/flaps, ISBN 1-58023-132-2 **$16.95**

The Rituals & Practices of a Jewish Life: A Handbook for Personal Spiritual
Renewal *Edited by Rabbi Kerry M. Olitzky and Rabbi Daniel Judson*
6 x 9, 272 pp, illus., Quality PB, ISBN 1-58023-169-1 **$18.95**

The Book of Jewish Sacred Practices: CLAL's Guide to Everyday & Holiday
Rituals & Blessings *Edited by Rabbi Irwin Kula and Vanessa L. Ochs, Ph.D.*
6 x 9, 368 pp, Quality PB, ISBN 1-58023-152-7 **$18.95**

Science Fiction/
Mystery & Detective Fiction

Mystery Midrash: An Anthology of Jewish Mystery & Detective Fiction
Edited by Lawrence W. Raphael. Preface by Joel Siegel.
6 x 9, 304 pp, Quality PB, ISBN 1-58023-055-5 **$16.95**

Criminal Kabbalah: An Intriguing Anthology of Jewish Mystery & Detective Fiction
Edited by Lawrence W. Raphael. Foreword by Laurie R. King.
6 x 9, 256 pp, Quality PB, ISBN 1-58023-109-8 **$16.95**

More Wandering Stars: An Anthology of Outstanding Stories of Jewish Fantasy and
Science Fiction *Edited by Jack Dann. Introduction by Isaac Asimov.*
6 x 9, 192 pp, Quality PB, ISBN 1-58023-063-6 **$16.95**

Wandering Stars: An Anthology of Jewish Fantasy & Science Fiction
Edited by Jack Dann. Introduction by Isaac Asimov.
6 x 9, 272 pp, Quality PB, ISBN 1-58023-005-9 **$16.95**

Spirituality

The Alphabet of Paradise: An A–Z of Spirituality for Everyday Life
By Rabbi Howard Cooper
In twenty-six engaging chapters, Cooper spiritually illuminates the subjects of our daily lives—A to Z—examining these sources by using an ancient Jewish mystical method of interpretation that reveals both the literal and more allusive meanings of each.   5 x 7¾, 224 pp, Quality PB, ISBN 1-893361-80-2 **$16.95** *(A SkyLight Paths book)*

Does the Soul Survive?: A Jewish Journey to Belief in Afterlife, Past Lives & Living with Purpose   *By Rabbi Elie Kaplan Spitz. Foreword by Brian L Weiss, M.D.*
Spitz relates his own experiences and those shared with him by people he has worked with as a rabbi, and shows us that belief in afterlife and past lives, so often approached with reluctance, is in fact true to Jewish tradition.
6 x 9, 288 pp, Quality PB, ISBN 1-58023-165-9 **$16.95**; Hardcover, ISBN 1-58023-094-6 **$21.95**

First Steps to a New Jewish Spirit: Reb Zalman's Guide to Recapturing the Intimacy & Ecstasy in Your Relationship with God
By Rabbi Zalman M. Schachter-Shalomi with Donald Gropman
An extraordinary spiritual handbook that restores psychic and physical vigor by introducing us to new models and alternative ways of practicing Judaism. Offers meditation and contemplation exercises for enriching the most important aspects of everyday life.   6 x 9, 144 pp, Quality PB, ISBN 1-58023-182-9 **$16.95**

God in Our Relationships: Spirituality between People from the Teachings of Martin Buber   *By Rabbi Dennis S. Ross*
On the eightieth anniversary of Buber's classic work, we can discover new answers to critical issues in our lives. Inspiring examples from Ross's own life— as congregational rabbi, father, hospital chaplain, social worker, and husband— illustrate Buber's difficult-to-understand ideas about how we encounter God and each other. 5½ x 8½, 160 pp, Quality PB, ISBN 1-58023-147-0 **$16.95**

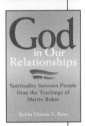

The Jewish Lights Spirituality Handbook: A Guide to Understanding, Exploring & Living a Spiritual Life   *Edited by Stuart M. Matlins*
What exactly is "Jewish" about spirituality? How do I make it a part of my life? Fifty of today's foremost spiritual leaders share their ideas and experience with us.
6 x 9, 456 pp, Quality PB, ISBN 1-58023-093-8 **$19.95**; Hardcover, ISBN 1-58023-100-4 **$24.95**

Bringing the Psalms to Life: How to Understand and Use the Book of Psalms
By Dr. Daniel F. Polish
6 x 9, 208 pp, Quality PB, ISBN 1-58023-157-8 **$16.95**; Hardcover, ISBN 1-58023-077-6 **$21.95**

God & the Big Bang: Discovering Harmony between Science & Spirituality
By Dr. Daniel C. Matt 6 x 9, 216 pp, Quality PB, ISBN 1-879045-89-3 **$16.95**

Godwrestling—Round 2: Ancient Wisdom, Future Paths
By Rabbi Arthur Waskow 6 x 9, 352 pp, Quality PB, ISBN 1-879045-72-9 **$18.95**

One God Clapping: The Spiritual Path of a Zen Rabbi   *By Rabbi Alan Lew with Sherril Jaffe*
5½ x 8½, 336 pp, Quality PB, ISBN 1-58023-115-2 **$16.95**

The Path of Blessing: Experiencing the Energy and Abundance of the Divine
By Rabbi Marcia Prager 5½ x 8½, 240 pp., Quality PB, ISBN 1-58023-148-9 **$16.95**

Six Jewish Spiritual Paths: A Rationalist Looks at Spirituality   *By Rabbi Rifat Sonsino*
6 x 9, 208 pp, Quality PB, ISBN 1-58023-167-5 **$16.95**; Hardcover, ISBN 1-58023-095-4 **$21.95**

Soul Judaism: Dancing with God into a New Era
By Rabbi Wayne Dosick 5½ x 8½, 304 pp, Quality PB, ISBN 1-58023-053-9 **$16.95**

Stepping Stones to Jewish Spiritual Living: Walking the Path Morning, Noon, and Night   *By Rabbi James L. Mirel and Karen Bonnell Werth*
6 x 9, 240 pp, Quality PB, ISBN 1-58023-074-1 **$16.95**; Hardcover, ISBN 1-58023-003-2 **$21.95**

There Is No Messiah... and You're It: The Stunning Transformation of Judaism's Most Provocative Idea   *By Rabbi Robert N. Levine, D.D.*
6 x 9, 192 pp, Hardcover, ISBN 1-58023-173-X **$21.95**

These Are the Words: A Vocabulary of Jewish Spiritual Life   *By Dr. Arthur Green*
6 x 9, 304 pp, Quality PB, ISBN 1-58023-107-1 **$18.95**

Spirituality/Lawrence Kushner

The Book of Letters: A Mystical Hebrew Alphabet
Popular Hardcover Edition, 6 x 9, 80 pp, 2-color text, ISBN 1-879045-00-1 **$24.95**
Deluxe Gift Edition with slipcase, 9 x 12, 80 pp, 4-color text, Hardcover, ISBN 1-879045-01-X **$79.95**
Collector's Limited Edition, 9 x 12, 80 pp, gold foil embossed pages, w/limited edition silkscreened print, ISBN 1-879045-04-4 **$349.00**

The Book of Miracles: A Young Person's Guide to Jewish Spiritual Awareness
All-new illustrations by the author
6 x 9, 96 pp, 2-color illus., Hardcover, ISBN 1-879045-78-8 **$16.95** *For ages 9–13*

The Book of Words: Talking Spiritual Life, Living Spiritual Talk
6 x 9, 160 pp, Quality PB, ISBN 1-58023-020-2 **$16.95**

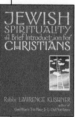

Eyes Remade for Wonder: A Lawrence Kushner Reader
Introduction by Thomas Moore
6 x 9, 240 pp, Quality PB, ISBN 1-58023-042-3 **$18.95;** Hardcover, ISBN 1-58023-014-8 **$23.95**

God Was in This Place & I, i Did Not Know
Finding Self, Spirituality and Ultimate Meaning
6 x 9, 192 pp, Quality PB, ISBN 1-879045-33-8 **$16.95**

Honey from the Rock: An Introduction to Jewish Mysticism
6 x 9, 176 pp, Quality PB, ISBN 1-58023-073-3 **$16.95**

Invisible Lines of Connection: Sacred Stories of the Ordinary
5½ x 8½, 160 pp, Quality PB, ISBN 1-879045-98-2 **$15.95**

Jewish Spirituality—A Brief Introduction for Christians
5½ x 8½, 112 pp, Quality PB Original, ISBN 1-58023-150-0 **$12.95**

The River of Light: Jewish Mystical Awareness
6 x 9, 192 pp, Quality PB, ISBN 1-58023-096-2 **$16.95**

The Way Into Jewish Mystical Tradition
6 x 9, 224 pp, Hardcover, ISBN 1-58023-029-6 **$21.95**

Spirituality/Prayer

Pray Tell: A Hadassah Guide to Jewish Prayer
By Rabbi Jules Harlow, with contributions from Tamara Cohen, Rochelle Furstenberg, Rabbi Daniel Gordis, Leora Tanenbaum, and many others
A guide to traditional Jewish prayer enriched with insight and wisdom from a broad variety of viewpoints—from Orthodox, Conservative, Reform, and Reconstructionist Judaism to New Age and feminist. Offers fresh and modern slants on what it means to pray as a Jew, and how women and men might actually pray. 8½ x 11, 400 pp, Quality PB, ISBN 1-58023-163-2 **$29.95**

My People's Prayer Book Series
Traditional Prayers, Modern Commentaries
Edited by Rabbi Lawrence A. Hoffman
Provides diverse and exciting commentary to the traditional liturgy, helping modern men and women find new wisdom in Jewish prayer, and bring liturgy into their lives.

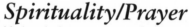

Each book includes Hebrew text, modern translation, and commentaries from all perspectives of the Jewish world.

Vol. 1—The *Sh'ma* and Its Blessings
7 x 10, 168 pp, Hardcover, ISBN 1-879045-79-6 **$23.95**
Vol. 2—The *Amidah*
7 x 10, 240 pp, Hardcover, ISBN 1-879045-80-X **$24.95**
Vol. 3—*P'sukei D'zimrah* (Morning Psalms)
7 x 10, 240 pp, Hardcover, ISBN 1-879045-81-8 **$24.95**
Vol. 4—*Seder K'riat Hatorah* (The Torah Service)
7 x 10, 264 pp, Hardcover, ISBN 1-879045-82-6 **$23.95**
Vol. 5—*Birkhot Hashachar* (Morning Blessings)
7 x 10, 240 pp, Hardcover, ISBN 1-879045-83-4 **$24.95**
Vol. 6—*Tachanun* and Concluding Prayers
7 x 10, 240 pp, Hardcover, ISBN 1-879045-84-2 **$24.95**
Vol. 7—Shabbat at Home
7 x 10, 240 pp, Hardcover, ISBN 1-879045-85-0 **$24.95**

Spirituality/The Way Into... Series

The Way Into... Series offers an accessible and highly usable "guided tour" of the Jewish faith, people, history and beliefs—in total, an introduction to Judaism that will enable you to understand and interact with the sacred texts of the Jewish tradition. Each volume is written by a leading contemporary scholar and teacher, and explores one key aspect of Judaism. *The Way Into...* enables all readers to achieve a real sense of Jewish cultural literacy through guided study.

The Way Into Encountering God in Judaism *By Neil Gillman*
6 x 9, 240 pp, Hardcover, ISBN 1-58023-025-3 **$21.95**

Also Available: **The Jewish Approach to God: A Brief Introduction for Christians**
By Neil Gillman 5½ x 8½, 192 pp, Quality PB, ISBN 1-58023-190-X **$16.95**

The Way Into Jewish Mystical Tradition *By Lawrence Kushner*
6 x 9, 224 pp, Hardcover, ISBN 1-58023-029-6 **$21.95**

The Way Into Jewish Prayer *By Lawrence A. Hoffman*
6 x 9, 224 pp, Hardcover, ISBN 1-58023-027-X **$21.95**

The Way Into Torah *By Norman J. Cohen*
6 x 9, 176 pp, Hardcover, ISBN 1-58023-028-8 **$21.95**

Spirituality in the Workplace

Being God's Partner
How to Find the Hidden Link Between Spirituality and Your Work
By Rabbi Jeffrey K. Salkin. Introduction by Norman Lear.
6 x 9, 192 pp, Quality PB, ISBN 1-879045-65-6 **$17.95**

The Business Bible: 10 New Commandments for Bringing Spirituality & Ethical
Values into the Workplace *By Rabbi Wayne Dosick*
5½ x 8½, 208 pp, Quality PB, ISBN 1-58023-101-2 **$14.95**

Spirituality and Wellness

Aleph-Bet Yoga
Embodying the Hebrew Letters for Physical and Spiritual Well-Being
By Steven A. Rapp. Foreword by Tamar Frankiel, Ph.D., and Judy Greenfeld. Preface by Hart Lazer
7 x 10, 128 pp, b/w photos, Quality PB, Layflat binding, ISBN 1-58023-162-4 **$16.95**

Entering the Temple of Dreams
Jewish Prayers, Movements, and Meditations for the End of the Day
By Tamar Frankiel, Ph.D., and Judy Greenfeld
7 x 10, 192 pp, illus., Quality PB, ISBN 1-58023-079-2 **$16.95**

Minding the Temple of the Soul
Balancing Body, Mind, and Spirit through Traditional Jewish Prayer, Movement, and
Meditation *By Tamar Frankiel, Ph.D., and Judy Greenfeld*
7 x 10, 184 pp, illus., Quality PB, ISBN 1-879045-64-8 **$16.95**
Audiotape of the Blessings and Meditations: 60 min. **$9.95**
Videotape of the Movements and Meditations: 46 min. **$20.00**

Spirituality/Women's Interest

Lifecycles, Vol. 1: Jewish Women on Life Passages & Personal Milestones
Edited and with introductions by Rabbi Debra Orenstein
6 x 9, 480 pp, Quality PB, ISBN 1-58023-018-0 **$19.95**

Lifecycles, Vol. 2: Jewish Women on Biblical Themes in Contemporary Life
Edited and with introductions by Rabbi Debra Orenstein and Rabbi Jane Rachel Litman
6 x 9, 464 pp, Quality PB, ISBN 1-58023-019-9 **$19.95**

Moonbeams: A Hadassah Rosh Hodesh Guide *Edited by Carol Diament, Ph.D.*
8½ x 11, 240 pp, Quality PB, ISBN 1-58023-099-7 **$20.00**

ReVisions: Seeing Torah through a Feminist Lens *By Rabbi Elyse Goldstein*
5½ x 8½, 224 pp, Quality PB, ISBN 1-58023-117-9 **$16.95**

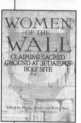

White Fire: A Portrait of Women Spiritual Leaders in America
By Rabbi Malka Drucker. Photographs by Gay Block.
7 x 10, 320 pp, 30+ b/w photos, Hardcover, ISBN 1-893361-64-0 **$24.95** *(A SkyLight Paths book)*

Women of the Wall: Claiming Sacred Ground at Judaism's Holy Site
Edited by Phyllis Chesler and Rivka Haut
6 x 9, 496 pp, b/w photos, Hardcover, ISBN 1-58023-161-6 **$34.95**

The Women's Haftarah Commentary: New Insights from Women Rabbis on
the 54 Weekly Haftarah Portions, the 5 Megillot & Special Shabbatot
Edited by Rabbi Elyse Goldstein 6 x 9, 560 pp, Hardcover, ISBN 1-58023-133-0 **$39.95**

The Women's Torah Commentary: New Insights from Women Rabbis on the 54
Weekly Torah Portions *Edited by Rabbi Elyse Goldstein*
6 x 9, 496 pp, Hardcover, ISBN 1-58023-076-8 **$34.95**

The Year Mom Got Religion: One Woman's Midlife Journey into Judaism
By Lee Meyerhoff Hendler
6 x 9, 208 pp, Quality PB, ISBN 1-58023-070-9 **$15.95**; Hardcover, ISBN 1-58023-000-8 **$19.95**

See Holidays for *The Women's Passover Companion: Women's Reflections on
the Festival of Freedom* and *The Women's Seder Sourcebook: Rituals &
Readings for Use at the Passover Seder.*

Travel

Israel—A Spiritual Travel Guide: A Companion for the Modern Jewish Pilgrim
By Rabbi Lawrence A. Hoffman 4¾ x 10, 256 pp, Quality PB, illus., ISBN 1-879045-56-7 **$18.95**
Also Available: **The Israel Mission Leader's Guide** ISBN 1-58023-085-7 **$4.95**

12 Steps

100 Blessings Every Day
Daily Twelve Step Recovery Affirmations, Exercises for Personal Growth &
Renewal Reflecting Seasons of the Jewish Year
By Rabbi Kerry M. Olitzky. Foreword by Rabbi Neil Gillman.
Using a one-day-at-a-time monthly format, this guide reflects on the rhythm of
the Jewish calendar to help bring insight to recovery from addictions and com-
pulsive behaviors of all kinds. Its exercises help us move from *thinking* to *doing*.
4½ x 6½, 432 pp, Quality PB, ISBN 1-879045-30-3 **$14.95**

Recovery from Codependence: A Jewish Twelve Steps Guide to Healing Your Soul
By Rabbi Kerry M. Olitzky 6 x 9, 160 pp, Quality PB, ISBN 1-879045-32-X **$13.95**

Renewed Each Day: Daily Twelve Step Recovery Meditations Based on the Bible
By Rabbi Kerry M. Olitzky and Aaron Z.
Vol. 1—Genesis & Exodus:
6 x 9, 224 pp, Quality PB, ISBN 1-879045-12-5 **$14.95**
Vol. 2—Leviticus, Numbers & Deuteronomy:
6 x 9, 280 pp, Quality PB, ISBN 1-879045-13-3 **$14.95**

Twelve Jewish Steps to Recovery
A Personal Guide to Turning from Alcoholism & Other Addictions—Drugs, Food,
Gambling, Sex...
By Rabbi Kerry M. Olitzky and Stuart A. Copans, M.D. Preface by Abraham J. Twerski, M.D.
6 x 9, 144 pp, Quality PB, ISBN 1-879045-09-5 **$14.95**

Theology/Philosophy

Aspects of Rabbinic Theology
By Solomon Schechter. New Introduction by Dr. Neil Gillman.
6 x 9, 448 pp, Quality PB, ISBN 1-879045-24-9 **$19.95**

Broken Tablets: Restoring the Ten Commandments and Ourselves
Edited by Rachel S. Mikva. Introduction by Lawrence Kushner. Afterword by Arnold Jacob Wolf.
6 x 9, 192 pp, Quality PB, ISBN 1-58023-158-6 **$16.95**; Hardcover, ISBN 1-58023-066-0 **$21.95**

Creating an Ethical Jewish Life
A Practical Introduction to Classic Teachings on How to Be a Jew
By Dr. Byron L. Sherwin and Seymour J. Cohen
6 x 9, 336 pp, Quality PB, ISBN 1-58023-114-4 **$19.95**

The Death of Death: Resurrection and Immortality in Jewish Thought
By Dr. Neil Gillman 6 x 9, 336 pp, Quality PB, ISBN 1-58023-081-4 **$18.95**

Evolving Halakhah: A Progressive Approach to Traditional Jewish Law
By Rabbi Dr. Moshe Zemer
6 x 9, 480 pp, Quality PB, ISBN 1-58023-127-6 **$29.95**; Hardcover, ISBN 1-58023-002-4 **$40.00**

Hasidic Tales: Annotated & Explained
By Rabbi Rami Shapiro. Foreword by Andrew Harvey, SkyLight Illuminations series editor.
5½ x 8½, 240 pp, Quality PB, ISBN 1-893361-86-1 **$16.95** *(A SkyLight Paths Book)*

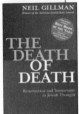

A Heart of Many Rooms: Celebrating the Many Voices within Judaism
By Dr. David Hartman
6 x 9, 352 pp, Quality PB, ISBN 1-58023-156-X **$19.95**; Hardcover, ISBN 1-58023-048-2 **$24.95**

Judaism and Modern Man: An Interpretation of Jewish Religion
By Will Herberg. New Introduction by Dr. Neil Gillman.
5½ x 8½, 336 pp, Quality PB, ISBN 1-879045-87-7 **$18.95**

Keeping Faith with the Psalms: Deepen Your Relationship with God Using the
Book of Psalms *By Daniel F. Polish*
6 x 9, 272 pp, Hardcover, ISBN 1-58023-179-9 **$24.95**

The Last Trial
On the Legends and Lore of the Command to Abraham to Offer Isaac as a Sacrifice
By Shalom Spiegel. New Introduction by Judah Goldin.
6 x 9, 208 pp, Quality PB, ISBN 1-879045-29-X **$18.95**

A Living Covenant: The Innovative Spirit in Traditional Judaism
By Dr. David Hartman 6 x 9, 368 pp, Quality PB, ISBN 1-58023-011-3 **$18.95**

Love and Terror in the God Encounter
The Theological Legacy of Rabbi Joseph B. Soloveitchik
By Dr. David Hartman
6 x 9, 240 pp, Quality PB, ISBN 1-58023-176-4 **$19.95**; Hardcover, ISBN 1-58023-112-8 **$25.00**

Seeking the Path to Life
Theological Meditations on God and the Nature of People, Love, Life and Death
By Rabbi Ira F. Stone 6 x 9, 160 pp, Quality PB, ISBN 1-879045-47-8 **$14.95**

The Spirit of Renewal: Finding Faith after the Holocaust
By Rabbi Edward Feld 6 x 9, 224 pp, Quality PB, ISBN 1-879045-40-0 **$16.95**

Tormented Master: *The Life and Spiritual Quest of Rabbi Nahman of Bratslav*
By Dr. Arthur Green 6 x 9, 416 pp, Quality PB, ISBN 1-879045-11-7 **$19.95**

Your Word Is Fire: The Hasidic Masters on Contemplative Prayer
Edited and translated by Dr. Arthur Green and Barry W. Holtz
6 x 9, 160 pp, Quality PB, ISBN 1-879045-25-7 **$15.95**

I Am Jewish
Personal Reflections Inspired by the Last Words of Daniel Pearl
Almost 150 Jews—both famous and not—from all walks of life, from all around
the world, write about Identity, Heritage, Covenant/Chosenness and Faith,
Humanity and Ethnicity, and *Tikkun Olam* and Justice.
Edited by Judea and Ruth Pearl
6 x 9, 304 pp, Hardcover, ISBN 1-58023-183-7 **$24.95**

JEWISH LIGHTS BOOKS ARE AVAILABLE FROM BETTER BOOKSTORES. TRY YOUR BOOKSTORE FIRST.

About Jewish Lights

People of all faiths and backgrounds yearn for books that attract, engage, educate, and spiritually inspire.

Our principal goal is to stimulate thought and help all people learn about who the Jewish People are, where they come from, and what the future can be made to hold. While people of our diverse Jewish heritage are the primary audience, our books speak to people in the Christian world as well and will broaden their understanding of Judaism and the roots of their own faith.

We bring to you authors who are at the forefront of spiritual thought and experience. While each has something different to say, they all say it in a voice that you can hear.

Our books are designed to welcome you and then to engage, stimulate, and inspire. We judge our success not only by whether or not our books are beautiful and commercially successful, but by whether or not they make a difference in your life.

For your information and convenience, at the back of this book we have provided a list of other Jewish Lights books you might find interesting and useful. They cover all the categories of your life:

Bar/Bat Mitzvah
Bible Study / Midrash
Children's Books
Congregation Resources
Current Events / History
Ecology
Fiction: Mystery, Science Fiction
Grief / Healing
Holidays / Holy Days
Inspiration
Kabbalah / Mysticism / Enneagram

Life Cycle
Meditation
Parenting
Prayer
Ritual / Sacred Practice
Spirituality
Theology / Philosophy
Travel
Twelve Steps
Women's Interest

Stuart M. Matlins, Publisher

Or phone, fax, mail or e-mail to: **JEWISH LIGHTS Publishing**
Sunset Farm Offices, Route 4 • P.O. Box 237 • Woodstock, Vermont 05091
Tel: (802) 457-4000 • Fax: (802) 457-4004 • www.jewishlights.com
Credit card orders: (800) 962-4544 (8:30AM–5:30PM ET Monday–Friday)
Generous discounts on quantity orders. SATISFACTION GUARANTEED. Prices subject to change.

For more information about each book, visit our website at www.jewishlights.com